Encyclopedia of Optography

The Shutter of Death

Derek Ogbourne

Encyclopedia of Optography,
The Shutter of Death

This publication is made possible by the
Gallerie Brigitte Schenk, Cologne, David Ryder
Susana Medina, Bill Cisneros,
Ali Hossaini and Hoor Al Qasimi

Encyclopediia of Optography,
The Shutter of Death
Copyright © Derek Ogbourne, 2008
Muswell Press, 2008
ISBN 0-9547959-4-6
First Published August 2008

ISBN 0-9547959-4-6

Muswell Press 2008

Encyclopedia of Optography

The Shutter of Death

Note: It is hoped that further editions of this volume will be printed that will contain two extra essays by Margarida Medeiros and Andrea Goulet, entitled respectively *Body, mind, machine: 19th century ideas of automation* and Death and the Retina: Claire Lenoir, L'Accusateur, and Les Frères Kip.

Contents

Optogram /op·to·gram/ (op´to-gram) The retinal image formed by the bleaching of visual purple under the influence of light.

www.thefreedictionary.com

Optography \Op*tog"ra*phy\, n. [Optic + -graphy.] (Physiol.) The production of an optogram on the retina by the photochemical action of light on the visual purple; the fixation of an image in the eye. The object so photographed shows white on a purple or red background. See Visual purple.

www.dict.die.net

The Shutter of Death

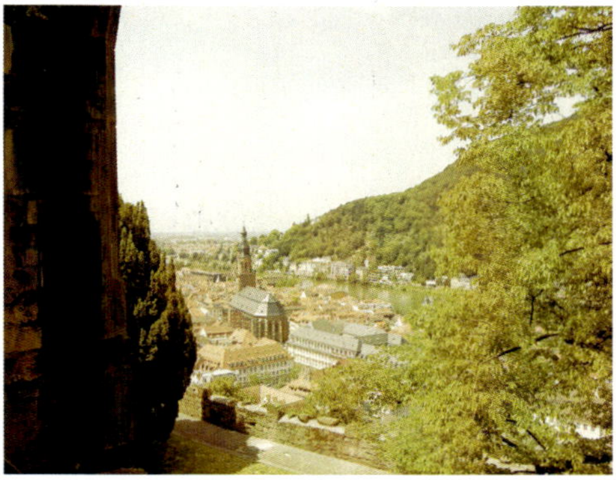

Heidelberg 2007

It all started seven years ago, a small article in a Time-Life book got me obsessed with optography:

A Jesuit friar called Christopher Schiener made an amazing observation in the mid 17th Century whereby he had observed an image laid bare on the retina of a frog, a faint, fleeting record of what the eye had been fixed on at the moment its owner had died. It was rumoured it became possible to fix this image and create what is termed an Optogram. (Time-Life, 1970)

Soon after reading the above, I contacted the Institute of Ophthalmology, London. They knew nothing about the phenomena but this did not stop me wanting to know more about optography. To my amazement, I found very little at the time. Although the image of the killer in the dead man's eye has held steady within popular myth since the 1860's and James Joyce, amongst other writers, makes reference to optography in Ulysses, the Internet had only one article: 'Optograms and Fiction' by Dr. Arthur B Evans, featured in this book. This still left me unsure up until very recently as to whether these strange traces of the external world could be produced at all.

Just prior to my new interest in all things optographic, I had been working on a project with the artist Brian Williams called 'Frankenstein's Kitchen', an art project that was about making a living self-sustaining sculpture, or a form that had properties that behaved like a living system. This gravitation towards the organic was a natural evolution from my painting The organic, the physical, the close up, as well as the persistent fascination with very small units of time, all clearly present in my recent drawings and videos.

I came to a dead end with my research and my desire to actually produce optograms, mainly on ethical grounds in dealing with grant bodies and institutions. At that point, my grant applications were alluding to an intent to actually produce optograms. My recent acquisition of two rabbits, Jessica and Cinnamon, now offers tantalising possibilities, but I have a conflict of intent, I don't think you should kill for art's sake.

Six or so years passed, and many video works.

In June 2005, I was in an show at the Brigitte Schenk Gallery, Cologne. On I was telling one of my fellow participating artists, Thom Kubli, about optography, by some sort of morphic resonance it turned out that his mother had met the scientist Dr. Alexandridis when he had had a crash in the snow with some friends right in front of her house in Heidelberg.

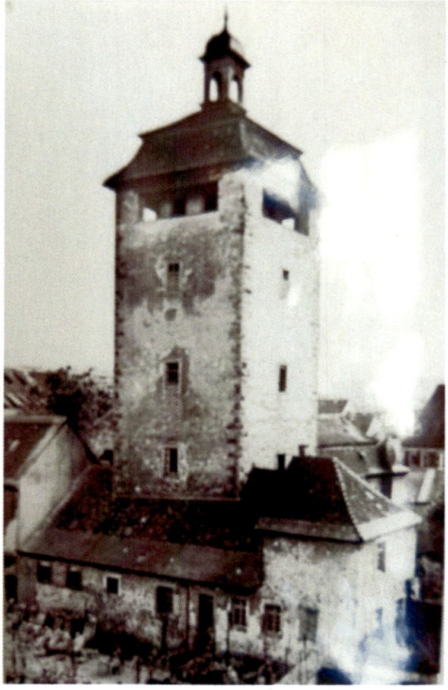

Old Bruchsal Prison 1880's

This rekindled my interest in optography, after a few years of sabbatical. I wrote to Dr. Alexandridis, probably the only person alive who has actually produced optograms. He kindly agreed to see me with Thom in Heidelberg. We were now fans (see conversation on page 48).

The Physiologist Wilhelm Kühne hadmade the first and most successful visually identifiable optograms recorded as drawings in the late 1870's in Heidelberg. He had also obtained the only known 'Human Optogram' in a nearby town of Bruchsal (see page 22).

My trip was set at long last. I was an artist explorer, a detective bringing form to the formless. Being a romantic I wanted to go where it had all happened.

In June 2006, I made a visit to the University City of Heidelberg with the intention of documenting further my research into optography and its main protagonists.

My mission in Heidelberg was twofold: to visit Dr. Alexandridis in order to establish once and for all whether it was really possible to produce optograms and to investigate 'The Human Optogram', a rather amorphous drawing recovered by George Wald in 1953. This led me to the small town of Bruchsal where a young man (I now know his name was Erhard Gustav Reif) was executed in 1880 for murder. His retina was extracted by Kühne and the optogram revealed. I traced down the old prison and the site where the guillotine was placed and I interviewed Dr. Erich Viehöfer, the curator of a prison museum nearby in Ludwigsburg, and local historian, Thomas Moos, in Bruchsal. I learnt that the process of obtaining optograms was straightforward and more akin to an amateur photographic lab with red safe light. I left with a borrowed set of four optograms made in 1975 by Dr. Alexandridis that appear in my 'Museum of Optography' shows. The Human Optogram Story was and still is a detective story about a man, Erhard Gustav Reif, who after his wife's death he'd killed his two children in the Old Rhine and faced his death without any idea that an artist a hundred and twenty-seven years later would be remotely viewing his last moments and seeing the last thing he saw as he, with remorse of his crime, ceased to be. His retina, drawn by William Kühne, appears in this book and is the only human optogram available.

My research has continued in London with the generous assistance of Alexandra Veith, a librarian at The Medical Library in Heidelberg, who passes me little gems of archival material every now and then.

The 'Museum of Optography' is a series of art shows that explore optography's visual extrapolations, playing with myth, romanticism, science and perception towards a body of work that constitutes a visual and auditory archive, some elements of which appear in this book.

The optogram exists within the fine line between being and not being. It is within every gaze that contemplates death. We imagine death, we imagine when and where. This project is about imagination and death. As a poetic metaphor, optography suggests a series of associations: the eye is a camera; the eyelid, the shutter, the moment of retreat into the internal, the virtual and eventually, a real death moment. It was apt that the mode of execution in Bruchsal was by guillotine, the fall of the blade echoing the fall of the shutter. The dying gaze captured in the instant of separation of head from body. How close was Barthes to the truth with his Camera Lucida, where he equated photography with death.

To produce optograms now is to kill the myth. The ambiguity becomes more interesting, although as I have mentioned earlier the process is very simple, albeit unpredictable.

The Shutter of Death, Encyclopedia of Optography started as an alternative way of presenting the hundred and forty retinal drawings I had produced in two sketchbooks for the first of my Museum of Optography shows at the Brigitte Schenk Gallery, Cologne. Books have to go to press and research is continuous, so this is a snapshot from varied disciplines approaching the same subject, a subject that is complicit in the blink of an eye. These insights into the various histories that form the myth and the reality of the optogram are from the following contributors: Dr. Evangelos Alexandridis, Dr. Arthur B. Evans, Olly Beck, Bill Jay, Professor Richard Kremer; Dr. Ali Hossaini; Dr. Susana Medina, and artists Paul Sakoilsky and Thom Kubli. Thanks to all for contributing to this book.

Derek Ogbourne, 2007

Addendum to the Museum of Optography

There is often a confusion as to what an optogram actually is, firstly this book contains photographs of optograms, yet no optograms actually exist due to the fleeting and difficult to capture nature of the image, further, as regards to preservation it is unclear as to whether the image could have been permanently 'fixed' with the technology the 1970's by Evangelos Alexandridis, if not today. An analogy I often use is this - when your arm is pressed up against a textured object the imprint temporarily marks the flesh. Your flesh has memory of its natural form. It is the unconscious involuntary function of the brain that puts things right. The eye containing the retina is, in comparison a complex organ considered at some evolutionary point as being part of, or an extension of the brain, maybe evolving from voluntary to involuntary working as a receptor of light. The image is formed on the retina regardless of what our brain tells us is in front of us. We close our eyes consciously or as motor reflex depending on the situation. When we go to sleep we place the lens cap on until another day. In this way the eye resembles the camera.

Photographing the fundus of the eye is standard practice in the living and dead person. Of course here we do not get an optogram. However with a laser scanning ophthalmoscope it is possible to watch what is watched by the subject in real time. An experiment was conducted where a Disney film was projected onto a child's retina and simultaneously viewed via a laser scanning ophthalmoscope on a TV monitor. I have seen the type of image produced by this method, it resembled security camera footage and is unremarkable from an artists point of view.

In 1974, Dr. Uday B Sheorey (now at the Indian Institute of Technology, Mumbai) while working at the Institute of Ophthalmology, London, developed a photographic technique to assess the spatial distribution of Rhodopsin (the photosensitive pigment within the photoreceptor cells) available In the human retina. In his paper 'Clinical Assessment of Rhodopsin in the Eye' (Brit. J. Ophthalmology, 1976, Vol.60), he described the technique whereby a standard fundus camera was modified to take a photograph of the distribution of rhodopsin in the fundus of subjects after a strip of the fundus was bleached by a short intense flash of light. The reflectometric image of the bleached fundus and the adjacent unbleached regions were recorded through a set of calibrated strips of neutral density filters immediately

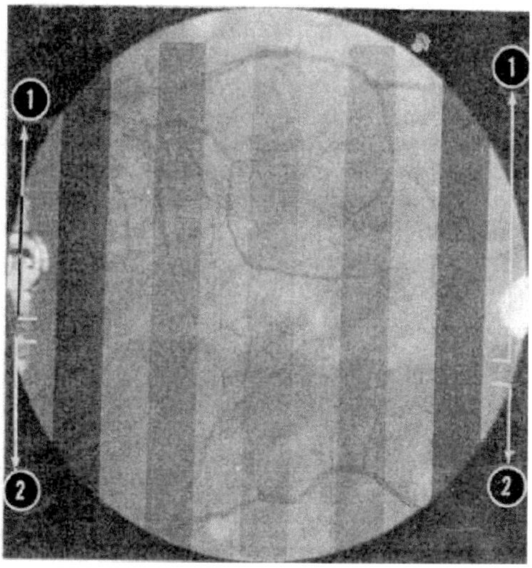

Dr. Uday B Sheorey, 1974

after the bleaching. This was pure capture of the afterimage.

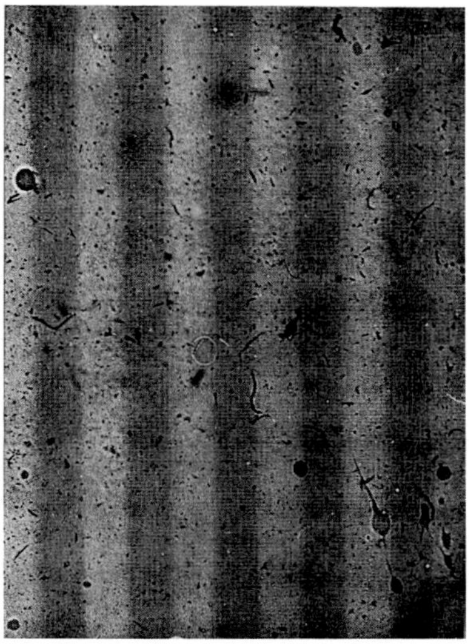

George Wald, Circa 1950

Rhodopsin or Visual Purple used as photographic emulsion as analogous to silver halide was first demonstrated by George Wald and two associates where he had extracted the light sensitive red pigment of rod vision from the retinas of cattle. It was mixed with gelatine, spread on celluloid, dried and then exposed to a pattern of black and white stripes. When the film was wetted in the dark with hydroxylamine, the rhodopsin bleached in the same pattern.

As we well know the photographic image presents us with the idea of the death moment of time (Barthes) and it acts also to remind us of a past time of life with cold objectivity. It is a challenge for the photographer to bring life in the mind to the lifeless. Optography shares the same cold objectivity, a lab experiment involving a device to capture light with the image 'fixed' with chemicals under a coloured light, potassium hydroxide used rather than developer and fixer. However the power of the idea of Optography transcends the Turin shroud. The primitive results it produces brings us a sort of wish fulfilment connected with mortality of our living existence. A myth we would like to believe because it acknowledges our existence in our minds eye.

Raw digital data in rows of binary numbers are the first stage of computer software processing. The retina acts in a similar way, the translation being done by the brain. The computer computes the code into recognisable forms based on learning inputted by man. (see Ali Hossaini's text about convergent technologies). The image on the retina is photographed. The photograph gives us a rough interpretation of what was seen by the eye. The printed image has gone through multiple stages of processing whether on a computer screen or in the form of a photograph to take it further away from the how the brain originally interpreted the scene; from Brain to Brain via all over the place. A journey that distorts the truth, no straight line. The Ideas explored in the Encyclopedia of Optography, The Shutter of Death follow the same process. The tale of optography, needs a private eye, a subjective eye, an objective eye and most importantly an active imagination. The extrapolations are endless. What is an optogram? Well this is the least absorbing thing about optography, it is how the mind continues the tale or edits the myth we have, as most evident with the French Gothic literature of the 19th century, worldwide press coverage (at the time) and its close ties with criminology all blend fact, fiction and imagination.

Derek Ogbourne, 2008

Alexandridis, Prof. Dr. Med. Evangelos

Dr Alexandridis worked at the Department of Clinical and Experimental Ophthalmology at the University of Heidelberg, Eye Clinic, Heidelberg, Germany and is now retired.

In 1975 he was approached by the German police to re-examine the possibility of extracting an optogram to aid forensic investigations. He 'fixed' a number of retinal images from rabbits that appear in this book. He has authored and contributed to numerous Journals and Books including *The Pupil and Electro Diagnostic Ophthalmology.*

Optography

'Optography' results from the bleaching of the rhodopsin in those areas of the retina that have been directly affected by light. Rhodopsin is a light sensitive chemical substance by which the rods of the retina can distinguish in twilight between bright and dark. Bright spots in an optogram correspond to the area where the rhodopsin has been bleached by light. Dark spots designate the sector in which the rhodopsin is still intact. Unlike photography where the film is produced as a negative, optography generates a positive. A bright object appears bright, whereas darker motifs result darker because of the lower bleaching effect of dark colours.

About 130 years ago, the physiologist Willy Kühne (1837-1900) from the University of Heidelberg discovered this phenomenon by accident. On the retina of a frog, he was able to detect the image of a gas flame the frog had been staring at for a while before it was killed in the laboratory. To confirm his observation, Kühne conducted subsequent experiments with rabbits. In a dark room, he placed the animals in front of a bright window for a short amount of time, killed them and removed – still in the dark – their eye bulb. The image of the window appeared clearly on the isolated retina as a bright quadrangular spot. Kühne called this image 'optogram'.

By the middle of the 20th century other scholars were also able to obtain optograms on animal retinas. The possibility to uncover previously seen objects on the retina of a creature especially inspired the imagination of criminologists. In the mid-1970s they contacted the ophthalmic hospital of the University of Heidelberg requesting "whether and to what extent it would be possible to detect objects or men on the retina of a murdered person, what this person had seen immediately before being killed." We considered this to be a very interesting question and revived Kühne's research to clarify the conditions on which an optogramm could be obtained.

Like Kühne, we also used rabbits for our experiments. We anaesthetised the animals and located them in front of a screen on which patterns rich in contrast were projected. After a certain amount of time we killed the animals in the dark, only using illumination available in a photographic darkroom. We quickly removed their eye bulbs and detached the anterior part of the eye and the vitreous.

The rear part of the bulb with the retina was put into a 14% potassic alum solution for 24 hours. After that we isolated the retina, tightened it on a ball that had the same dimensions as the eye bulb, and let it dry in the dark.

The original optograms are not very light-resistant. Therefore we took photographs of the results that show the patterns the rabbits had been looking at. For this experiment we also used a portrait of Salvador Dalí as pattern that I had drawn with a black 1,5mm pencil on white paper. In this case we took a coloured photograph of the optogram.

The criminologists, however, had to abandon their hope of seeing the image of a murderer on the retina of his or her victim. Although this remains a theoretical possibility, it is impossible to obtain an optogram that would be usable for forensic purposes. The creation of a 'readable' optogram depends on a multitude of prerequisites that can be provided only in a laboratory. And how many murderers oblige their prosecutors by working under laboratory conditions?

Evangelos Alexandridis, Heidelberg, 2007

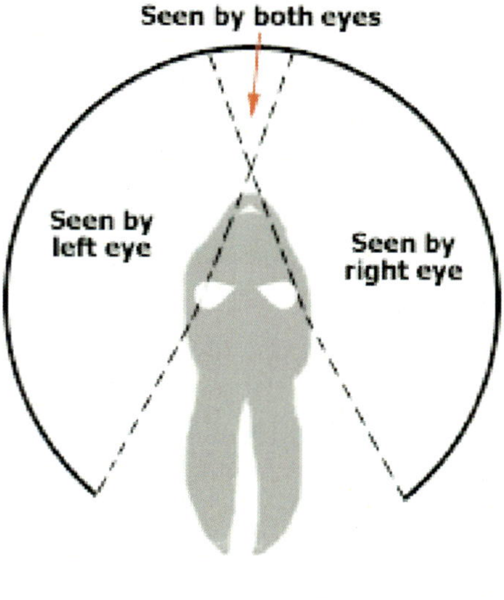

The Optograms of Dr. Evangelos Alexandridis, Heidelberg, 1975

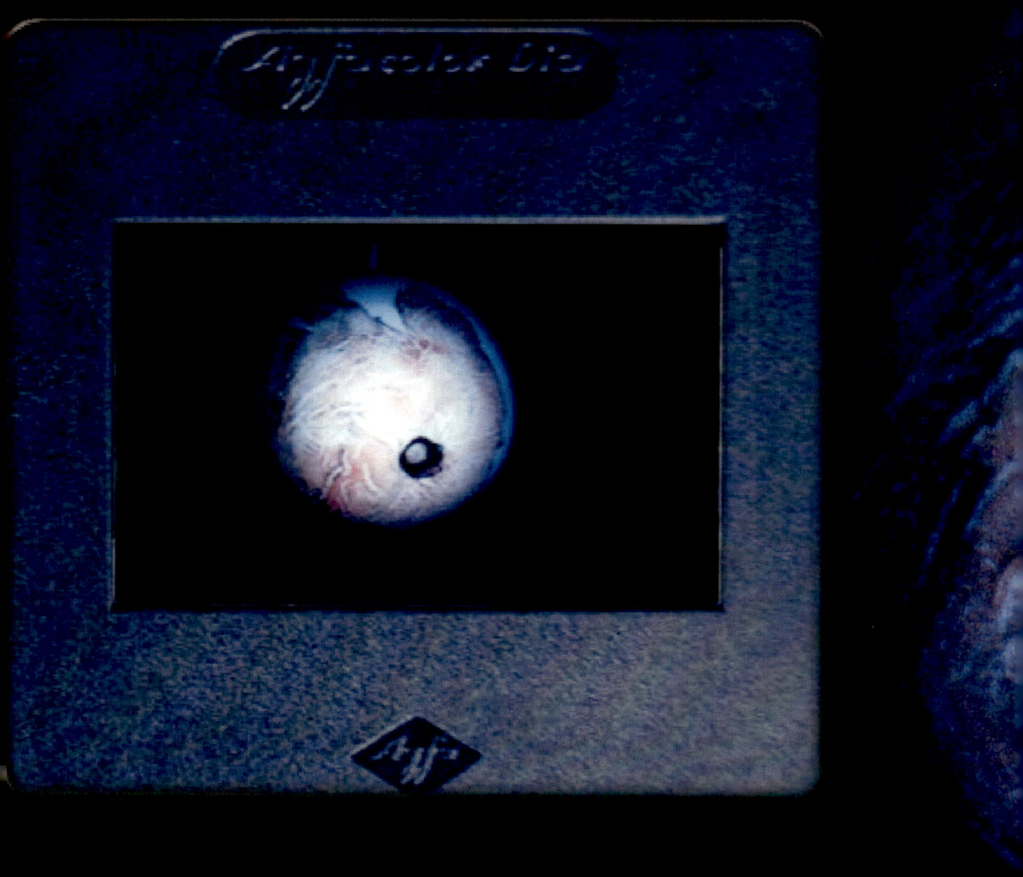

Optogram 1
'75'

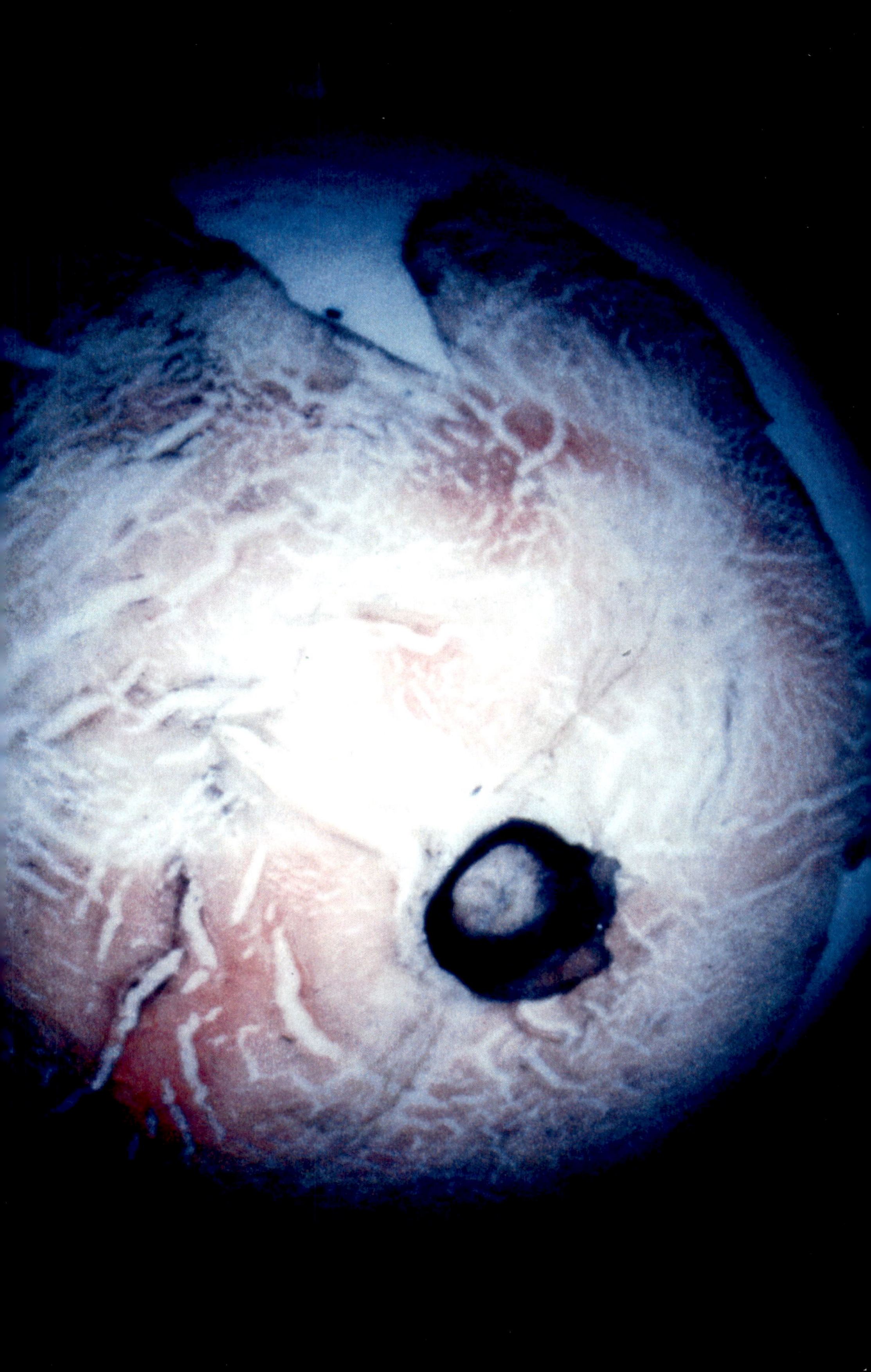

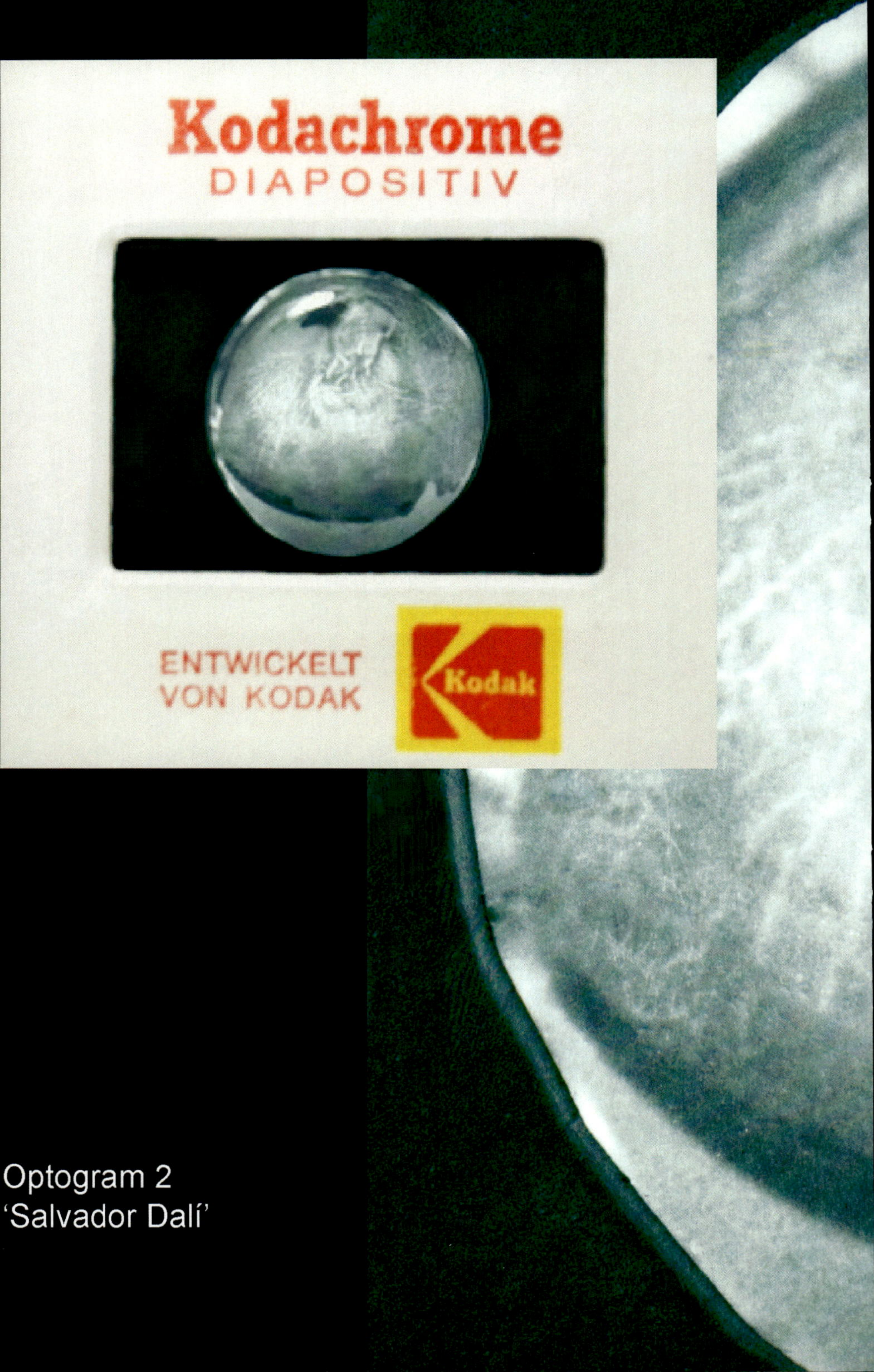

Optogram 2
'Salvador Dalí'

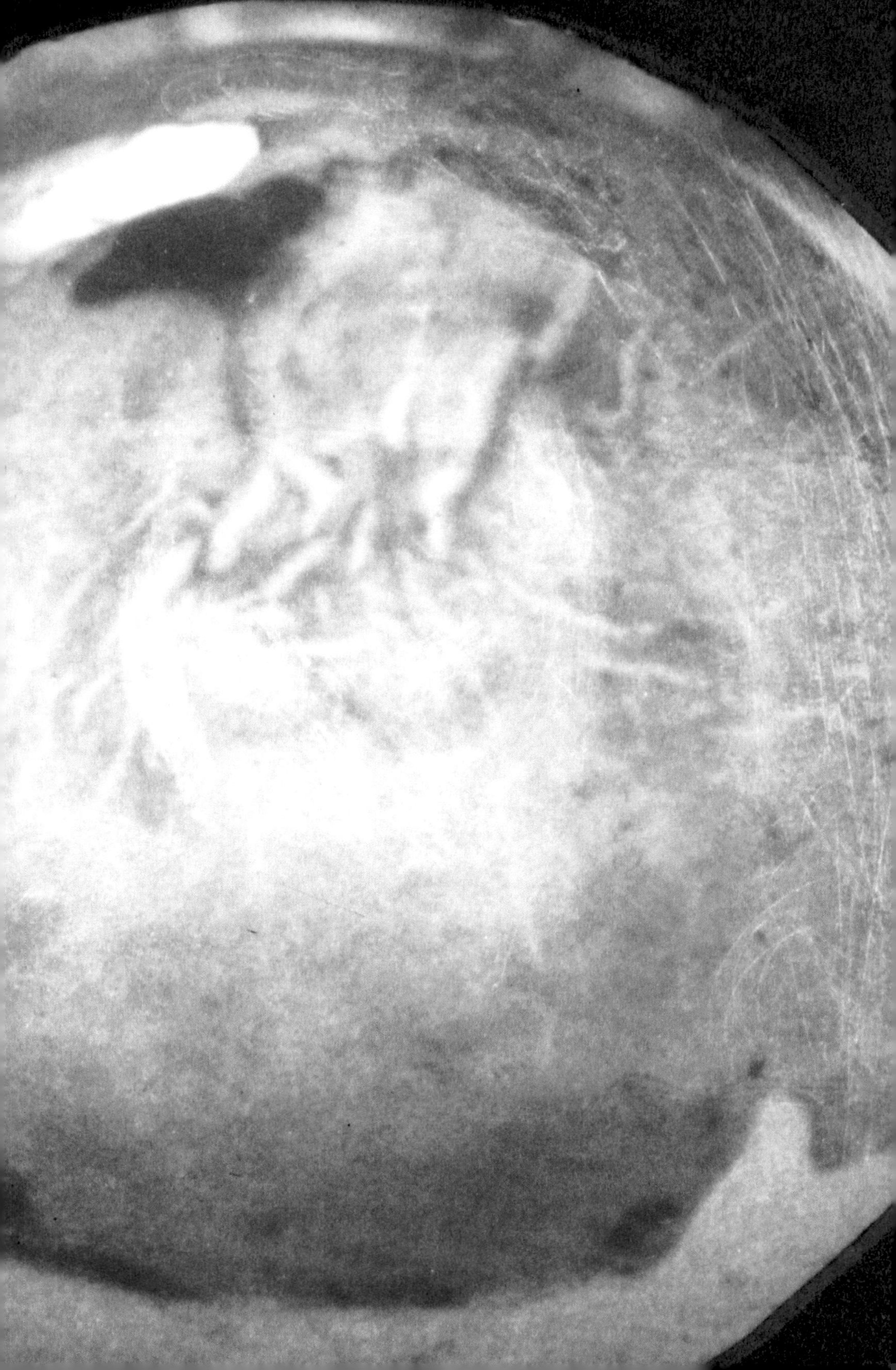

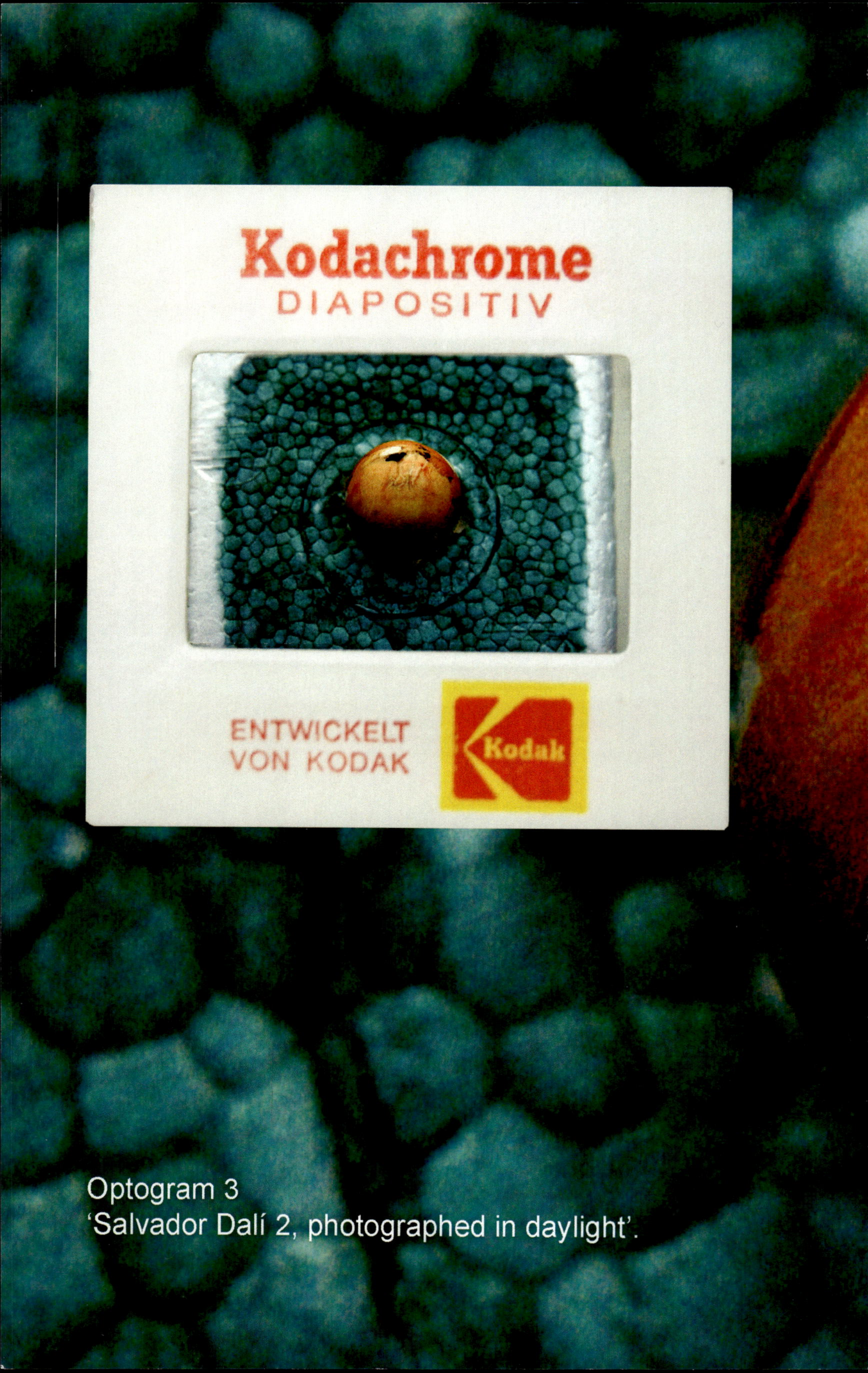

Optogram 3
'Salvador Dalí 2, photographed in daylight'.

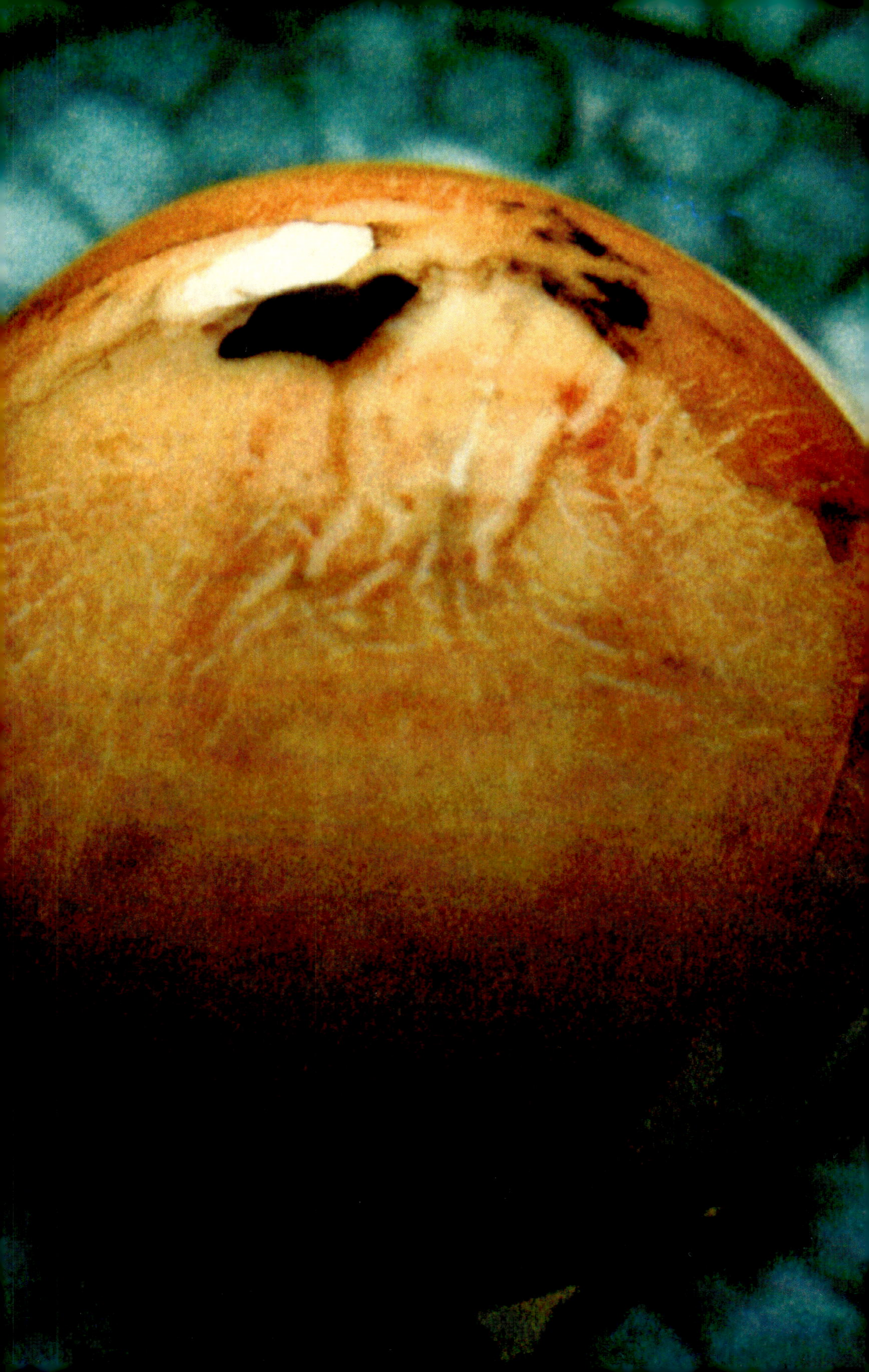

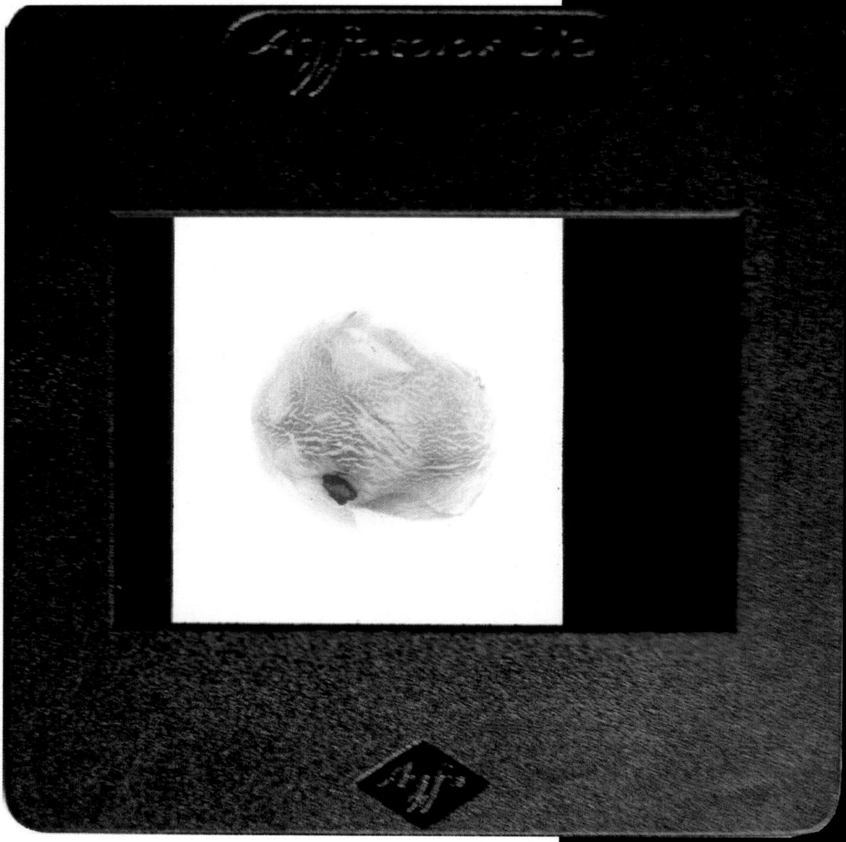

Optogram 4
'Checkerboard Pattern'

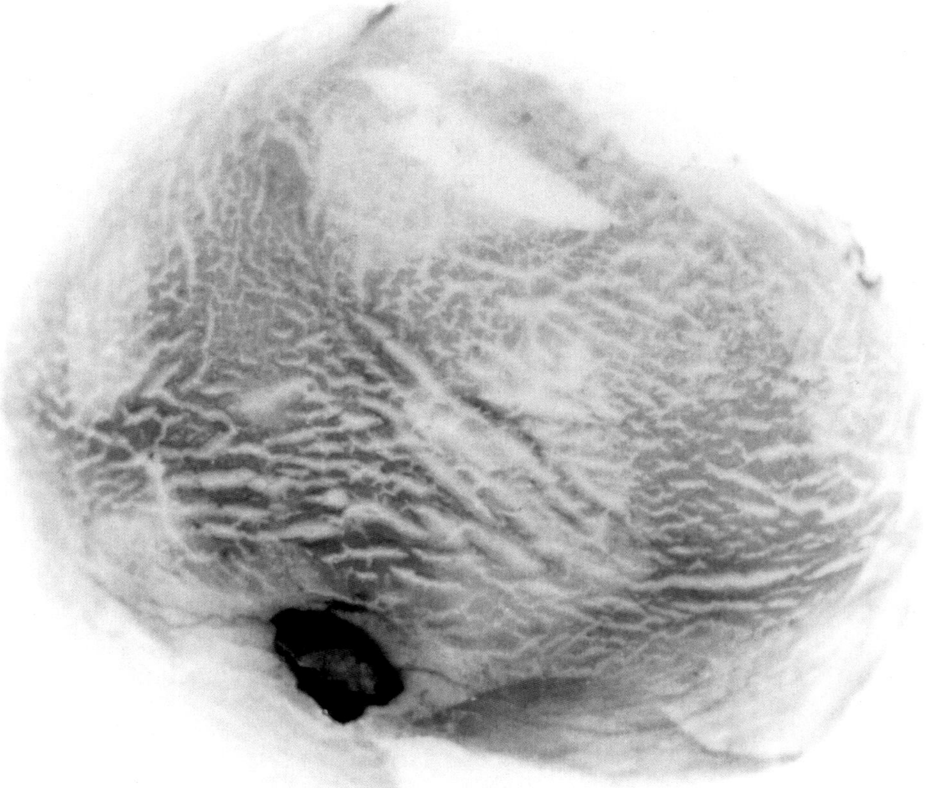

The Human Optogram

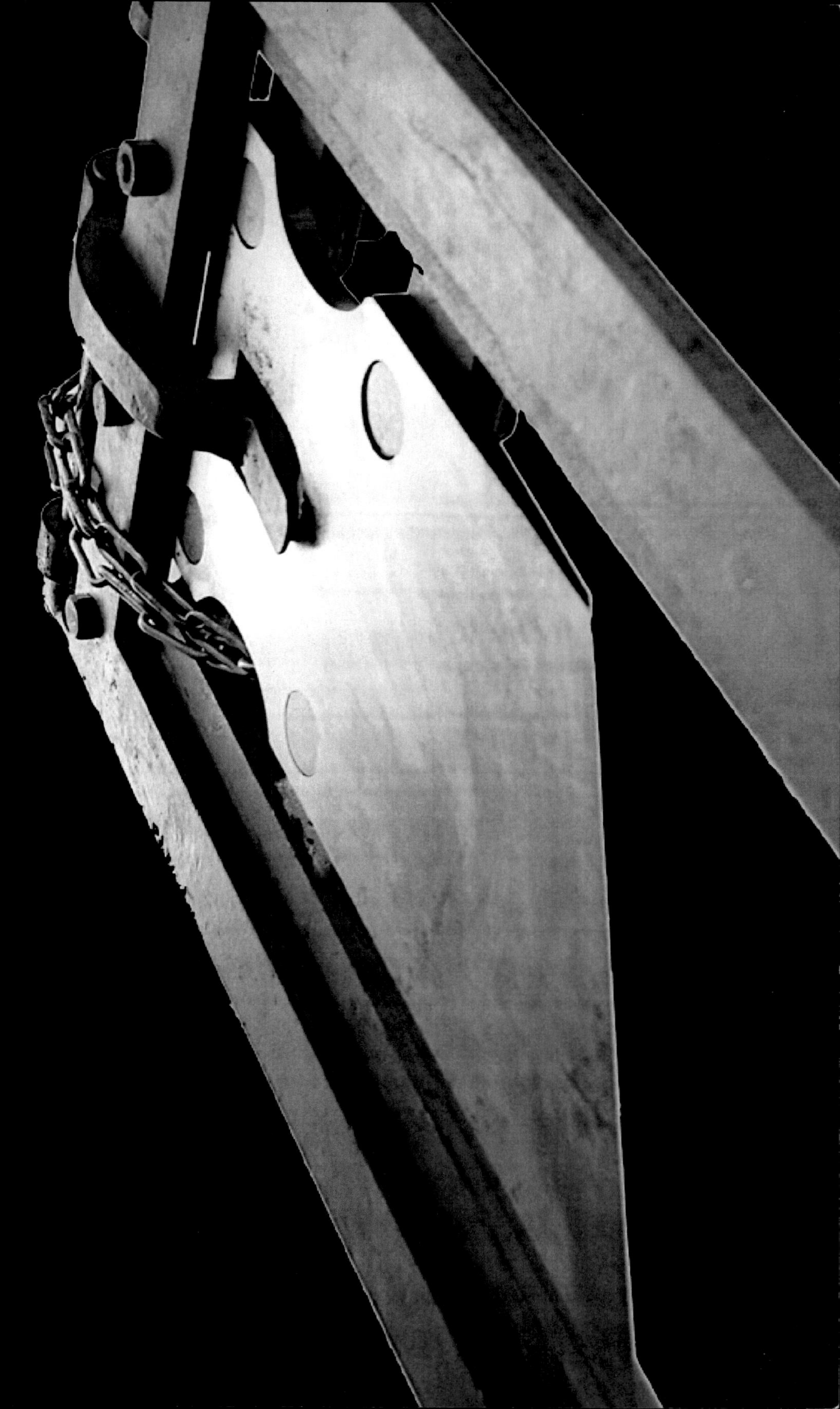

The Human Optogram

George Wald, 1953

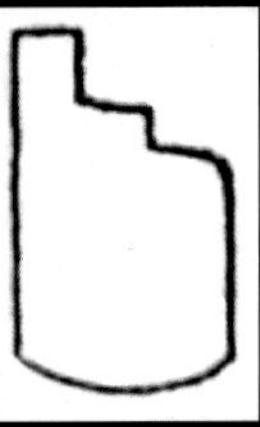

In the nearby town of Bruchsal on November 16, 1880, a young-man was beheaded by guillotine. Wilhelm Kuhne had made arrangements to receive the corpse. He had prepared a dimly lighted room screened with red and yellow glass to keep any rhodopsin left in the eyes from bleaching further. Ten minutes after the knife had fallen he obtained the whole retina from the left eye and had the satisfaction of seeing and showing to several colleagues a sharply demarcated optogram printed upon its surface. Kühne's drawing of it is reproduced here. To my knowledge it is the only human optogram on record. Kühne went to great pains to determine what this optogram represented. He says: "A search for the object which served as a source for this optogram remained fruitless, in spite of a thorough inventory of all the surroundings and reports for many witnesses. The delinquent had spent the night awake by the light of a tallow candle; he slept from four to five o'clock in the morning; and had read and written, first by candlelight until dawn, then by feeble daylight until eight o'clock. When he emerged in the open, the sun came out for an instant, according to a reliable observer, the sky became somewhat brighter during the seven minutes prior to the bandaging of his eyes and his execution, which followed immediately. The delinquent, however, raised his eyes only rarely.

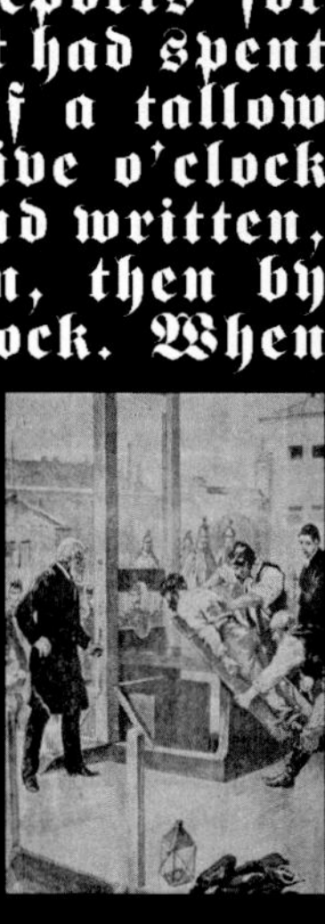

Investigations from the Physiological Institute of
The University of Heidelberg.
William Kühne, 1881.

eichmäßig hellrosa, etv
n im unteren, äußerer
ıd vor mehreren Colleg
ar diese 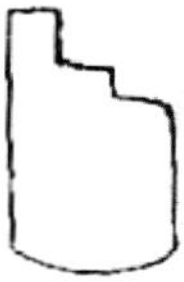 bei 2 ur
nerhalb der farb
ch um kein Psc
ıs Bild etwa 5 Min. s
Die mikroskopisch
ückfläche ohne Druck

Portion of text from the chapter: Anatomical and physiological observations of the retina showing the human optogram.

Staats- Ministerium.

Verbrechen.

(Mord)

Lit. R.

Betreff: J.A.S.

gegen

Erhard Gustav Reiß von Hausen

wegen mehrfachen Mords

Kast. —,

Fach. —,

Vol. —,

Fasc. —,

Jahr 1880.

bis 188[illegible]

The opening page of the trial of Erhard Gustav Reif in Karlsruhe, Germany, 1880 for murder.
The 31 year old from Hausen was beheaded by guillotine on the 16th November at 8am in Bruchsal Prison courtyard, in front of a crowd of 70 people. After the death of his wife he had drowned his two youngest children in the Old Rhine at Maxau, Germany.
Ten minutes after the blade had severed Reif's head from his body, Wilhelm Kühne extracted the left eye to reveal the only known human
optogram.

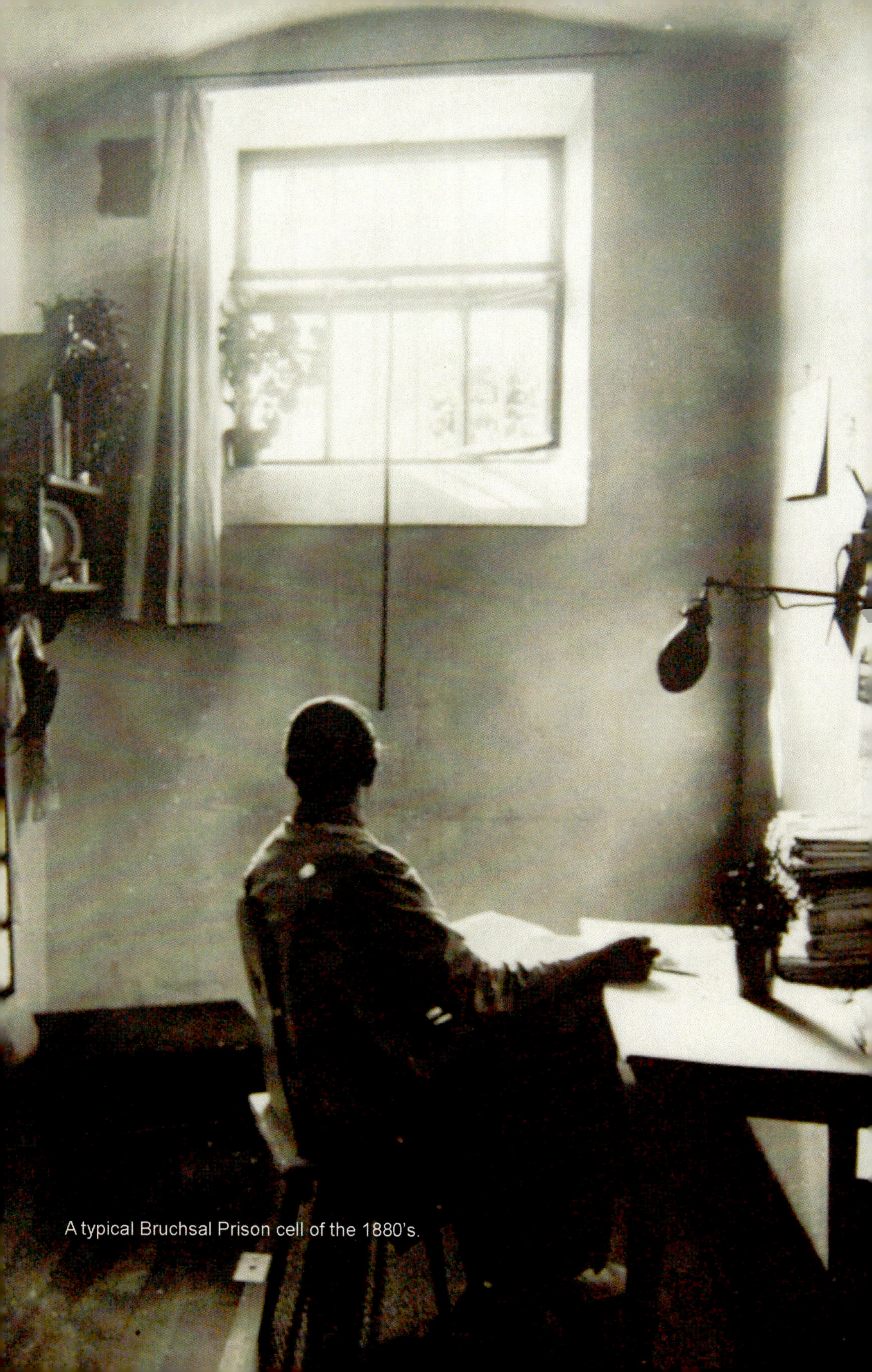

A typical Bruchsal Prison cell of the 1880's.

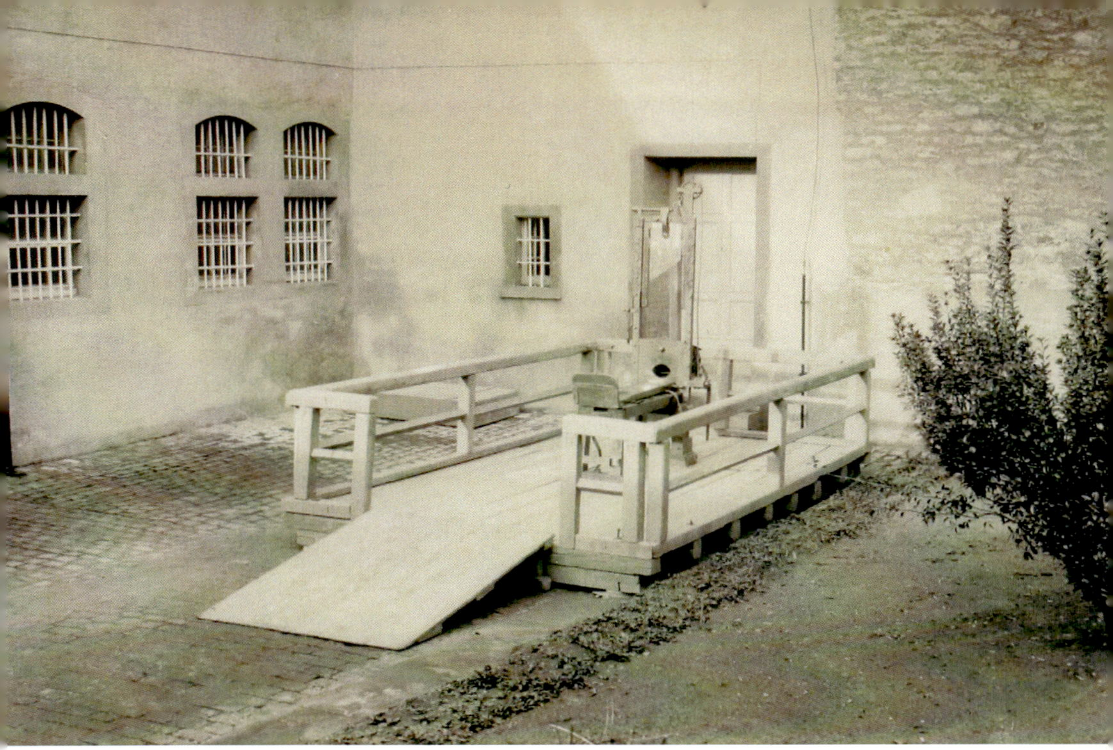

(Above) The Guillotine that was used on Erhard Reif.

(Below) Bruchsal Old Prison today.

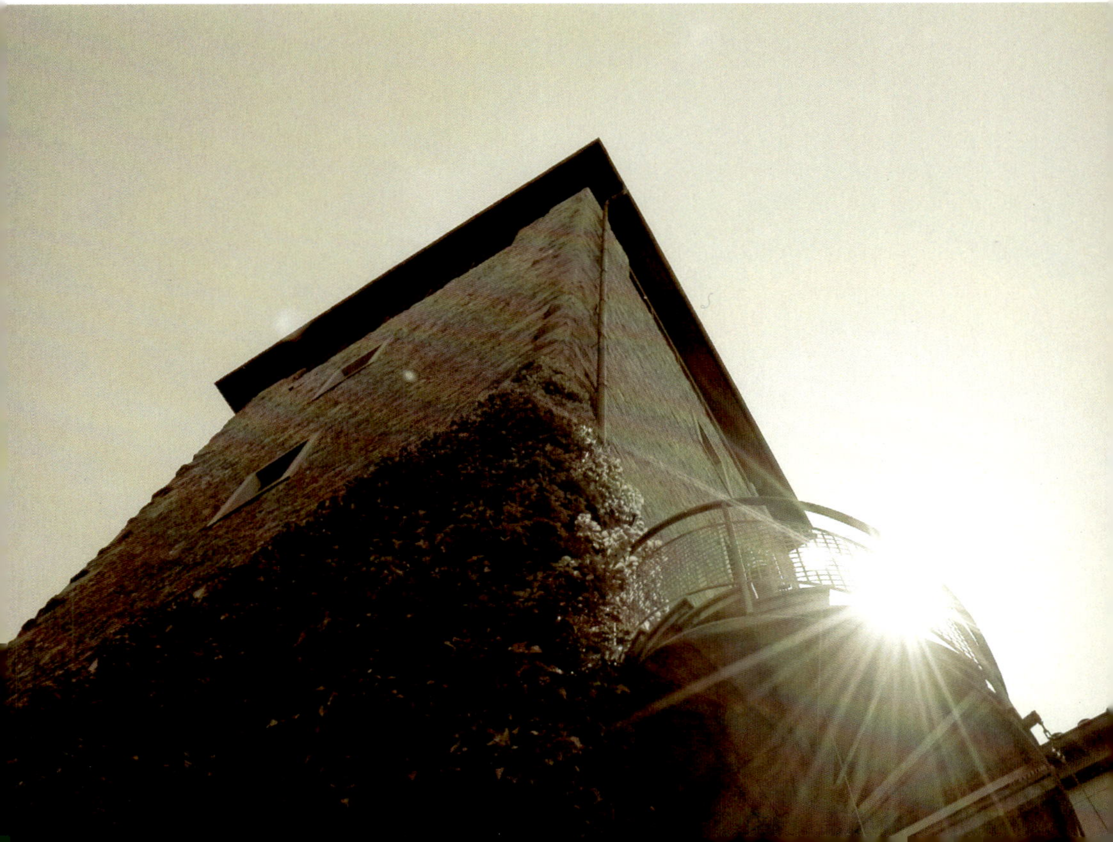

Ausschnitt
aus
der Karlsruher Zeitung
Nr 271
v. Dienstag den 16. November 1880.

Badische Chronik.

† Karlsruhe, 14. Nov. Durch Urtheil des Schwurgerichts Karlsruhe vom 30. September d. J. ist Erhard Gustav Reif von Hausen, welcher am 27. Juli d. J. seine beiden jüngsten Kinder im Altrhein bei Maxau ertränkt hat, wegen mehrfachen Mords zur Todesstrafe verurtheilt worden. Nach früherer gesetzlicher Bestimmung bedurfte jedes Todesurtheil zu seiner rechtlichen Giltigkeit der landesherrlichen Bestätigung. Diese Bestimmung ist durch die seit 1. Oktober 1879 in Wirksamkeit getretene Reichs-Strafprozeßordnung aufgehoben; die Vollstreckung ist jedoch erst zulässig, wenn die Entschließung des Staatsoberhaupts ergangen ist, von dem Begnadigungsrecht keinen Gebrauch machen zu wollen. In dem oben erwähnten Schwurgerichts-Falle ist nun die entscheidende Frage, ob in den Verhältnissen des Verbrechers, in den Motiven und Umständen seiner entsetzlichen That Gründe dafür zu finden sind, der Forderung des Kriminalgesetzes und dem Urtheil des Gerichtes gegenüber Gnade für Recht ergehen zu lassen, verneint und laut höchster Staatsministerial-Entschließung vom 9. d. M. dem Begnadigungsgesuche des Reif keine Folge gegeben worden. Diese Entschließung wurde dem Reif am heutigen Tage eröffnet; die Vollstreckung des Todesurtheils wird am Dienstag den 16. d. M., Morgens 8 Uhr, im Hofraume des Amtsgefängnisses zu Bruchsal stattfinden.

Cutting of the Karlsruhe newspaper no. 271 of Tuesday November 16th, 1880.

Chronicle of Baden

Karlsruhe, Nov. 14th. Through the sentence of the Assize Court of Karlsruhe Sept. 30th 1880, Erhard Gustav Reif of Hausen, who on July 27th 1880 drowned his two youngest children in the Old-Rhine at Maxau, was sentenced to the death penalty for double murder. According to former ordained law corresponding to this country each death penalty needs its validity by rule of law corresponding to its sovereign county. These provisions are annihilated by the Reich- Strafprozeßordnung[1] that has come into effect since October 1st, 1879 as criminal procedure, now the execution is only permitted once the resolution has been dictated by the Head of State not to make use of the prerogative of mercy. In the above mentioned Assize Court the case heard by a court jury is now the decisive question, if in the social circumstances of the criminal, in the acts and circumstances of this horrible crime a reason can be found to apply mercy instead of the law in face of the claims of criminal jurisdiction and the judgement of the court, has been negated and according to the highest decision of the Ministry of State on the 9th of this month, the petition for mercy by Reif has not been followed. This decision was communicated to Reif today. The execution of the death penalty will be effected on Tuesday 16th of this month, at 8 o'clock in the morning, in the courtyard of the jail of Bruchsal.

[1]After October 1, 1879 there was a new code of criminal procedure which was called Reichs-Strafprozeßordnung.

Karlsruhe, 17. Nov. Die Hinrichtung des wegen mehrfachen Mordes zum Tode verurtheilten Eisengießers Erhard Reif von Hausen erfolgte am 16. November d. J., Morgens 8 Uhr, im umschlossenen Hofe des Amtsgefängnisses zu Bruchsal. Der Vollzug richtete sich nach der Verordnung vom 12. April 1856, insoweit dieselbe nicht durch die Bestimmungen der deutschen Strafprozeßordnung abgeändert erscheint. Dem Akte wohnten die in § 486 St.P.O. bezeichneten Personen an. Die Leitung lag in Händen der Staatsanwaltschaft.

Punkt 8 Uhr betraten die zur Mitwirkung berufenen Personen einen erhöhten Platz in unmittelbarer Nähe des Schaffots, wohin Erhard Reif, vom Geistlichen begleitet, vorgeführt wurde. Reif, welcher in letzter Zeit eine aufrichtige Reue über seine That gezeigt hatte, erschien ruhig und gefaßt und hörte, ohne eine Miene zu verziehen, die nochmalige Verlesung des Urtheils nebst den auf die Begnadigung bezüglichen Staatsministerialerlassen an. Hierauf ergriff der Staatsanwalt einen schwarzen Stab, zerbrach denselben und warf ihn vor die Füße Reif's mit den Worten: „Ihr Leben ist verwirkt, Gott sei Ihrer Seele gnädig!"

Der Geistliche betete alsdann mit Reif und ermahnte ihn, wie entsetzlich auch seine That sein möge, auf Gottes Barmherzigkeit zu vertrauen. Hierauf übergab der Staatsanwalt den Reif dem Scharfrichter mit dem Befehle, das Todesurtheil zu vollziehen. Reif betrat festen Schrittes das Schaffot und ließ auch während des Anschnallens auf das Brett und Vorschieben desselben keinen Klagelaut vernehmen. Der Geistliche stund ihm betend zur Seite, bis das Beil gefallen war.

Der ganze Akt, welcher etwa eine Viertelstunde dauerte und während dessen eine Glocke läutete, wurde mit einem Gebete geschlossen. — Außer den Gerichtspersonen waren etwa 70 Personen anwesend.

Karlsruhe Newspaper, November 1880

Karlsruhe, Nov. 17th. The execution due to repeated murder and sentenced of death of the iron founder Erhard Reif from Hausen, took place on Nov.16th at 8 o'clock in the morning in the courtyard of the jail of Bruchsal. The execution was according to the decree of April 12th 1856 to the extent that the regulations had not been cancelled by the German Code of Criminal procedure. The act assisted by paragraph 486 St.V.D. of the criminal procedure of designated persons. The administration was in the hands of the Public Prosecutors office.

Punctually at 8 o'clock the assigned participants entered, getting to an elevated position right next to the guillotine, while Erhard Reif entered accompanied by a priest. Reif who lately had shown a sincere regret about his crime, seemed tranquil, prepared and listened, without any expression, to the repeated reading of his sentence which included the prerogative of mercy by the Ministerial Head of State. Afterwards, the public processor took a black bar, broke it in two and threw it at Reif's feet with the words: "Your life has finished, may God protect your soul."

The priest prayed with Reif and told him that however horrible his crime had been, he should trust in God's mercifulness. Then the public processor passed Reif on to the executioner with the order to effect the death penalty. Reif stepped firmly on to the guillotine without making a sound of pain or complaint while he was buckled to the board. The priest stood beside him until the hatchet had fallen.

The whole act, which lasted about a quarter of an hour, while a bell rang, was closed with a prayer. Apart from the court personalities, 70 persons were present.

Investigations from the Physiological
Institute of
The University of Heidelberg.
William Kühne, 1881.

Beobachtungen zur Anatomie und Physiologie der Retina.

Von

W. Kühne.

1. Netzhaut des Menschen.

Nach einer am 16. November 1880 in Bruchsal vollzogenen Hinrichtung eines 31jährigen gesunden Mannes fand sich Gelegenheit eine Netzhaut frisch zu untersuchen, deren Verwendung zum Sehen bis zum Tode genau festgestellt worden war. Drei Minuten nachdem das Fallbeil den Kopf unterhalb der Medulla oblongata getrennt hatte, waren am Körper keine Reflexe mehr zu erzeugen, auch nicht das Kniephänomen, während sich bei der Enucleation des Auges noch starke Bewegungen der Umgebung störend bemerklich machten. Die Präparation geschah in einem schwach erhellten Raume, hinter einem Schirme von rothem und gelbem Glase. Etwa 10 Min. nach dem Tode war die Retina des linken Auges (das rechte wurde andern Zwecken vorbehalten), nach Ausbohrung der Papille und Entfernung des unter Salzwasser auffallend locker haftenden Glaskörpers, bis zum Aequatorialschnitte vollkommen erhalten, mit der Rückseite nach oben freigelegt. Mit Ausnahme der Macula lutea und deren nächster Umgebung erschien die Stäbchenfläche gleichmäßig hellrosa, etwas heller als bei Dunkelaugen, indeß intensiv genug, um im unteren, äußeren Theile ein scharfbegrenztes Optogramm erkennen und vor mehreren Collegen demonstriren zu können. Die Form des Bildchens war diese 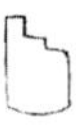 bei 2 und 3—4 mm Seitenlänge; da der Stäbchenbesatz sich innerhalb der farblosen Fläche überall erhalten zeigte, so handelte es sich um kein Pseudooptogramm. An dem trüben Herbstmorgen blieb das Bild etwa 5 Min. sichtbar.

Die mikroskopische Untersuchung der gegen ein Deckglas mit der Rückfläche ohne Druck angelegten Netzhaut ergab an einigen Stellen Besatz durch kleine Gruppen von Pigmentepithelien, und das Anhaften einer solchen, schon makroskopisch erkannten Zellgruppe grade hinter der fovea centralis. Es hatte dies besonderes Interesse, weil man sehen konnte, daß jeder der an diesem Orte bekanntlich besonders kleinen Epithelzellen groß genug war, um eine beträchtliche Anzahl von Zapfenaußengliedern zu um-

Observations
for Anatomy and Physiology of the Retina

by

W. Kühne

1. Retina of Humans

On Nov.16th 1880 in Bruchsal after the execution was carried out on a healthy 31 year old man there was the opportunity to explore a fresh retina, whose function was proved exactly before death. Three minutes after the hatchet had dropped and separated the head below the medulla oblongata, no more reflexes were produced by the body, not even a sudden contraction of the anterior muscles of the thigh, (knee phenomenon). During the enucleation of the eye, violent and disturbing movements surrounding the eye still could be seen. The preparation happened in a weakly illuminated room, behind a screen of red and yellow glass. About 10 min. after death, the retina of the left eye (the right eye was reserved for other purposes) and after drilling the pupil and after removing under saltwater the remarkably loosely clasped vitreous humour, until the equatorial cuts were completely preserved, with the back side turned towards the top side. With the exception of the macula lutea and its nearest surroundings appeared the bacillus level evenly light pink, a little lighter as with dark eyes, though intense enough, to recognize in the lower outside parts, a sharp-limited Optogram, which could be demonstrated before several colleagues. The form of the tiny picture was like this, of 2 and 3-4 mm side length; as the rod cell which showed itself entirely within the colourless space, suggesting that this is not a Pseudooptogram. On this cloudy autumn morning the figure remained visible for about 5 min.

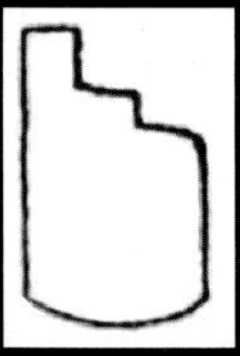

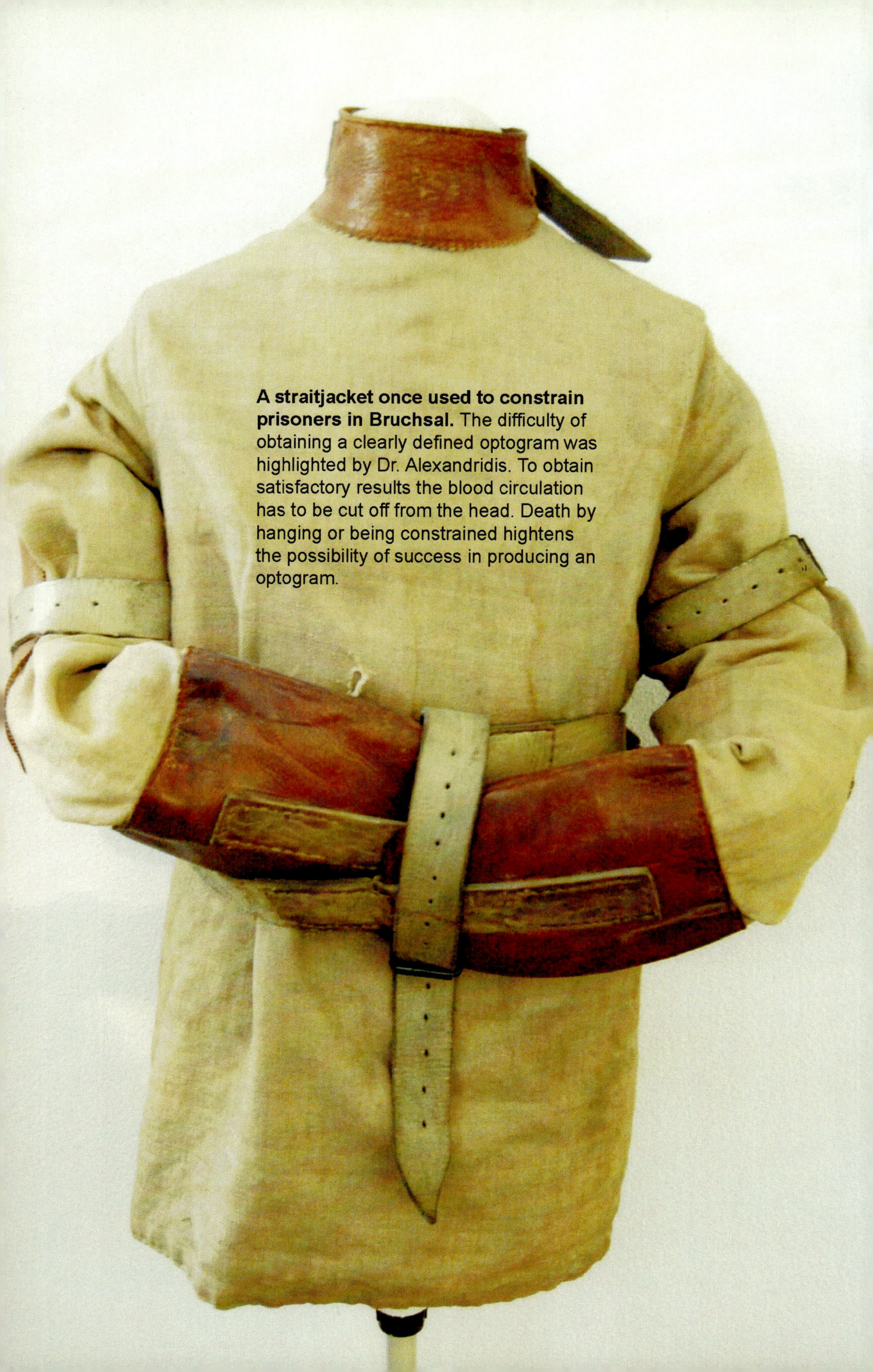

A straitjacket once used to constrain prisoners in Bruchsal. The difficulty of obtaining a clearly defined optogram was highlighted by Dr. Alexandridis. To obtain satisfactory results the blood circulation has to be cut off from the head. Death by hanging or being constrained hightens the possibility of success in producing an optogram.

The Human Optogram Device

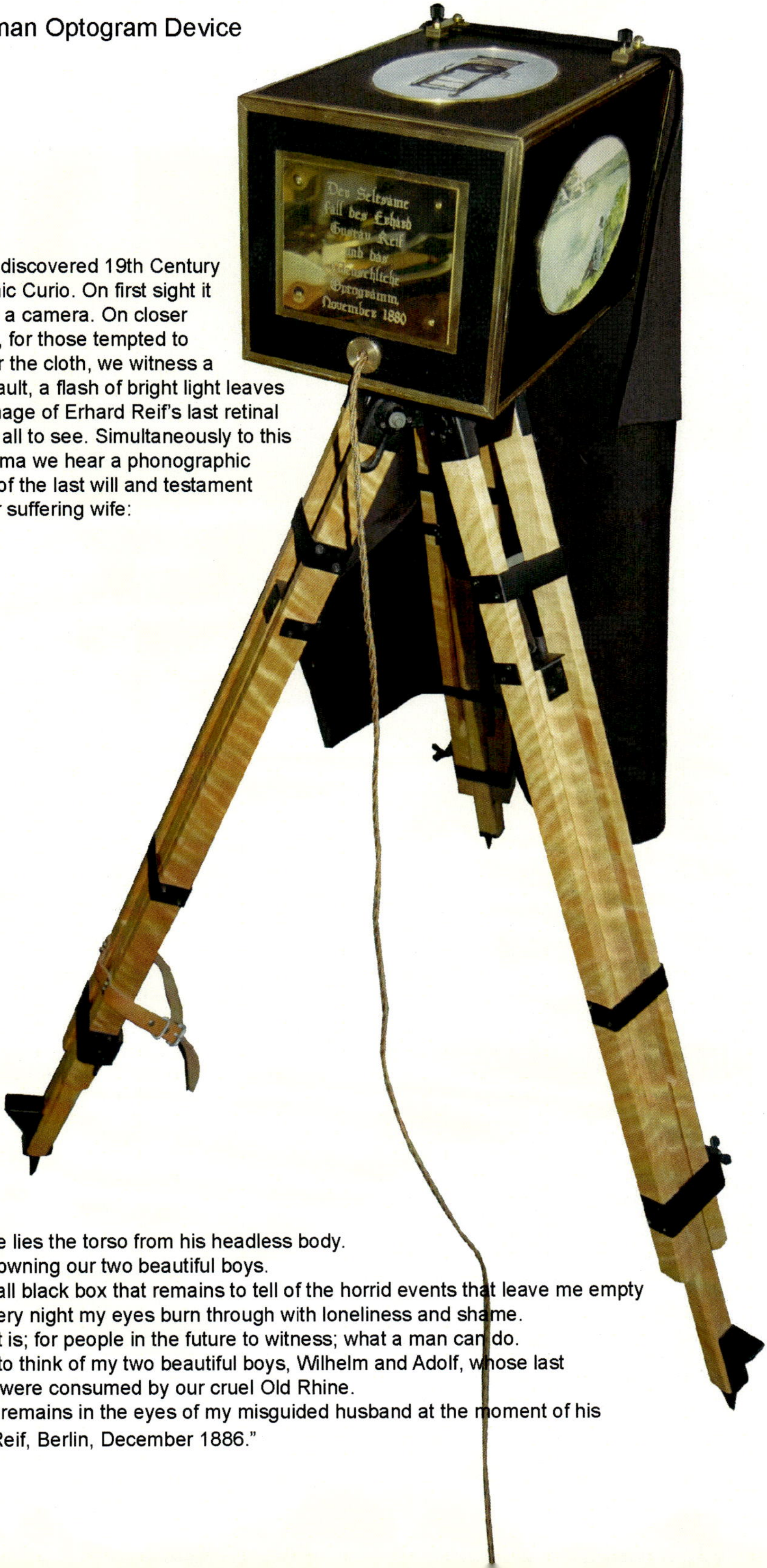

A recently discovered 19th Century Optographic Curio. On first sight it resembles a camera. On closer inspection, for those tempted to peer under the cloth, we witness a visual assault, a flash of bright light leaves an after image of Erhard Reif's last retinal imprint for all to see. Simultaneously to this visual trauma we hear a phonographic recording of the last will and testament of his poor suffering wife:

"Well, here lies the torso from his headless body.
Cruelly drowning our two beautiful boys.
And a small black box that remains to tell of the horrid events that leave me empty inside; every night my eyes burn through with loneliness and shame.
So, here it is; for people in the future to witness; what a man can do.
I ask you to think of my two beautiful boys, Wilhelm and Adolf, whose last moments were consumed by our cruel Old Rhine.
And what remains in the eyes of my misguided husband at the moment of his death. A Reif, Berlin, December 1886."

Evans, Dr. Arthur B

Professor of French at DePauw University

Dr. Arthur B. Evans is a professor of French at DePauw University, managing editor of the scholarly journal Science Fiction Studies, and general editor of Wesleyan University Press's *Early Classics of Science Fiction* book series. He has published numerous books and articles on Jules Verne and early French science fiction, including the award-winning Jules Verne Rediscovered (Greenwood, 1988). His personal website is located at: http://academic.depauw.edu/~aevans

The aim of Dr Evans' article is to examine this pseudoscientific literary motif, its origins and evolution, and to show how science fact can sometimes become science fiction and take on a life of its own in the popular imagination.

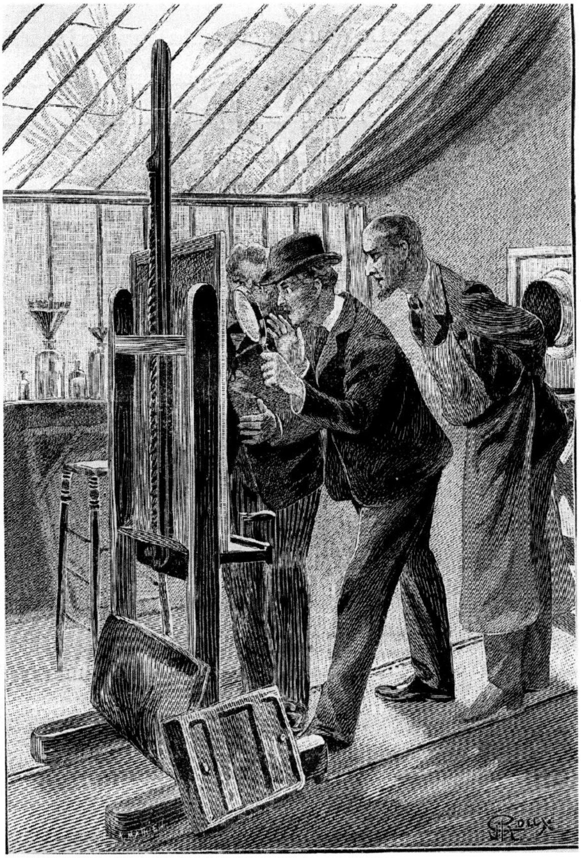

Arthur B. Evans

Optograms and Fiction: Photo in a Dead Man's Eye

Science Fiction Studies
#61 = Volume 20, Part 3 = November 1993

They looked. Murderer's ground. It passed darkly. Shuttered, tenantless, unweeded garden. Whole place gone to hell. Wrongfully condemned. Murder. The murderer's image in the eye of the murdered. They love reading about it.—James Joyce, *Ulysses* (§6:205)

One of Jules Verne's later *Voyages Extraordinaires* entitled Les *Frères Kip* (The Kip Brothers, 1902) features in its conclusion a somewhat curious scientific concept—yet one which was quite popular during the latter half of the nineteenth century and the early years of the twentieth: the notion that the image of the last thing seen at the moment of death remains imprinted upon the retina of the eye.

The fictional setting in Verne's novel where this theory comes into play is as follows:

A certain Captain Harry Gibson of the English freighter *James Cook* has been stabbed to death. On the strength of circumstantial evidence, two brothers named Karl and Pieter Kip are promptly arrested and imprisoned for the crime. Photos of the dead body are taken; in particular, snapshots of the victim's head (with eyes open). An acquaintance of the victim asks the photographer for an enlargement of the head photo as a memento of his dead friend. The photographer agrees and makes several copies of the portrait, giving one to the victim's family as well. Upon seeing the enlarged photo of his slain father, the young Nat Gibson is seized with grief and bends over to kiss it—and suddenly discerns two small points of light in the eyes of the photo. He examines these with a strong magnifying glass and discovers therein the faces of the real murderers: two villainous sailors from the *James Cook* whom the police had initially suspected but against whom no hard evidence could be found. The real culprits are now arrested and condemned; the Kip brothers are vindicated; and the novel concludes with Justice served and the status quo happily re-established.

In his final chapter, Verne (always the pedagogue) explains to the reader the "scientific" basis for this pivotal discovery:

> For some time now it has been known—as a result of various interesting ophthamological experiments done by certain ingenious scientists, authoritative observers that they are—that the image of exterior objects imprinted upon the retina of the eye are conserved there indefinitely. The organ of vision contains a particular substance, retinal purple, on which is imprinted in their exact form these images. They have even been perfectly reconstituted when the eye, after death, is removed and soaked in an alum bath. (§16:556)

It is likely that Verne gleaned this tidbit of ocular physiology from any one of the various newspapers, scientific journals, or encylopedias available to him in fin-de-siècle France—like the *Gazette Médicale*, for example, or the *L'Encyclopédie française d'ophtalmologie* by Lagrange and Valude—which offer detailed descriptions of this phenomenon (the latter which, in particular, bears some resemblance to Verne's own).[1]

Whatever the case, the experiments leading up to this scientific discovery were relatively well-known during Verne's time. The following is a brief summary by the noted biochemist George Wald (winner of the Nobel Prize for Medicine in 1967) in his article called "Eye and Camera":

> In 1876 Franz Boll of the University of Rome discovered in the rods of the frog retina a brilliant red pigment. This bleached in the light and was resynthesized in the dark, and so fulfilled the elementary requirements of a visual pigment. He called this substance visual red; later it was renamed visual purple or rhodopsin. This pigment marks the point of attack by light on the rods: the absorption of light by rhodopsin initiates the train of reactions that end in rod vision.
>
> Boll had scarcely announced his discovery when Willy Kühne, professor of physiology at Heidelberg, took up the study of rhodopsin, and in one extraordinary year learned almost everything about it that was known until recently. In his first paper on retinal chemistry Kühne said: "Bound together with the pigment epithelium, the retina behaves not merely like a photographic plate, but like an entire photographic workshop, in which the workman continually renews the plate by laying on new light-sensitive material, while simultaneously erasing the old image."
>
> Kühne saw at once that, with this pigment which bleaches in the light, it might be possible to take a picture with the living eye. He set about devising methods for carrying out such a process, and succeeded after many discouraging failures. He called the process *optography* and its products *optograms*.
>
> One of Kühne's early optograms was made as follows. An albino rabbit was fastened with its head facing a barred window. From this position the rabbit could see only a gray and clouded sky. The animal's head was covered for several minutes with a cloth to adapt its eyes to the dark and to let rhodopsin accumulate in its rods. Then the animal was exposed for three minutes to the light. It was immediately decapitated, the eye removed and cut open along the equator, and the rear half of the eyeball containing the retina laid in a solution of alum for fixation. The next day Kühne saw, printed upon the retina in bleached and unaltered rhodopsin, a picture of the window with the clear pattern of its bars. (563-64)

Franz Boll reported his findings on rhodopsin to the Berlin Academy on November 12, 1876. Willy Kühne's optographic experiments were presented to the Naturhistorisch-Medizinischen of Heidelberg on January 5, 1877 and they were later published in the 1877 and 1878 issues of the *Untersuchungen aus dem Physiologischen Institut der Universität Heidelberg*. English translations of these articles appeared in England in 1878 in Michael Foster's *On the Photochemistry of the Retina and on Visual Purple.*[2] Subsequently, Boll's and Kühne's discoveries were featured in a variety of newspapers and international journals offering "current events" columns on science like *Fortnightly, Nature, Athenaeum, and the Nineteenth Century* in England, t*he Musée des Familles, Les Merveilles de la Science, Année scientifique et industrielle,* and the *Revue des Deux Mondes* in France, and in American periodicals like *Harper's Weekly*, *Scientific American,* and *The Chautauquan*.

Undoubtedly, the rapid technological advances made in (and the growing popularity of) photography throughout this period served to highlight these discoveries and to introduce them into public awareness.[3]

After all, the lesson seemed simple and very straightforward: the retina functioned like the photographic plate of a camera, therefore the final image viewed before death should remain fixed forever—like a photo—within the dead person's eyes. It also came to be believed (as a logical extension of this hypothesis) that if death were to occur at a moment when the pupils of the eyes were hugely dilated—e.g., because of fear, surprise, anger or some other strong emotion—the retinal optograms of the deceased would be even clearer, more detailed, and easier to "develop."[4]

Popular belief in these "facts" became so widespread during the final decades of the nineteenth century and the beginning of the twentieth that some police departments began to take close-up photographs of the eyes of murder victims in the hope of identifying their murderers. The most celebrated of such cases involved Scotland Yard's investigation of the infamous Jack-the-Ripper murders in Whitehall, London in 1888. One historian, in describing these events, notes:

> In an attempt to be scientific, the police pried open Annie Chapman's dead eyes and photographed them, in the hope that the retinas had retained an image of the last thing she saw. But no images were found. (Stewart-Gordon 121)

And another adds:

> The comparatively new science of forensic photography was called upon, and scene-of-crime photographs were admitted in evidence. ...
> Later, the curious ritual of photographing the victim's eyes was carried out. There was a theory that was to last well into the first quarter of the twentieth century that in cases of violent death the last images were fixed permanently to the retina of the eye. A photograph taken when the eye had been drawn a little way out of the socket could thus, it was believed, identify the killer.
> It was nonsense, of course, but it was a superstition that reached right into our own century... (Sharkey 83-4).

Murderers, in their turn, sometimes destroyed the eyes of their victims for fear that their image might be recorded therein. The case involving the murder of a certain Constable P.C. Gutteridge in England in 1927 was one of many such instances. As described by Richard Harrison in his book *Scotland Yard*:

> In the early hours of September 27, 1927, occurred a crime that shocked England with its brutality...
> In the very act of doing his duty Constable P.C. Gutteridge of the Essex constabulary was shot down. He was found by the roadside with four bullet wounds in his head, each fired from a distance of about ten inches. A shot had been fired through each eye, and it was believed by some at the time that the murderer had done this out of superstition. There is an old belief that a picture of the murderer is imprinted in the victim's eyes. (§5:74).

And in Brussels, in 1955, a court condemned to death two men who murdered the wife of one so that the other's daughter could then marry him. The remaining wife, a conspirator in the crime, was given three years in prison because she had "sewn the head-cape which was to prevent the victim from seeing her assassin and conserving his image on the retina of her eyes..." (Bornecque 62, n.1).

Finally, it would seem that this belief—at least in some sectors of the population—continues to persist even today. Witness, for example, the following article appearing in the August 1992 *Reader's Digest* about the Russian mafia in New York City:

> Police often found themselves powerless to intervene. Few refugee-immigrants dared to report crimes, much less identify those responsible. Reprisals, even againstfamily members, could be brutal. In one instance, the wife of a man who had crossed rival gangsters was stabbed to death. Then, in keeping with an ancient Russian custom, the killer gouged out her eyes in the belief that his image would be recorded in them. (Adams 34-5)

Or consider the February 22, 1993 television broadcast of the NBC *Today show*, where an American author is being interviewed about his newly-published book on a notorious Russian serial killer:

> BRYANT GUMBEL, co-host: When the Soviet Union fell, one of the most frightening stories to emerge was that of Andrei Chikatilo, the most savage serial killer in history. In all, Chikatilo murdered, mutilated, and cannibalized more than 50 women and children in a dozen years in and around the town of Rostov. Issa Kostoev, a special investigator, spent five years stalking Chikatilo, finally helping to bring him into custody in November of 1990 and gaining a full and gruesome confession nine days later when Chikatilo admitted to at least 52 murders—there were probably more. The murders, the manhunt, and confession are all detailed in *Hunting the Devil* by Richard Lourie....
>
> RICHARD LOURIE: He would gouge out the eyes of his victims. He hated eyes and genitals. That was part of his mania. And then there's a Russian superstition that the last thing that the victim sees, which is the image of the murderer, is imprinted on the eyes of the dying victim.5

Accordingly, in the light of such news items, it seems no exaggeration to assert that this particular belief has, for well over a century, continued to remain deeply rooted in the popular imagination.

Jules Verne was neither the first or last writer to use (or misuse) this piece of "scientific" data in his fiction. But he was one of the first [6] to incorporate it realistically—that is to say, without unduly spiritualizing it with metaphysics, twisting it to serve an ideological message, or extrapolating it into futuristic high-tech brain-scans.

The first literary work, to my knowledge, to use optograms was by the *décadent* French author Villiers de l'Isle-Adam in his short story "Claire Lenoir" (first published in 1867, later expanded into his 1887 novel called *Tribulat Bonhomet*)—a narrative described by Huysmans as having been "obviously derived from the tales of Edgar Poe."[7] With a satiric intent, Villiers portrays a self-assured positivist doctor called Tribulat Bonhomet who sets out to visit an old friend named Césaire Lenoir and his wife Claire near Saint-Malo. En route, he befriends a young English naval lieutenant named Henry Clifton who has recently had a brief affair with a married woman whose description seems strangely similar to that of Claire Lenoir. Dr Bonhomet and Henry Clifton part company; the former to spend a few weeks visiting the Lenoirs, while the latter ships out to the South Seas to cure himself of his ill-fated love. Bonhomet arrives in Saint-Malo, pauses to rest in a local café, and discovers a strange article in a newspaper which someone has left behind:

> I took up a newspaper that lay on the table—a local paper, dirty, torn, dated I know not how long ago....
> As I turned over the pages I saw a short article, inserted between a case of intrusion on the part of the Clergy and some recent recipe, which ran:
> "L'Académie des Sciences de Paris has stated the authenticity of certain surprising facts. It can be asserted that the animals destined to our nourishment—such as sheep, lambs, horses and cats, conserve in their eyes, after the butcher's death stroke, the impression of the objects they have seen before they die. It is a photograph of pavements, stalls, gutters, of vague figures, among which one almost always distinguishes that of the man who has slaughtered them; this endures until their decomposition. As one sees, our ignorance in this matter ought to be lessened by so curious a discovery." (§4:42)

Later that day, settled in at the Lenoir residence, Bonhomet and his hosts have lengthy philosophical discussions about life, death, reality, afterlife, and the nature of the soul. Césaire Lenoir suddenly falls ill. Just before his death, he somehow learns of his wife's infidelity, and he swears vengeance on his rival in the hereafter. One year later, Bonhomet and the widow Claire Lenoir meet. She is now on her deathbed, driven there by guilt and by persistent nightmares about her deceased husband who is standing in an exotic land, dressed as a bloodthirsty savage, and awaiting the arrival of his fated victim. Bonhomet is shocked: a few days earlier, he had received word that Henry Clifton had been brutally murdered, beheaded in Polynesia by a particularly ferocious member of a tribe of cannibals! The widow Lenoir then expires. Noticing a blurry image remaining in her eyes, Bonhomet examines them with the aid of his ophthalmoscope and discovers therein a horrific sight:

> In examining the eyes of the dead woman, I saw, distinctly, at first detach itself, as a frame, the stripe of violet paper that encircled the top of the wall. And, in this frame, reverberated in this fashion, I perceived a picture which no language, dead or alive...could, under the sun and under the moon, express in its unimaginable horror. ...
> I saw the skies, the far-off floods, a great rock, the night and the stars! And upright, on the rock, larger in height than the living, a man, like one of the natives of the Dangerous Sea, stood. Was he a man, this ghost? He lifted with one hand, towards the abyss, a bloody head, with dripping hair. With such a howl as I have never heard, but the horror of which I divined in the ignivomous distension of the hugely opened mouth, he seemed to devote himself to the destructiveness of shadow and space. In his other hand that hung, he held a stone cutlass, disgusting and red.

Around him, the horizon seemed to me endless—the solitude for ever accursed! And, under the expression of a supernatural fury, under the spasm of vengeance, of solemn wrath and of hate, I recognized instantly on the face of the Ottysor-Vampire, his *inexpressible resemblance* to *Césaire Lenoir* before his death and, in the severed head, the features, frightfully obscured, of the young man I had known, Sir Henry Clifton, the lost lieutenant!
Stumbling, arms extended, shivering like a child, I recoiled.
My reason fled from me: hideous, confused conjectures maddened and stupefied me. I was no more than a living chaos of anguish, a human rag, a brain as withered as chalk, pulverized under the immense menace! And Science, the old queen-sovereign with clear eyes, with perhaps too disinterested a logic, with her infamous embrace, sneered in my ear that she was not, she also, more than a lure of the Unknown that spies on us and waits for us—inexorable, implacable! (§20:219-22)8

The first reference to optograms quoted here (read in a newspaper by Bonhomet) is anecdotal and authoritatively scientific. It foreshadows and sets the stage for the second (witnessed by Bonhomet) which is spiritualistic and heavy with metaphysical implications. And, considered together, the author's narrative strategy becomes very apparent. Villiers, an avowed anti-science idealist and firm believer in the supernatural, has prepared and sprung a trap on his pompous anti-hero Bonhomet. This deathbed hallucination imprinted in Claire Lenoir's eyes—this "photo" of her vision—is well beyond the power of Science to explain. Yet it exists. Faced with this reality, Doctor Bonhomet's entire value system is abruptly shaken to its roots, reducing him to "a living chaos of anguish." And it is important to note that the story concludes at this point—Bonhomet is purposefully left hanging in existential crisis. His plight thus represents a dramatic consummation of his creator's satiric purpose, a kind of literary vengeance by Villiers on the hated philosophy of Positivism. It is obvious that Villiers' use of retinal images in "Claire Lenoir," brimming with irony and mysticism, stands in marked contrast to Verne's later more conservative portrayal. Villiers' approach, polemical rather than expository, is tailored to send a strong ideological message: that Science is wholly incapable of understanding the higher planes of human consciousness and the true nature of the universe.[9]

Another such "metaphysical" portrayal of optographic images occurs in Rudyard Kipling's 1891 short story titled "At the End of the Passage" (included in his collection *Life's Handicap*). The fictional setting is India during the 1880s. In the searing summer heat of India's provinces, three British civil servants get together every Sunday to play whist at the home of one of their countryman, a certain Doctor Spurstow. One of them, Hummil, complains of sleepless nights and bad dreams. The following week, he is found dead in his bed with a look of horror frozen upon his face. Doctor Spurstow examines the dead man and, noticing gray blurs in the pupils of his eyes, decides to photograph them for later study. Although the cause of his death remains uncertain, Hummil is buried. After the burial, his friends continue to wonder how he died:

> After breakfast, they smoked a pipe in silence to the memory of the dead. Then Spurstow said absently—
> "Tisn't in medical science."
> "What?"
> "Things in a dead man's eye."
> "For goodness' sake leave that horror alone!" said Lowndes. "I've seen a native die of pure fright when a tiger chivvied him. I know what killed Hummil."
> "The deuce you do! I'm going to try to see." And the doctor retreated into the bath-room with a Kodak camera. After a few minutes there was the sound of something being hammered to pieces, and he emerged, very white indeed.
> "Have you got a picture?" said Mottram. "What does the thing look like?"
> "It was impossible, of course. You needn't look, Mottram. I've torn up the films. There was nothing there. It was impossible."
> "That," said Lowndes very distinctly, watching the shaking hand striving to relight the pipe, "is a damned lie."
> Mottram laughed uneasily. "Spurstow's right," he said. "We're all in such a state now that we'd believe anything. For pity's sake let's try to be rational."
> There was no further speech for a long time. The hot wind whistled without, and the dry trees sobbed. Presently the daily train, winking brass, burnished steel, and spouting steam, pulled up panting in the intense glare. "We'd better go on that," said Spurstow. "Go back to work. I've written my certificate. We can't do any more good here, and work'll keep our wits together. Come on."
> No one moved. It is not pleasant to face railway journeys at mid-day in June. Sprustow gathered up his hat and whip, and, turning in the doorway, said—
> "There may be Heaven; there must be Hell.
> Meantime, there is our life here. We-ell?"
> Neither Mottram nor Lowndes had any answer to the question. (265-69)

Kipling's narrative suddenly ends at this point. The "things" in the dead man's eyes are never explained nor even described in detail. The reader is told only of the Doctor's horror when viewing the developed photographs and his immediate destruction of them. But, once again, the metaphysical implications of these photographic images—as astounding as they are understated in this story—cannot be denied: just as in Villiers' "Claire Lenoir" (which may well have served as Kipling's intertextual model), Hummil witnessed an "impossible" vision which terrified him and caused his death. And this nightmarish hallucination left its physical imprint upon the retinas of his dead eyes—either from within or, even more inexplicably, from without (having somehow become corporeal and exteriorized). Doctor Spurstow's initial reactions—similar to Doctor Bonhomet's—are disbelief, shock, and fear. But, unlike the fate of Villiers' protagonist, Kipling's character is allowed to overcome his crisis. Adopting a kind of Voltairian "cultivate one's garden" attitude, Spurstow suggests that they all simply "Go back to work" because "work'll keep our wits together." And it is now the reader who is left hanging—and wondering . . . .

Yet another unrealistic use of this scientific concept—this time twisting it to serve the needs of racist propaganda—occurs in Thomas Dixon, Jr.'s *The Clansman*, a novel published in 1905, which later served as the basis for D.W. Griffith's film, *The Birth of a Nation.* The narrative is set in the

Carolinas during the post-Civil War period of 1865-70 and, at one point, concerns the double suicide of a white mother (named, very suggestively, *Mrs. Lenoir*) and her daughter after they have been raped by a rampaging band of black men. The coroner's jury reports that they were killed by accidentally falling over a steep cliff known as Lovers' Leap, but Doctor Cameron—a friend of the family—suspects foul play. In a chapter entitled "*The Hunt for the Animal*," he decides to conduct an experiment:

> When the bodies reached the home, Doctor Cameron placed Mrs. Cameron and Margaret outside to receive visitors and prevent any one from disturbing him. He took Ben into the room and locked the doors.
> "My boy, I wish you to witness an experiment." He drew from its case a powerful microscope of French make.
> "What on earth are you going to do, sir?"
> The doctor's brilliant eyes flashed with a mystic light as he replied: "Find the fiend who did this crime—and then we will hang him on a gallows so high that all men from the rivers to the ends of the earth shall see and feel and know the might of an unconquerable race of men."
> "But there's no trace of him here."
> "We shall see," said the doctor, adjusting his instrument. "I believe that a microscope of sufficient power will reveal on the retina of these dead eyes the image of this devil as if etched there by fire. The experiment has been made successfully in France. ... "
> Ben watched him with breathless interest.
> He first examined Marion's eyes. But in the cold azure blue of their pure depths he could find nothing. "It's as I feared with the child," he said. "I can see nothing. It is on the mother I rely. In the splendour of life, at thirty-seven she was the full-blown perfection of womanhood with every vital force at its highest tension..."
> He looked long and patiently into the dead mother's eye, rose and wiped the perspiration from his face.
> "What is it, sir?" asked Ben.
> Without reply, as if in a trance, he returned to the microscope and again rose with the little quick nervous cough he gave only in the greatest excitement, and whispered: "Look now and tell me what you see."
> Ben looked and said: "I can see nothing."
> "Your powers of vision are not trained as mine," replied the doctor, resuming his place at the instrument.
> "What do you see?" asked the younger man, bending nervously.
> "The bestial figure of a negro—his huge black hand plainly defined—the upper part of his face is dim, as if obscured by a gray mist of dawn—but the massive jaws and lips are clear—merciful God!—it's Gus!" (§4.1:312-14)

Subsequently, the black man named Gus is located. He is bound and gagged, beaten, and dragged to a cave in the mountains by the white-cloaked members of the local chapter of the Ku Klux Klan (of whom Dr. Cameron is the secret leader). That night he is judged before a flaming cross, confesses his crimes, and is summarily executed by this "Order of the Invisible Empire" —who, incidentally, describe themselves as "an institution of Chivalry, Humanity, Mercy, and Patriotism: embodying in its genius and principles all that is chivalric in conduct, noble in sentiment, generous in manhood, and patriotic in purpose" (320).

While the blatant racism which oozes from the pages of this novel is very unsettling, the use of Science toward this end is perhaps even more disturbing. This particular episode illustrates how the popularization of certain scientific theories might be exploited to serve the needs of extremist propaganda. Doctor Cameron supposedly saw an image of the villainous Gus in Mrs. Lenoir's dead eyes—despite the fact that, scientifically, this image could not possibly have existed there. The reason is obvious: Gus's face was not the final thing Mrs Lenoir saw before dying! Consider the chronology of the event: immediately after the crime, "the mother cleaned and swept the room, piled the torn clothes and cord in the fireplace and burned them, dressed herself as for a walk, softly closed the doors, and hurried with her daughter along the old pathway through the moonlit woods" to the cliff (§3.12:305); and, there, the two victims exchanged last words of love and Christian faith before plunging to their deaths. Was the author of this novel unaware of his error? Or, in a more sinister twist, did he fully understand the science of optograms but chose instead to purposefully gloss over such annoying details—counting on the fact that the public's belief in the possibility of such retinal images would guarantee his Doctor's credibility? In either case, the reference to optograms in this text performs an invaluable function: to provide a believable "scientific" justification for hunting down and executing the black "devil" who was identified thereby.

As mentioned earlier, by the 1920s, the public's unquestioning belief in optograms began to wane—perhaps in part because of their continuously unrealistic portrayal in literature but, more importantly, because of their total lack of success in police murder investigations where they had been repeatedly searched for and never found. The very idea of post-mortal retinal images found itself demoted to the status of a mere "superstition" or a "legend." Witness, in this regard, the treatment given to it by the French author Maurice Renard in his very popular novel Les Mains d'Orlac (The Hands of Orlac) published in 1921.[10] After the mysterious murders in Paris of two noted spiritualists, the French police question the coroner who had performed the autopsies:

> Doctor Frouardet had performed the autopsies on both cadavers.
> "No," he was saying, "there was not the slightest indication, external or internal...."
> "And did you discover anything in the eyes?" asked M. Lambert-Gondat.
> "No, I found nothing in the eyes—although I did look—oh, I'm not hiding it—I did look. You know ... my many observations have led me to believe that a person who is killed does not retain, photographed on his retina, the picture of his last vision, which might furnish the means of discovering the murderer. In my opinion this is a legend." (§25:318-19)

During the 1920s, a relatively new literary genre was beginning to take root in the United States—offering futuristic stories which depicted not only "hard" science but also fictionalized science. It was through this new genre called science fiction that a modernized variant of the (now discredited) optogram eventually emerged: the necroscopic brain-scan. In this updated version, the location of the post-mortal images is now the brain itself instead of the eyes; a complex electronic instrument replaces the old-fashioned box camera as the device for extracting them; and (in some narratives) the reconstituted "last vision" no longer takes the form of a simple photograph, but is rather a motion picture or a hologram which can be played back like a video by the scientists.

An early precursor to this more extrapolative, science-fictional rendering of optograms can be found in an 1899 novel called *Dr. Berkeley's Discovery* by Richard Slee and Cornelia Pratt. The story goes like this:

An American physiologist named Dr. Berkeley makes a truly amazing discovery: by removing a piece of human brain from a recently-deceased person, dipping it in a fixative solution to prevent deterioration, briefly implanting it in an animal brain to reactivate it, and then examining it on a slide under a very powerful microscope, he succeeds in "developing" as photographs the visual images that the brain received just before death. He calls their source "memory cells."[11] About this time, a brutal crime occurs in New York: a young woman is found stabbed to death, and the alleged murderer is put on trial. The court has asked Dr. Berkeley to use his new procedure on the dead woman's brain and to offer testimony in the case:

> Being requested to describe the nature of his evidence, he rehearsed briefly but with absolute lucidity his theory of the memory cells, and the progress of his work, to prove that theory. ...
>
> When Berkeley had concluded the account of his experiments, he stated that he had brought with him a number of sections from the brain of Mme. Massoneau, feeling that his evidence would best be presented to the court in the same form in which it had come to him. ...
>
> He stated that, as the memory cells were visible only with the aid of a microscope of the highest power, which required an expert to manipulate it, he had photographed some of the brain sections, and would attach the resulting slides to a stereopticon. If the Court would order the room darkened, he would throw the pictures that the slides held upon the white wall, where they could be seen by all. ...
>
> It flashed upon the wall, and the crowd saw against the background of a commonplace room, identical in all points with the photograph of that hotel parlour where the murder had taken place, the prisoner's figure.
>
> As it wavered to its place on the screen, it seemed by some odd illusion to be moving down toward them from the wall. The face was distorted with a blind, unreasoning fury, and in one hand was the daggar, raised to strike. ...
>
> The tumult grew uncontrollable. Such scenes had never been known in that grave room before. Only the quickness of the sheriff and his deputies prevented the crowd from falling upon the senseless man, and tearing him to pieces. The case of the State vs. Massoneau was over, and the verdict rendered by popular acclaim. (§14:192-200)

The idea that a person's memory is carried in the brain as photographs within "memory cells" may seem somewhat quaint to those of us living in the late twentieth century. But it is instructive to note that, even today, modern science still has no clear understanding of how human memory works. Despite decades of major technological advances like the development of EEGs (electroencephalograms), CAT scans (computerized axial tomography), MRI scans (magnetic resonance imaging), and PETT scans (positron emission transaxial tomography), brain scientists are still far from agreeing as to exactly how this organ processes, stores, and retrieves memories. Laboratory experiments from the 1950s seem to have shown that memory cannot be localized in any specific part of the brain. But, beyond this, the biological mystery of how memory operates in the human brain continues to be largely unresolved. Witness, for example, what a few scientific experts have recently said on this topic:

> The mechanism of memory remains far from clear. (Hart 153)
>
> We are just beginning to gain some understanding of the brain systems that code and store these various aspects of memory. (Thompson 303)
>
> At present the world of brain science is in the middle of...a revolution. Scientists now regard the brain as a hormonally driven gland, not an electrically driven computer. ... As gravity is the great unknown in physics, memory is the great enigma of brain science. (Bergland 93, 120)
>
> ...a mass of conflicting evidence in a bitterly contested field. (Rose 200)

Most modern hypotheses for how the brain creates memory can be divided into two basic groups: electricity-based theories (modifiable synapses, hologramic distribution, network redundancies, etc.) and molecular-hormonal theories (proteins, peptides, RNA, etc.). To adequately outline these various hypotheses would require much more time and space than can be afforded here. But it is important to simply point out that human memory is not yet fully understood, and that it will undoubtedly someday prove to be a complex combination of both neurological and molecular-hormonal functions working together within the brain.

In SF, one of the earliest 20th-century portrayals of a high-tech memory scanner seems especially interesting in this regard—all the more so since it occurs in a trilogy of novels published during the heyday of radio and (perhaps not coincidentally) around the time of the development of the EEG in 1929-34. This curious piece of technology, called a "mechanical educator," appears (repeatedly) in Edward E. Smith's famous *Skylark* series of 1928-1935. It is not only capable of reading the accumulated memories of both the living and the recently dead but also of transferring those memories directly into the brain of the examiner or onto an external "record" for later play-back. This device was first developed by a certain

Dunark, the Kofedix or Crown Prince of the nation of Kondal, on the green planet called Osnome thousands of light-years from Earth. The novel's hero Dick Seaton, after travelling there with his companions in his spheroid spaceship "Skylark," borrows this technology and improves upon it. He explains how this extraordinary machine works:

> "This is an improved model—it has quite a few gadgets of my own in it. Now, Mart, as to how it works—it isn't so funny after you understand it—it's a lot like a radio in that respect. It operates on a band of frequencies lying between the longest light and heat waves and the shortest radio waves. This thing here is the generator of those waves and a very heavy power amplifier. The headsets are stereoscopic transmitters, taking or receiving a three-dimensional view. Nearly all matter is transparent to those waves; for instance bones, hair, and so on. However, cerebin, a cerebroside peculiar to the thinking structure of the brain, is opaque to them. Dunark, not knowing chemistry, didn't know why the educator worked or what it worked on—he found out by experiment that it did work; just as we found out about electricity. This three-dimensional model, or view, or whatever you want to call it, is converted into electricity in the headsets, and the resulting modulated wave goes back to the educator. There it is heterodyned with another wave—this second frequency was found after thousands of trials and is, I believe, the exact frequency existing in the optic nerves themselves—and sent to the receiving headset. Modulated as it is, and producing a three-dimensional picture, after rectification in the receiver, it reproduces exactly what has been 'viewed,' if due allowance has been made for the size and the configuration of the different brains involved in the transfer. ...
>
> I had a big advantage in knowing that cerebrin was the substance involved, and with that knowledge I could carry matters considerably farther than Dunark could in his original model. I can transfer the thoughts of somebody else to a third party or to a record. Dunark's machine couldn't work against resistance—if the subject wasn't willing to give up his thoughts he couldn't get them. This one can take them away by force. In fact, by increasing the plate and grid voltages in the amplifier, I can pretty nearly burn out a man's brain. Yesterday, I was playing with it, transferring a section of my own brain to a magnetized tape—for a permanent record, you know—and found out that above certain rather low voltages it becomes a form of torture that would make the best efforts of the old Inquisition seem like a petting party." (Smith, Skylark Three, §4:33-35)

As the interplanetary plot unfolds, the narratological importance of the "mechanical educator" in these novels becomes instantly apparent. With its use Seaton succeeds in transferring to his own mind—and to the ship's permanent "record"—a wealth of knowledge from highly advanced alien civilizations, gleaned directly from the brains of their most enlightened scientists and rulers. And he is later able to discover secret invasion plans from both the living and newly-dead brains of a viciously bellicose race called the Fenachrone who are seeking to conquer the galaxy, but whom Seaton and his allies manage to defeat in the end. Another much less "space-opera" variant of such brain-reading devices occurs in Stanislaw Lem's 1967 SF novel *The Invincible*. The crew of the spaceship Invincible has landed on the desert planet Regis III in a far sector of the galaxy. They have come to investigate the sudden disappearance of their sister ship

Condor. After an extensive search of the planet, they finally locate the remains of the *Condor*: the ship is intact, but its interior has been ransacked, its bulkheads strangely pock-marked, and its entire crew killed. One crewmember's body, however, is found to be perfectly preserved; he had apparently stumbled into the ship's hibernator during the crisis and had frozen to death. *The Invincible's* physician Dr. Nygren, assisted by the neuro-physiologist Sax, examines the victim's body along with the ship's navigator Rohan. They attempt to "read" the dead crew member's brain:

> Nygren...picked up a small black satchel off the floor, opened it and pulled out that apparatus about which Rohan had heard so much but which he had never seen until now. With slow, almost pedantic movements, Sax began to untangle the cords whose ends had flat electrodes attached to them. He placed six electrodes against the dead man's skull and fastened them with an elastic band. Then he crouched down and pulled three pairs of headphones out of the satchel. He put on one of these and kept testing the buttons of the machine inside a plastic case. His eyes were closed, his face bore an expression of deepest concentration. ...
>
> This apparatus was referred to by the space crews as the "corpse-spy." With it one could "auscultate the brain" of recently deceased persons, or those dead in whom decay had not yet set in, or a body like this one that had been preserved by very low temperatures. Long after death had occurred one could ascertain what the last conscious thoughts and emotions had been.
>
> The apparatus sent electrical impulses into the brain; there they followed the path of least resistance, moving along those nerve tendrils that had formed one functional entity during the preagonal phase. The results were never too reliable, but it was said to have obtained extraordinarily significant data on many occasions. In cases like the present one, use of the "corpse-spy" was clearly indicated. (§3:52-3)

The "corpse-spy" does its job, and the final scenes viewed by the dead crew member are retrieved and observed. But (in typical Lemian fashion) the results are far from definitive:

> At first he heard nothing but the humming of the current...he tightly squeezed his eyelids together.
>
> Suddenly he could perceive clearly...It looked like one of the corridors inside the *Condor*; there were pipes running along the ceiling. The passage was totally blocked by human bodies that seemed to move. But it was only the image that was waving to and fro. The people were half-naked; shreds of clothing barely covered them. Their skin was unnaturally white and was sprinkled with dark spots like some kind of a rash. Perhaps these spots were not on the skin but were a peculiar visual phenomenon, for they were scattered everywhere: tiny black dots on the floor and the walls. The entire image seemed to fluctuate like a blurred photograph taken through a deep layer of flowing water. The picture seemed to stretch, then contracted again, billowing and swaying. ...
>
> [Rohan] stammered: "But what did that mean?"
>
> Sax unzipped his protective suit. ..."I don't know any more than you do," he answered. "Maybe even less." (§3:54-5)

It is important to note that, in Lem's portrayal of the necroscopic brain-scan, the reconstituted images are perceived *within the brains* of the examiners themselves (rather than, for example, on an external viewing screen). As such, they are prone to subjective interference—a kind of automatic "uncertainty principle" ignored by most earlier SF works. In fact, unlike all the previous narratives we have examined, here the victim's final vision proves useless: it solves no mystery, incriminates no one, and provides no immediate answer to the riddle facing the protagonists. Of course, this episode occurs near the beginning of the novel, and it would be narratologically self-defeating to do otherwise. But, Lem seems also to be offering in this passage an ironic commentary on the value of technology as it relates to human comprehension: "The results were never too reliable..." "I don't any more than you do...Maybe even less."

That is to say, it is still the human brain which is ultimately responsible for the "meaning" of the images procured. It is only when the brain interprets the visual images captured (by the machine, as by the eye) that real perception occurs. And it is at this crucial juncture—the point of interface between the objective and the subjective—that all "scientific" explanations for phenomena observed in the "real" world take place: in the human brain. Thus, what Lem appears to be underscoring in this episode (as elsewhere in his oeuvre) recalls a similar epistemological question once raised by Flaubert in his highly satirical *Bouvard et Pécuchet*. After receiving a lengthy lesson in astronomy from his science-enthralled friend Pécuchet, the naïve Bouvard suggests quite simply: "Science is constructed according to data furnished by only one corner of space. Perhaps it doesn't fit in with the remainder that we are unaware of and cannot discover" (779).

Much less postmodern in tone (although still able to generate a certain "sense of wonder") are the necroscopic brain-scans portrayed in much SF cinema and television of the latter 20th century. For example, Roy Ward Baker's 1968 British film *Five Million Years to Earth* features an "unconscious vision machine" which successfully reads the multimillion-year old racial memories of a locust-like alien found in a spacecraft beneath the city of London. Douglas Trumbull's 1983 film *Brainstorm* depicts a team of scientists who develop an electronic mechanism that (à la E.E. Smith) records directly from the brain and stores on magnetic tape the totality of an individual's sensorial perceptions—which can then be transferred to another who experiences them as if they were his/her own. The British SF television series *Doctor Who* aired a segment in 1975 titled "The Ark in Space" wherein a scientist removes a portion of the brain from a dead insect-like alien called a Wirran and stimulates it to recapture memories of the creature's last thoughts. And, as recently as this past year, during the CBS television broadcast premiere of *Space Rangers* on January 6, 1993, the hero Captain Boon and Fort Hope's science officer Mimmer recreate a 3-D hologram of the final moments of a murdered man by "reading" the dead man's cerebral cortex with a high-tech scanner that is sensitive to certain residual radioactive elements in the brain.

There are doubtlessly many other films and TV serials containing this particular topos, but one which I find exemplary is William Castle's *Project X*, a grade-B SF film from 1968 based on Leslie P. Davies' two novels The *Artificial Man* (1965) and *Psychogeist* (1967). The year is 2118. The world's geopolitical future is precariously balanced between the Western powers and Sino-Asia, both of whom, wishing to avoid thermonuclear war, have agreed to an uneasy truce but continue to search for other weapons to destroy their rivals and expand their empires. A certain Doctor Crowther, who had earlier developed a serum to erase a soldier's memory in the event of his capture, is now asked by the Western government to reverse this process and recover
the lost memories of one of their top spies, Hagan Arnold, who was captured by the Sino-Asians but then managed to escape. Arnold's final message to the West at the moment of his capture was: "The West will be destroyed in fourteen days...repeat...fourteen days..." Dr. Crowther assembles a team of scientists, and they construct a "laser pictograph" to reconstitute Arnold's lost memories. The procedure is explained as follows:

> Dr. Tarbin: These holograms are images or pictures to be transmitted by laser beam instead of short wave or microwave. We can send any image or we can record any image. These images appear to the eye to be in solid form, although they are not.
>
> Dr. Crowther: Before he left on his Sino-Asian mission, Arnold took a crash course in the Oriental language. For several months, he was shown symbols as a method of instruction. This instruction has conditioned his mind to receive holograms. So we are going to transmit the facts we have in the hope that, when we get to the episode we don't know about, our action will reactivate his memory. The laser pictograph, as Dr. Tarbin has indicated, will be our means of input and it will also show us exactly what is going on in Hagan Arnold's mind.

Electrodes are attached to Arnold's head and the memory-stimulation procedure begins. Several "lost" memories of Arnold's activites in Sino-Asia are recovered—including his rescue of another Western agent named Gregory Gallea (who had been presumed dead) and their subsequent escape from their captors. But at this point in the memory play-back, Arnold's brain suddenly resists—projecting into the laboratory a huge ectoplasmic apparition of his face, hovering above them and screaming. Unable to continue the experiment, Dr. Crowther searches for a rational explanation for this unexpected apparition, saying to his superiors:

> Dr. Crowther: The lines on these EEGs are impulses, aren't they? Impulses which we measure electrically—in other words, energy.
>
> Col. Collins: All right.
>
> Dr. Crowther: Then you do admit that the brain is capable of producing a form of energy?
>
> Col. Collins: Yes, I understand all that but . . .
>
> Dr. Crowther: Ah, then why cannot this energy, under certain circumstances, become so strong that it develops its own motive power?

Col Collins: To move at its own will?

Dr. Crowther: Yes, why not? There is still one third of the brain that is an absolute mystery to us, Colonel. I submit to you that the phenomenon that we saw in that room was really a form of energy created by Arnold's brain.

Col. Collins: Next you'll be talking about the Id and the Superego.

Dr. Crowther: Call it anything you like. I believe that our holograms released an energy, and that now that energy stands between us and the truth. We have failed.

During this time Gregory Gallea joins the group and accuses Dr. Crowther of treason and complicity with the Sino-Asians in having purposefully sabotaged the experiment. In response, Colonel Collins demands that the laser pictograph's prodding of Arnold's memory continue, regardless of his subconscious resistance (and that of his exteriorized psychic projection) to their efforts. Dr. Crowther protests strenuously, but is forced to comply. Predictably, the ghostly apparition appears again and prevents any further brain-scan but, this time, it kills Gregory Gallea. The experiment now seems to have failed utterly. One of the West's top espionage agents is dead, the other has incurable amnesia, and an attack by the Sino-Asians' secret weapon is imminent. But Dr. Crowther suddenly has an inspiration:

Col. Cowen: All right, Dr. Tarbin, cremate the body.

Dr. Crowther: No, don't! Don't destroy that body! This may be our chance!

Col. Cowen: Chance? For what?

Dr. Crowther: Gallea and Arnold were together. They shared the secret.

Col. Cowen: Doctor, this man is dead—he's stone dead!

Dr. Crowther: Wait! The body is clinically dead—that's correct, Colonel. But the brain cells are still alive!

Dr. Tarbin: If we operate quickly, there's a chance, Colonel. A slim chance!

Dr. Crowther: Look at it this way, Colonel. You have nothing to lose. If necrosis hasn't set in, if the skull fracture hasn't destroyed too much tissue, we may succeed.

Col. Cowen: In getting a dead man's brain to reveal information?

Dr. Crowther: Yes, by the same use of holograms.

Gallea's brain is extracted, set into a spheroid-shaped nutrient bath, hooked up to the laser pictograph's electrodes, and his memories are perused. It is discovered, to everyone's astonishment, that Gallea himself was the real traitor—during their arranged "escape," he had injected Arnold with the Sino-Asians' secret weapon: "a bacterial culture combining all the plague diseases of the Middle Ages" designed to decimate the West's population who, for decades, have had no knowledge of sickness. Worse, they had all been exposed to this lethal bug during the experiment itself! As panic grows, Dr. Crowther quarantines the area. Then he realizes that, since the dying Hagan Arnold had been cryonically frozen for a week immediately after his return to the West and had been revived only when his injuries were no longer life-threatening, they had seven days left before the virus would activate—time enough to develop an effective antidote! The antidote is quickly created and distributed, Hagan Arnold is "programmed" for a new life, Dr. Crowther is vindicated, the West is saved, and (in a final irony) Gregory Gallea's brain is preserved in the hope of revealing other bio-military secrets of Sino-Asia!

Obviously, this particular SF tale combines a number of primary and secondary characteristics which have become common in this sort of fiction since the nineteenth century: the mysterious presence of metaphysical, exteriorized psychic projections (Villiers, Kipling), the politico-legalistic motivations for attempting such memory retrieval in the first place (Verne, Slee), the xenophobia (Dixon), and the use of high-tech brain-scanners to record such latent memories (Smith, Lem), among others. In this regard, *Project X* stands as a kind of one-stop-shopping warehouse of topoi associated with this theme. But it might also be seen as representing something more: mingling together elements of SF, fantasy, the supernatural, horror, spy fiction, and detective fiction, it exemplifies a hybridized breed of narrative that, in many ways, seems quite symptomatic of the growing heterogeneity of these literary/cinematic genres during the past few decades of the late twentieth century.

From laboratory to legend to literature and cinema, optograms and their variants have, for almost one hundred and fifty years, continued to fascinate scientists, storytellers, and the public at large. From a photo in a dead man's eye to futuristic necroscopic brain-scans, the possibility of "reading the dead" with the aid of Science, albeit still unrealized, remains a surprisingly persistent notion—one which might even be called a deep-rooted obsession, given its enduring cognitive and affective appeal. But, for those interested in the history of SF and other forms of scientific narrative, it also provides a unique opportunity to witness how science can sometimes evolve into pseudo-science, become firmly anchored in popular belief, and then develop into a recurring touchstone for the fictional imagination.

NOTES

1. See Drougard, pp. 78-81. All translations are by me unless otherwise indicated. Many thanks to my co-editors of SFS, our editorial consultants, and all my "virtual" friends on the Humanist e-mail network for their advice and suggestions during my preparation of this article—in particular, Istvan Csicsery-Ronay Jr, Vivian Sobchack, Abbie Angharad Hughes, and Stan Kulikowski II.

2. See Shipley and Crescitelli, pp. 1252-1323.

3. In this regard, note the mini-portrait "carte-de-visite" craze of the 1850s, the wide popularity of "stereographs" throughout the 1860s and 1870s, and especially George Eastman's development of the first do-it-yourself "Kodak" camera in 1888 which brought inexpensive amateur photography (and a familiarity with photographic principles) to millions world-wide. See Lemagny and Rouillé, pp. 38-41, 80.

4. In reality, these popular assumptions go well beyond the facts. The retina does not act like a *permanent* photographic plate (as common belief would have it) but rather, in the words of Kühne, as an "entire photographic workshop, in which the workman continually renews the plate by laying on new light-sensitive material, while simultaneously erasing the old." Therein lies the crux of the problem. As further explained by one expert in the field:

> It is a very romantic idea but, for a start, under normal daylight conditions there is very little rhodopsin in the retina; it is only used for dawn, dusk, and night vision. It would be pointless to try to recover an image unless it had been formed under conditions of low illuminations, rod vision not cone vision, and there would have to have been no been no illumination of the eye from the moment the image was seen to the time of fixation on the retina. Even the best images that we can see by nocturnal vision actually depend on quite small local differences in the concentration of rhodospin which would be enormously difficult to measure without using the sensitive neural apparatus of the dead eye to detect it (don't even think it—the retinal nerve cells die within minutes of the cessation of blood flow). Further, our eyes are in continual motion, and the pigment is locally bleached and restored as we look from one place to another. The only image on the retina at death is the last one seen. Normally functioning eyes need an exposure time, as it were, of some ten milliseconds or so to see a new "picture," but experiments in the last century required several minutes to get a very crude image of a window on the completely stationary retina of a rabbit. Before that, the rabbit had been kept in the dark for a long time to maximize the amount of rhodospin. Only if a person has stared fixedly at a bright object for several minutes before death, or less hopefully a dark one on a light background, having previously been in the dark, would even crude imagery be available for development. If their eyes had shut at death, the amount of light coming through the lids would still be enough to bleach the image if the retina were not removed and fixed immediately. The fictional accounts are all fantasy. —Abbie Angharad Hughes, Institute of Advanced Studies, Canberra, e-mail message to me on July 3, 1993.

Of course, it is still *theoretically* possible—if all the proper conditions are met: e.g., if the individuals stared for a few minutes at a brightly lit object before dying, if they closed their eyes immediately upon death and remained in a darkened room, if their eyes were rapidly excised and the retinal tissue removed and bathed in an alum solution, etc.—i.e., if Kühne's experiments were systematically duplicated with a human eye. In fact, Kühne himself once attempted this. As explained by George Wald:

> In the nearby town of Bruchsal on November 16, 1880, a young man was beheaded by guillotine. Kühne had made arrangements to receive the corpse. He had prepared a dimly lighted room screened with red and yellow glass to keep any

rhodopsin left in the eyes from bleaching further. Ten minutes after the knife had fallen he obtained the whole retina from the left eye, and had the satisfaction of seeing and showing to several colleagues a sharply demarcated optogram printed upon its surface. To my knowledge it is the only human optogram on record. Kühne went to great pains to determine what this optogram represented. He says: "A search for the object which served as source for this optogram remained fruitless, in spite of a thorough inventory of all the surroundings and reports from many witnesses." (564)

5. I have asked a number of Russian and Slavic language professors about this supposedly "old Russian superstition," and none have ever heard of it. My guess, barring proof to the contrary, is that this belief did not originate in Russia and, in fact, did not predate the nineteenth century.

6. Another, also a murder mystery, is Cleveland Moffett's "On the Turn of a Coin" published in April 1900 in *The Black Cat*. And Moffett's tale is even more scientifically correct than Verne's in that the victim "closed her eyes with fright at the very moment when she saw the murderer, and never opened them since" (27) thereby, ostensibly, preserving the final image on her retinas for later inspection.

7. J.-K. Huysmans. *A Rebours* (Paris: UGE, 1975), p. 297. This controversial novel was originally published in 1884.

8. These two translations are from Villiers de l'Isle-Adam, Claire Lenoir (trans. Arthur Symons), NY: Albert & Charles Boni, 1925.

9. It is also interesting to note that Villiers' short story *"Claire Lenoir"* was originally written in 1867, or nine years before Boll's and Kühne's much-acclaimed discoveries. So what were his sources? *The Académie des Sciences de Paris* report on retinal images quoted by Villiers is pure fiction and never occurred. So how did Villiers come up with this idea almost a decade before it was to become common knowledge? The answer to this riddle might well be a French newspaper report published on September 26, 1863 in the *Publicateur des Côtes-du-Nord,* as cited in J. Bollery, *La Bretagne de Villiers de l'Isle-Adam* (Saint-Brieuc: Presses bretonnes, 1961), and translated as follows:

> An English photographer, Mr. Warner, has had the idea of reproducing on collodion the eye of a steer a few hours after its death. Examining this under the microscope, he perceived quite distinctly on the retina the lines of the cobblestone floor of the slaughterhouse, the last object viewed by the animal as its head was lowered to receive its deathblow. This experiment is even more successful, according to its author, if it is done at a moment closer to actual death. Therefore, if one reproduced by photography the eyes of a murdered person, and if one operated within 24 hours of the death, one could discern on the retinas with the aid of a microscope the last thing that was present before the eyes of the victim. (110)

Whether or not this particular newspaper report was the true source of Villiers' use of retinal images in "Claire Lenoir" is of less importance that the realization that experiments on this phenomenon were, in fact, being undertaken (by photographers, among others) apparently *long before* the "official" scientific explanations offered by Boll and Kühne in the late 1870s.

By way of corroboration, an even earlier indication comes from R.W. Hackwood (cited in Alexander Kelly's *Jack the Ripper*, 26) who, in an issue of Notes and Queries published on October 3, 1857, registers his surprise and scepticism about a then-recent article in the *New York Observer.* Hackwood quotes the article at length, saying:

> The astonishing and intensely interesting fact was recently announced in the English papers of a discovery, that the last image formed on the retina of the eye of a dying person remains impressed upon it as on a daguerrean plate. Thus it was alleged that if the last object seen by a murdered person was his murderer, the portrait drawn upon the eye would remain a fearful witness in death to detect

> the guilty, and lead to his conviction. A series of experiments have recently been made (Aug. 1857) by Dr. Pollock has made he has found that an examination of the retina of the eye with a microscope reveals a wonderful as well as beautiful sight, and that in almost every instance there was a clear, distinct, and marked impression. We put these facts upon record in the hope of wakening an interest in the subject, that others may be induced to enter upon these interesting experiments, and the cause of science be advanced. The recent examination of the eye of J.H. Beardsley, who was murdered in Auburn, conducted by Dr. Sandford, corresponds with those made elsewhere. The following is the published account of the examination: "At first we suggested the saturation of the eye in a weak solution of atrophine, which evidently produced an enlarged state of the pupil. On observing this we touched the end of the optic nerve with the extract, when the eye instantly became protuberant. We now applied a powerful lens, and discovered in the pupil the rude worn-away figure of a man with a light coat, beside whom was a round stone standing or suspended in the air, with a small handle stuck as it were in the earth. The remainder was debris, evidently lost from the destruction of the optic, and its separation from the mother brain. Had we performed this operation when the eye was entire in the socket, with all its powerful connection with the brain, there is not the least doubt that we should have detected the last idea and impression made on the mind and eye of the unfortunate man. The thing would evidently be entire, and perhaps we should have had the contour, or better still, the exact figure of the murderer." (268-69)

I have been unable to pursue these references any farther back than 1857. But it seems more than mere coincidence that many (if not all) of the earliest experiments on this phenomenon appear to have occurred during the years immediately following Hemholtz's invention of the *ophtalmoloscope* in 1850.

10. The quotation from this novel is taken from its English translation, *The Hands of Orlac*, trans. Florence Crewe-Jones (NY: E.P. Dutton, 1929), pp. 318-19. Another, somewhat later, reference of this sort occurs in Graham Greene's 1940 novel *The Power and the Glory*: "The priest sat hopelessly at the man's side: nothing now would shift that violent brain towards peace... There was a legend believed by many criminals that dead eyes held the picture of what they had last seen—a Christian could believe that the soul did the same..." (§2:254)

11. The inspiration for Dr. Berkeley's fictional "discovery" may well have been more than just a simple extrapolation of retinal optograms into brain "memory cells." An anonymous letter to the editor published on January 15, 1888 in the *New-York Daily Tribune* with the headline "Brain Pictures—A Photo-Physiological Discovery" discusses in detail the experiences of a doctor who claims to have found "curious markings which...did not belong to the ordinary structure" in the brain cells of a recently-deceased linguist who was "distinguished for his linguistic attainments." The markings were subsequently identified as "characters in the Ethiopic, ancient Seriac and Phoenician languages." The doctor's letter concludes:

> If anything practical shall result from this discovery, if for instance, future literary executors shall be able to extract from the distinguished dead posthumous poems, suppressed opinions, the contents of "burned letters," family secrets or the mysteries of life that are buried, it will be a truly remarkable achievement of science; but whole lives of patient experiment and profound study must be expended upon a perplexing field of investigation before such a marvellous result can be attained. My own business claims too much of my time to permit me to give the mysterious subject that attention it requires, but now that I have suggested its possibilities, there are without doubt others who will eagerly explore this hitherto unknown realm. New-York, Dec. 28, 1887. (6)

Perhaps not surprisingly, I have been unable to locate a record of any follow-up medical experiments to indicate that, in fact, "others" did "eagerly explore this hitherto unknown realm" after the publication of this letter.

WORKS CITED

Adams, Nathan M. *"Menace of the Russian Mafia," The Reader's Digest* (Aug. 1992), pp. 34-35.
Bergland, Richard. *The Fabric of Mind.* NY: Viking, 1985.
Bleiler, Everett F. *Science-Fiction: The Early Years.* Kent State UP: 1990.
Bornecque, Jacques-Henry. *Villiers de l'Isle-Adam: créateur et visionnaire.* Paris: Nizet, 1974.
"Brain Pictures." New-York Daily Tribune, Jan. 15, 1888: 6.
Brainstorm. Dir. Douglas Trumbull, MGS/United Artists, USA, 1983.
Davies, L.P. *The Artificial Man.* Garden City, NY: Doubleday, 1965.
————. *Psychogeist.* Garden City, NY: Doubleday, 1967.
Dixon, Thomas Jr. *The Clansman.* NY: Doubleday, Page & Co., 1905.
Drougard, E. Villiers de l'Isle-Adam, *Les Trois Premiers Contes (édition critique) tome II.* Paris: Ed. Belles Lettres, 1931.
Five Million Years to Earth (in England, *Quatermass and the Pit*). Dir. Roy Baker, Hammer Films, UK, 1968.
Flaubert, Gustave. *Bouvard et Pécuchet in Oeuvres complètes,* Paris: Gallimard, "Pléiade," 1952. Originally published in 1881.
Greene, Graham. *The Power and the Glory.* 1940. NY: Viking Press, 1951.
Hackwood, R.W. "Impressions on the Eye," Notes and Queries #92 (Oct. 3, 1857), pp. 268-69.
Harrison, Richard. *Scotland Yard.* Chicago/NY: Ziff-Davis Publishing Co., 1949. Originally published as *Whitehall* 1212 (London: Jarrolds Ltd., 1948).
Hart, Leslie. *How the Brain Works.* NY: Basic Books, 1975.
Huysmans, J.-K. *A Rebours.* Paris: UGE, 1975. Originally published in 1884.
Joyce, James. *Ulysses.* 1922. A Critical and Synoptic Edition. NY: Garland, 1984.
Kelly, Alexander. *Jack the Ripper: A Bibliography and Review of the Literature.* London: Assoc. of Asst. Librarians, 1984.
Kipling, Rudyard. "At the End of the Passage." *Life's Handicap: Being Stories of Mine Own People.* By Kipling. NY: Doubleday, Doran & Co., 1931. 244-69.
Lem, Stanislaw. *The Invincible.* NY: Penguin Books, 1976. First published in Polish as *Niezwyezony* (Cracow: Wydawnietwo, 1967).
Lemagny, Jean-Claude and André Rouillé, eds. *A History of Photography.* Trans. Janet Lloyd, NY: Cambridge UP, 1987.
Moffett, Cleveland. "On the Turn of a Coin," *The Black Cat* #55:22-28, April 1900.
NBC's Today television broadcast (transcript), Feb. 22, 1993, 7:00-9:00 AM.
Project X. Dir. William Castle, Paramount, USA, 1968.
Renard, Maurice. Les Mains d'Orlac. Verviers, Belgium: M
Renard, Maurice. *Les Mains d'Orlac.* Verviers, Belgium: Marabout, 1970. Originally published (in feuilleton format) in the daily newspaper *L'Intransigeant,* May 15 to July 12, 1920. Originally published (in volume): Paris: Nilson, 1921. Published in English as The *Hands of Orlac,* trans. Florence Crewe-Jones, NY: E.P. Dutton, 1929.
Rose, Steven. *The Conscious Brain.* NY: Knopf, 1975.
Sharkey, Terrence. *Jack the Ripper: 100 Years of Investigation.* NY: Dorset Press, 1987.
Shipley, T. and F. Crescitelli. *Visual Photochemistry: The Beginnings.* NY: Pergamon Press, 1979.
Slee, Richard & Cornelia Pratt. *Dr. Berkeley's Discovery.* NY: Putnam, 1899.
Smith, Edward E. *The Skylark of Space.* NY: Pyramid, 1970. Originally published in *Amazing Stories* (Aug.-Oct. 1928).
Skylark Three. NY: *Pyramid,* 1973. Originally published in *Amazing Stories* (Aug.-Sept. 1930).
Skylark of Valeron. NY: Pyramid, 1973. Originally published in *Astounding Stories* (Aug.-Feb. 1934-35).
Stewart-Gordon, James. *"The Enduring Mystery of Jack the Ripper,"* The Reader's Digest, June 1973: 119-23.

Thompson, Richard F. *The Brain: An Introduction to Neuroscience.* NY: Freeman 1991.
Verne, Jules. *Les Frères Kip*. Paris: Hetzel, 1902.
Villiers de l'Isle-Adam, Jean-Marie Philippe-Auguste, comte de. "Claire Lenoir" *Revue des Lettres et des Arts*, Oct. 13-Dec. 1, 1867. Later incorporated into his novel *Tribulat Bonhomet* (Paris: Tresse et Stock, 1887). English translation: *Claire Lenoir*, trans. Arthur Symons (NY: Albert & Chas. Boni, 1925).
Wald, George. "Eye and Camera," *Scientific American Reader.* NY: Simon & Schuster, 1953. 555-68.

Kremer, Dr.Richard

Associate Professor of History at Dartmouth College, Hanover, New Hampshire

Professor Kremer teaches courses in the history of science, medicine and technology. He earned his PhD in History of Science from Harvard and specializes in European science from the fifteenth through the nineteenth centuries. His books include *The Thermodynamics of Life and Experimental Physiology* (Garland 1990), a study of experiment in nineteenth-century medicine; *Letters of Hermann von Helmholtz to His Wife, 1849-1859* (Steiner 1990), an edition of early letters by a leading German physicist and cultural icon; and *The Practice of Alfonsine Astronomy in the Fifteenth Century* (forthcoming), an analysis of early printed almanacs. Kremer's current research examines responses to Copernican astronomy in astrological calendars printed between 1543-1630. His work has been supported by grants from the National Endowment for the Humanities, National Science Foundation, Humboldt Foundation, and the Howard Foundation.

Originally published, with notes, in *Biology integrating scientific fundamentals: Contributions to the history of interrelations between biology, chemistry, and physics from the 18th to the 20th centuries*, pp. 359-81. Ed. Brigitte Hoppe. Munich: Institut für Geschichte der Naturwissenschaften, 1997. Reprinted with permission.

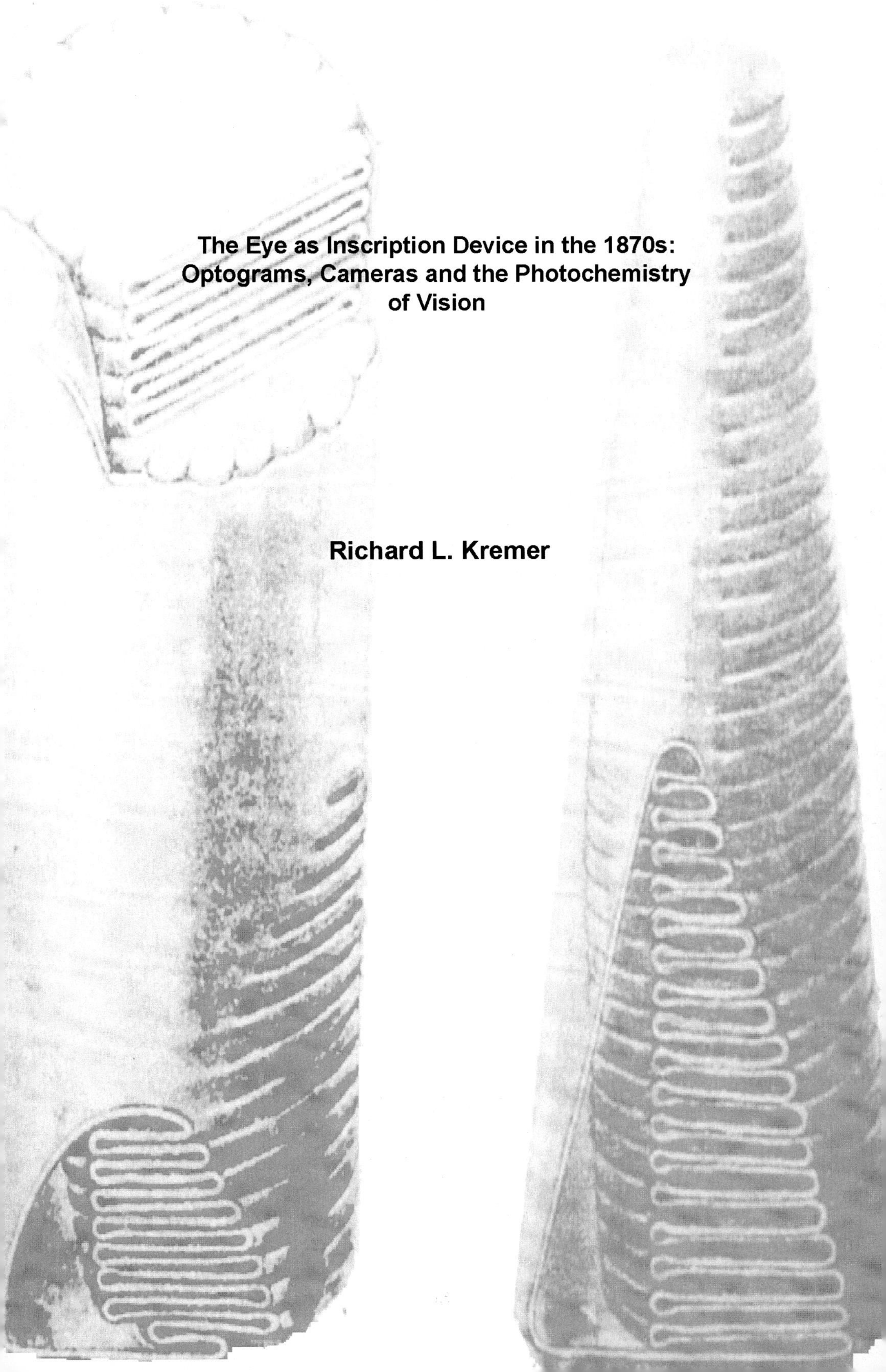

The Eye as Inscription Device in the 1870s: Optograms, Cameras and the Photochemistry of Vision

Richard L. Kremer

In April of 1877, the Berlin newspapers were filled with reports of a particularly gruesome murder. Frau von Sabatzky, a seventy-two year old widow, had been killed in her shop by someone who horribly mutilated her body and then escaped without leaving a clue as to motive or identity. By offering a large monetary reward, the police had persuaded bystanders to name many suspects who were duly arrested and questioned. But the newspapers also noted that an entirely new forensic technique had been used in the case: "To leave no stone unturned, the police photographed the eye of the body immediately after it was found, for as is known, scientific authorities claim that the final image seen before death is imprinted on the victim's eye. Despite particularly favorable circumstances, however, the image gave no clues." The case remained unresolved.

The new forensic tool, which apparently could not identify Sabatzky's murderer, was the recent discovery of what Willy Kühne called "optography." In the rods of the retina a colored pigment had been found which rapidly bleaches to become transparent when illuminated by light. Varying intensities of light produce varying degrees of bleaching, so that an image passing through the dioptric (lens) apparatus of the eye could literally be fixed on the retina, just as the film in a camera fixes the image arranged by its lens. The eye, in 1877, had become a complete camera, and not only the police were fascinated by the new technology. As R. Steven Turner has shown in a survey of nineteenth-century physiological optics, nearly ten percent of all publications in that field, from 1875 to 1879, were devoted to the study of this new pigment, called by Kühne "visual purple" (later rhodopsin). The optogram, or image fixed on the visual purple, had taken the worlds of police science and physiology by storm.

In this paper, I want to explore the significance of this discovery within the larger patterns of change in the life sciences of the nineteenth century. In addition to examining the reductionist intersections of physics, chemistry and physiology in this case study, I will suggest that especially Kühne's presentation of the discovery reveals two other equally important intersections: the long-standing effort to model physiological explanation on mechanical systems, and the emergence of a new "moral economy of science" in which a new type of objectivity is being imported into the practice of physiological optics. After the optogram, the eye became not only a camera, but also an inscription device, to use Bruno Latour's and Steve Woolgar's term, which could directly inscribe the phenomena of vision without the intervention of the subject whose eye was being investigated or the experimenter arranging the phenomenon. Before considering these latter two intersections, however, let me sketch briefly the steps by which visual purple and the optogram appeared on the stage of sensory physiology in 1876-77.

It was not Kühne but the young Franz Boll (1849-1879), since 1873 extraordinary professor of comparative anatomy and physiology in

Rome, who in November of 1876 announced the "best discovery that I have yet made"--a light-sensitive pigment in the retina. Boll's initial contexts were histological and physical reductionist. He had begun his university studies at Bonn under Max Schultze, the leading microscopist of the 1860s who had explored morphological structures of the retina, especially the rods and cones. From 1871-73, Boll had worked as an assistant to Emil Du Bois-Reymond in Berlin and had published important physical and histological studies of the electric torpedo fish. In addition, Boll had spent one semester (summer 1868) studying with Hermann Helmholtz in Heidelberg. In Bonn, Boll had explored microscopically the nerve endings in teeth and glands; in 1871, he tried by means of dioptric experiments on compound eyes of amphibians to determine where the light-sensitive layer is located in the retina. In 1876 he returned to these issues, seeking to confirm Heinrich Müller's 1853 suggestion that the rods and cones are the "end organs" of the optic nerve. Significantly, Boll in his early researches had devoted little attention to physiological chemistry.

While preparing frog retinas for these in vitro histological investigations, Boll accidently and to his considerable astonishment noticed a "purplish red" pigment which bleached transparent about 40 to 60 seconds after the retina had been removed from the living frog's eye. Microscopic examination revealed that only the rods contained the bleachable material. At first, Boll attributed the bleaching simply to the "death" of the retina. But after finding that the time required for complete bleaching varied dramatically between clear and cloudy days, he reversed himself and concluded that ambient light rather than death prompts the bleaching. Indeed, retinas removed from the eye and kept in complete darkness could preserve for up to twenty-four hours their reddish hue, which then would disappear in seconds upon exposure to bright sunlight. Boll also found that live frogs, placed in sunlight before being sectioned, had their retinal pigment bleached. Further experiments on live frogs, placed first in bright light and then in darkness before having their retinas removed, showed that the bleaching process was reversible, that the reddish color again appeared on rod ends which had been restored to darkness. As a final proof that the pigment in question was light-sensitive, Boll exposed only a narrow strip of a retina to sunlight, and found that only that strip, and not the entire retina, bleached transparent. In other words, he fixed an image on the retinal pigment, the process Kühne soon would christen as optography.

It is, however, not merely these findings but Boll's public presentation of his discovery that is especially important for our purposes. From the beginning Boll assumed that the "objective change of the rods by light unquestionably forms part of the [subjective] act of seeing." This was a very bold claim since Boll could not find any visual pigment in the cones, those retinal elements concentrated in the center of the eye where humans see most acutely. Furthermore, even the reality of a light-sensitive pigment might seem implausible, since as Boll admitted "numerous histologists" before him had failed to find the element in their studies of the retina. To legitimate his claims Boll thus sought to situate his discovery within several broader contexts: the so-called Young-Helmholtz theory of trichromatic colour vision, Du Bois-Reymond's physicalist program of physiological investigation, an epistemological tradition relating sensations to external objects, and an artistic tradition of histological illustration. These contexts provided not only the language and concepts but also the experimental space in which Boll initially presented and then experimentally explored his discovery.

First, Boll asked whether the bleaching process depends on the wavelength of the light striking the retina. Further experiments on frogs kept in variously coloured containers revealed that the longer the wavelength, the shorter the exposure time required for bleaching. Boll grouped his wavelengths into three sets of coloured lights, and suggested that these groups might be "identical" to the three basic colours of the Young-Helmholtz theory. In an unfinished essay published posthumously in 1881 by Du-Bois Reymond and Helmholtz, Boll began to work out a grand scheme for correlating three anatomical elements in the retina (rods, cones, pigment epithelium) with the tripartate colour sensors required for Helmholtz's theory of colour vision. By linking the bleaching pigments to the Young-Helmholtz theory then being hotly contested, Boll thus created a significance for his discovery which extended far beyond its immediate histological context.

Second, Boll asked whether the change in colour of the retinal pigment was a photochemical process, resulting from inherent chemical alteration of the material or a photophysical change arising from optical interference effects produced by the well-known layered platelets at the end of the rods. Boll's reported experiments seemed to favour the latter alternative: ultraviolet light did not bleach the retina, unlike the photochemical case where such rays do expose photographic film; physical pressure on the rods (simply squeezing the cover glass over the slide) could instantly erase the red colour; and Boll, admitting his general ignorance of physiological chemistry, found that he could not extract the active substance from the rods with any standard chemical reagent. Yet he also reported that a yellow pigment in oil droplets located in the retina appeared to regenerate the visual red, a fact which, he ambiguously stated, made "the photochemical theory of light sensation extremely probable." Despite these conflicting accounts of the mechanism behind the bleaching of the red pigment, Boll nonetheless concluded that he had proved for sensory organs, as had Du Bois-Remond for muscles, that "the physiological states of rest and activity correspond to very specific material, physical, chemical and anatomical changes." Boll thus explicitly linked his find to Du Bois-Reymond's program.

Boll also tied his discovery to the long-standing question of the relationship between material changes in sensory organs and the quality and nature of the sensation produced. According to what Boll called the "interpretation theory" of Johannes Müller and Helmholtz, the "objective nature of the sign and the way in which the mind interprets the sign" were not identical but only symbolically related. Yet the discovery of the retinal pigment, Boll asserted, seemed to support an "identity theory" in which a "definite and necessary relationship" existed between mental representation and material processes in the sensory organs. That is, Boll seemed at least implicitly to be aligning himself with Ewald Hering and against Helmholtz in the battle between "nativism" and "empiricism" which during the 1870s had been rocking sensory physiology. Although visual red might provide support for Helmholtz's theory of color vision, it also could reduce the role of "mind" which Helmholtz had made so central in his views of the visual process.

Finally, by means of the illustrations which accompanied his essays on the red pigment, Boll situated himself within an earlier anatomical and histological visual tradition which Lorraine Daston and Peter Galison recently have described as the presentation of "ideal images." Tracing this tradition through anatomical atlases of the eighteenth-century, Daston and Galison suggest that these image makers sought to depict not any particular individual but rather a normative, perfect, ideal speciman. By means of judgment and art, such enhanced images were intended to enable viewers to see the essentials or universals rather than the particulars of nature. These visual representations embodied both ontological and ethical commitments--about what "nature" is and about the responsibility of the observer to distill the ideal "nature" from the messiness of experience.

From the beginning Boll had worried about the credibility of his reports and about how to convey the essense of his discovery. He admitted that when attempting to demonstrate the pigment in freshly prepared frog's retinas to Berlin's scientific elite-- Helmholtz, Du Bois-Reymond and Nathanael Pringsheim--he had "sacrificed in vain" nearly half a dozen frogs before the desired phenomenon appeared. Boll called in other prominent witnesses also to authenticate his discovery. The Rome professor of physics, Pietro Blaserna, confirmed the hue of the colored glasses Boll used as filters to illuminate retinas with nearly monochromatic light. And Boll publicly thanked the well-known Berlin sculptor, Louis Sussmann-Hellborn, for "assisting in my experiments, and for completing the plate after the determination of the observed nuances of color." Writing privately to Du Bois-Reymond, Boll admitted that Sussmann-Hellborn could better identify the hues than could Boll, and that a "division of labor between preparer and artistic interpreter [künstlerischer Darsteller]" was required. Indeed so problematic was this determination of hue that Boll even changed his mind on the color of the retinal pigment, calling it "purplish red" in his first announcement and then "red" in his subsequent publications.

The illustration Boll presented with his paper reflects a similar concern to stabilize the experimental situation (see Fig. 1). On a single engraved plate he presented rectangular coloured swatches of the hues assumed by the retinal pigment at various stages of its bleaching process. He also offered drawings of cross sections of frog retinas, depicting microscopically magnified views of the rods (albeit in a rectangular rather than circular format which he would have seen through the microscope) and painted to show their colours after being illuminated by various monochromatic lights. Boll's images seemed designed to assist other histologists in seeing what he had seen under his microscope. Significantly, the "optograms" which Boll described in his text are not illustrated on the plate, and indeed congruent with his avoidance of chemical practice and language, Boll never employed the metaphors of photography to describe the visual pigment. Boll's illustrations, rather, remain firmly within the tradition of "ideal" visual representation. After viewing an unspecified numbers of frog retinas, Boll or his artist engraved diagrams to represent the "ideal" retina as it bleached during exposure to light. The histological context of such illustrations would have been immediately apparent to Boll's readers.

Given the prominence of the contexts into which Boll placed his discovery, his announcement not surprisingly unleashed a flood of publications on the light-sensitive pigment, the majority of which issued from Kühne's physiological institute in Heidelberg. Unlike Boll who saw himself as an histologist, Kühne was a leading physiological chemist. He had studied chemistry with Friedrich Wöhler in Göttingen and with Carl Lehmann at Jena, spent time in Paris with Claude Bernard, and explored the chemical nature of the protoplasm with Ernst Brücke and Carl Ludwig in Vienna. From 1861-68, he had directed the chemical laboratory in Virchow's Berlin institute for pathological anatomy and produced an important textbook on physiological chemistry. At Heidelberg since 1871 (as Helmholtz's successor), Kühne had devoted himself primarily to the chemistry of digestion, especially to a study of the enzymes (he coined the term in 1876) of the pancreas. Thus Kühne placed the coloured pigments of the retina within a photochemical rather than the more varied contexts of Boll. In the first reports of his research on Boll's discovery, appearing already in January of 1877, Kühne deployed the language and techniques of photography and made the "optogram" (or the "photogram"), which he soon learned to fix chemically so that it could be preserved and easily displayed in classroom demonstrations, the central feature of his public presentation of "optography."

Over the next several years, Kühne and his associates at Heidelberg thoroughly explored the behaviour of "visual purple" as they called the pigment, using chemical, spectrographic and comparative methods. Unlike Boll, they quickly managed to extract the active substance from the rods with a chemical reagent (bile salts). By closely following the bleaching process, they suggested that several additional light-sensitive substances are produced sequentially, each of which can be reconverted to visual purple by contact with oil particles located in the pigment epithelium of the retina. Furthermore, they systematically looked for visual purple in many vertebrate and invertebrate species, and found some species entirely lacking visual purple, the individuals of which nonetheless see quite well. Neither Kühne nor anyone else could find any light-sensitive coloured pigments in the outer layers of the cones. Furthermore, live frogs whose visual purple was completely bleached still seemed able to distinguish colours. Additionally, at Kühne's encouragement, the Swedish physiologist, Alarik Frithjof Holmgren (who also had studied with Du-Bois Reymond and Helmholtz) found that photochemical processes in the retina did not correlate with the electrical behaviour of the eye. Already in 1865 Holmgren, seeking to extend Du Bois-Reymond's claim that every stimulus of tissue linked to the nervous system produces a deviation in electric potential measured across that tissue, had measured what he called the "retinal current," a tiny electrical potential between the front and rear surfaces of the retina which varied when the tissue was abruptly bathed with light (work that had attracted no attention before Boll's discovery). In 1878 Holmgren found that such voltage deviations occur even in retinas with totally bleached visual purple, and that slowly bleaching retinas produce no variation in the potential. Physicalist that he was, Holmgren chose to privilege the electrical over the photochemical as the objective sign of subjective sensation, and concluded that visual purple could stand in "no essential connection" to the nerve impulses which begin the visual process.

All of these investigations forced Kühne, in a 1879 review article, to abandon his initial optimistic assertion that visual purple alone held the "key to the secret of nerve stimulus by light." Instead, he now proposed a more comprehensive and speculative "optochemical hypothesis" to describe how the arrival of light in the retina might initiate nervous stimulation. Essentially, Kühne hypothesized three types of substances to be sought in the retina: visual substances, visual excitants, and selective filters. Visual substances, which may or may not be coloured, are chemically decomposed by the action of light. Visual excitants, the products of these decompositions, stimulate the protoplasm of the visual cells (rods and cones) and thereby start nervous impulses. Other coloured pigments in the retina may act as selective filters by absorbing various wavelengths of incoming light before they reach the visual substances. The discovery of visual purple, Kühne concluded, had demonstrated the viability of such an optochemical hypothesis, even if one could no longer claim that visual purple was the only visual substance, or even if it was such a substance at all.

To develop this optochemical hypothesis, Kühne in 1879 proposed a comprehensive research program for analysing the behaviour of the illuminated retina. Its methods were to be exclusively "objective," even if the optogram itself as a technique of analysis would become significantly less important since some visual substances might be colourless and thus could not be explored via visual inspection. All subjective or self-observational techniques were to be abandoned. "However well our conscious sensation is suited to recognize and judge [ermessen] excitatory processes in the sensory organs, nonetheless all subjective investigation of sensation remains incomplete and one-sided until it is connected to objectively recognizable processes in the stimulated organ." For the next few years, many such "objective" studies issued from Kühne's Heidelberg laboratory: spectral studies of the hues of various chemical products in the retina; chemical analyses of substances produced in the active retina; and electrical measurements of currents in the retina under conditions of illumination and darkness. Kühne thus emphatically rejected "subjective" vision studies, that tradition which made human verbal reports about visual experience the essential phenomenon and extended from Helmholtz and Hering back to Johannes Müller, Jan Purkyne and Goethe. Indeed, despite the obvious similarities between his studies of bleaching and regeneration in visual purple and Hering's chemical theory of vision (based on chemical processes of "assimilation" and "dissimilation"), Kühne only once mentioned Hering's work and steadfastly refused to situate his work amidst the polemical discussions of Helmholtz's and Hering's theories of vision.

This desire for "objectivity" in the study of vision also appears in Kühne's public presentation of the optogram. Initially he offered only verbal reports rather than visual illustrations of his short-lived optograms, appealing to the authority of a "competent witness"--the Heidelberg chemist, Robert Bunsen--to bolster the veracity of his descriptions. In his first lengthy report, not published until May of 1877, Kühne described in great detail the experimental circumstances under which he could produce sharply-focused optograms and warned "even the most experienced" observers that they might well face difficulties in attempting to repeat Kühne's procedures. That is, Kühne freely admitted that optography, despite its promise of objectivity, represented a very unstable experimental situation. It was in the same paper that Kühne published the first optographic images, the crudeness for which he apologized. The illustrations could not be "exact [genau] as is desired for visual scientific representation" since no artist had been able to "guarantee the trustworthiness" of drawings of such rapidly changing phenomena. And when optograms were fixed chemically and dried, their convex surface made it technically impossible for a direct mechanical reproduction of the image onto a printed page. Unlike photography, which by the 1870s had developed techniques so that a single negative could produce myriads of identical positive images, Kühne's optogram (much like the original daguerreotype) could yield only one unique image which could not be mechanically multiplied. Kühne was thus forced to represent his optograms by employing an artist or making his own drawings. That is, he had to redraw his images for his readers, just as Boll had done for his microscopical cross-sections. As seen in Fig. 2, Kühne published only simple geometrical images captured on the retina, for which he again apologized: "It cannot be the duty of physiological optics to bring optography to such a perfection as it might acquire in the skilled hands of a professional photographer. I could not, however, deny myself the pleasure of treating optographically a few complicated objects, such as the garden side of the laboratory here and a human portrait." These latter optograms, however, Kühne never published.

Kühne's ambitious optochemical program met little success over the next several decades. After the initial burst of publications which explored the phenomena of visual purple, interest in the subject waned by the mid 1880s. Kühne himself abandoned the topic after 1882, directing his attention back to the chemistry of proteins and digestion. By 1900 a critical review of knowledge of "visual substances" concluded that the program outlined by Kühne twenty years earlier had reached a dead-end. No additional retinal pigments had been found which might be candidates for "visual substances." And searching for non-coloured visual substances, especially in the cones, seemed impossible because such variable and probably short-lived substances could not be easily observed. Light-induced morphological changes--phototropism--in the cones had been observed, but these could not be related to chemical changes. The reviewer in 1900 thus concluded that "in relation to knowledge of visual substances very little has been learned."

Despite this enigmatic state of Kühne's optochemical program by 1900 (only in the 1970s did the chemistry of photoreceptor cells in the retina again become a major research topic), the episode of visual purple reveals, I think, two important features of late nineteenth-century physiology. First, a kind of technological reductionism can be seen in Kühne's quest for optography. For Kühne, the organism and its internal processes operate not only according to physical and chemical laws but also like the machines of the nineteenth century. Many historians have noted, for example, how machines such as the steam engine, telegraph, or electrical induction apparatus became analogies for physical or physiological explanations. Kühne's optograms completed, very literally, the metaphor of the eye as a camera. Already in the seventeenth century, Kepler and Descartes had discussed the dioptric apparatus of the eye as a camera obscura and illustrations comparing the optical geometries of the eye and the camera obscura had appeared. And shortly after the invention of photography, some physicists had sought analogies between photochemical processes on silver iodide plates and retinal action. Now Kühne had added film to the camera-eye, or more precisely, an entire "photographic factory in which workers upon command repeatedly prepare new light-sensitive material for the film and simultaneously wipe out the old image." The language and the concepts of photography, for Kühne, became the language and concepts of optography.

Yet the camera was more than a conceptual metaphor for Kühne. To regularize and standardize the production of optograms, Kühne constructed a rough analogue of the camera obscura--a darkroom equipped with sodium lamps and a "light funnel" in the ceiling into which half-meter square glass plates bearing geometrical images (or even negatives of human portraits, reputedly Helmholtz's) could be inserted. With this device, Kühne could precisely control the light intensity, time interval, and images to which he exposed retinas, either in vivo or in vitro. Although the funnel held the image to be reproduced, unlike the opening in the camera obscura through which an externally produced image passes, Kühne's device nonetheless made the eye (with its dioptric apparatus and retina intact) a literal and active component in a large camera (see Figs. 3 and 4). Unlike the more abstract cases recently analysed by Norton Wise in which nineteenth-century machines "mediate" in various ways between societal contexts and the generation of scientific knowledge, in Kühne's darkroom the phenomenon under scrutiny was inserted directly into a machine and became a "working object" only as part of that mechanical system. In this sense, no conceptual analogies were required to mediate between Kühne's optograms and the camera obscura.

Yet at least one moral structure implicit in the camera obscura did appear in Kühne's quest for optography. As Jonathan Crary has argued, since the seventeenth century the camera obscura represented a discursive order of "objectivity" in which images were considered to resemble their objects perfectly and observers were sovereign, private and completely separated from the external world of objects. As noted above, Kühne emphatically sought to enter this discursive order. His "objective" physiological optics represented a dramatic break from the "subjective" approach to that discipline which had become increasingly dominant during the course of the nineteenth century. Starting perhaps with Goethe's Farbenlehre (1810), continuing through the often non-reproducible self-observations of Purkyne and canonized finally by Helmholtz's widely influential Handbuch der physiologischen Optik (1856-67), the subjective approach had made the study of human vision paramount in physiological optics, for only human subjects can report what they see. In this tradition, the principal "working object" was the verbal report of human sensory experience, the final product of a series of steps: external stimulus - visual system - subject's "mind" - verbal report. Even though observers tried to reduce the terminological ambiguities in verbal reports to a minimum (e.g., instead of saying "I see red" one would say "this hue appears identical to that hue"), words alone increasingly became too problematic for evaluating the ever more complex theories of vision generated in the Helmholtz-Hering controversies of the 1860-70s. Kühne's proposed solution was to remove the human subject, to replace the verbal report with the inscripted diagram produced directly by the visual system of an animal. In optography, the phenomena "draw themselves" without human intervention.

Indeed, Kühne's repeated exhortations to convert the study of sensory physiology to "determinations of objectively verifiable reactions in the stimulated organ" nicely mirror what Daston and Galison have called the turn to "noninterventionist or mechanical objectivity" in nineteenth-century science. The scientific observer in this new moral regime withdraws in self-restraint from all judgment, interpretation or even sensory testimony, so that nature can "speak for itself," safe from all frauds, system builders or idealisers. Kühne's optogram, I think, represents this "non-interventionist objectivity" on two levels. He sought to remove the subject's mind from the study of vision, so that visual processes could be explored without verbal intervention by the subject. And by inscribing itself directly onto a graphic trace, the visual pigment could be recorded without any intervention by the experimenter. Like Ludwig's recording kymograph or Marey's grapho-cinematographic methods, Kühne's optograms captured and fixed in time and space fleeting phenomena--chemical transformations of the active retina.

The photograph, as Daston and Galison note, became the nineteenth-century emblem of non-interventionist objectivity, a new moral regime which 'swept through' the sciences, both physical and social (witness the importance of photographs in Cesare Lombroso's so-called "criminal anthropology"). In the final paper he published on photochemistry, Kühne described a sharply-focused optogram he had found traced on the retinal pigment of a criminal executed by guillotine. Yet to his dismay, Kühne could not relate the image preserved on the eye to anything the unfortunate man may have seen immediately prior to his death. Criminology once again did not benefit from optography. Nonetheless, Kühne's ascetism was complete at least within the physiological and moral realms. Unlike Ludwig's and Marey's technologies, which required complex techno-mechanical devices to mediate between "nature" and the graphic trace, Kühne's optography required no intermediate machine. The eye, for Kühne, had become its own inscription device, creating a visible trace directly on itself. Rather than "mechanical" objectivity, Kühne's moral regime might more accurately be called "physico-chemical" objectivity, a place where neither the experimenter nor the experimenters's apparatus intrudes. The optogram had become the supreme emblem of noninterventionist objectivity.

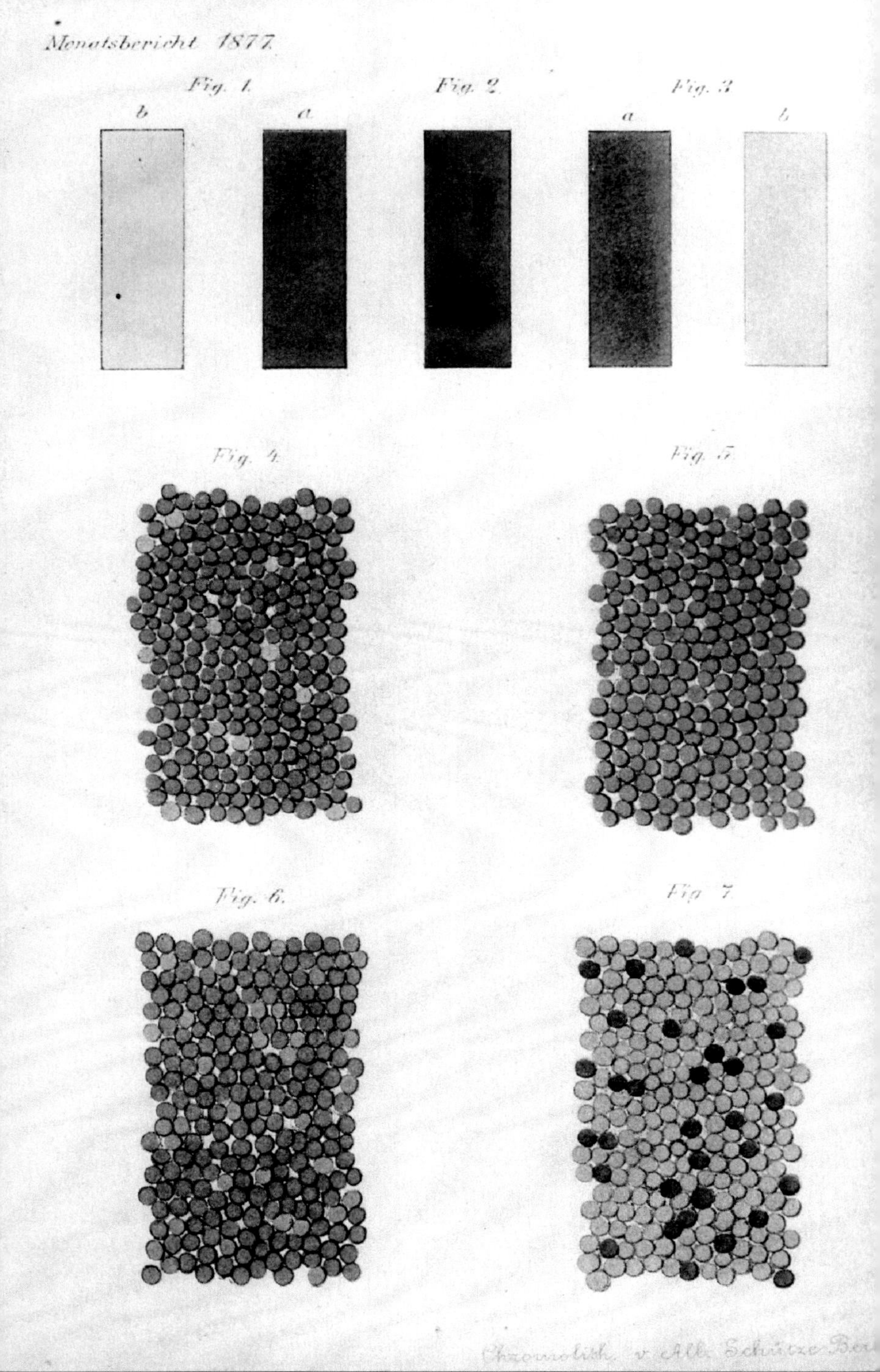

Fig. 1: Boll's swatches (Figs. 1-3) and illustrations of retinal cross-sections (Figs. 4-7), coloured in the original. Reprinted from Boll, 1877a (fn. 8), between pp. 2-3.

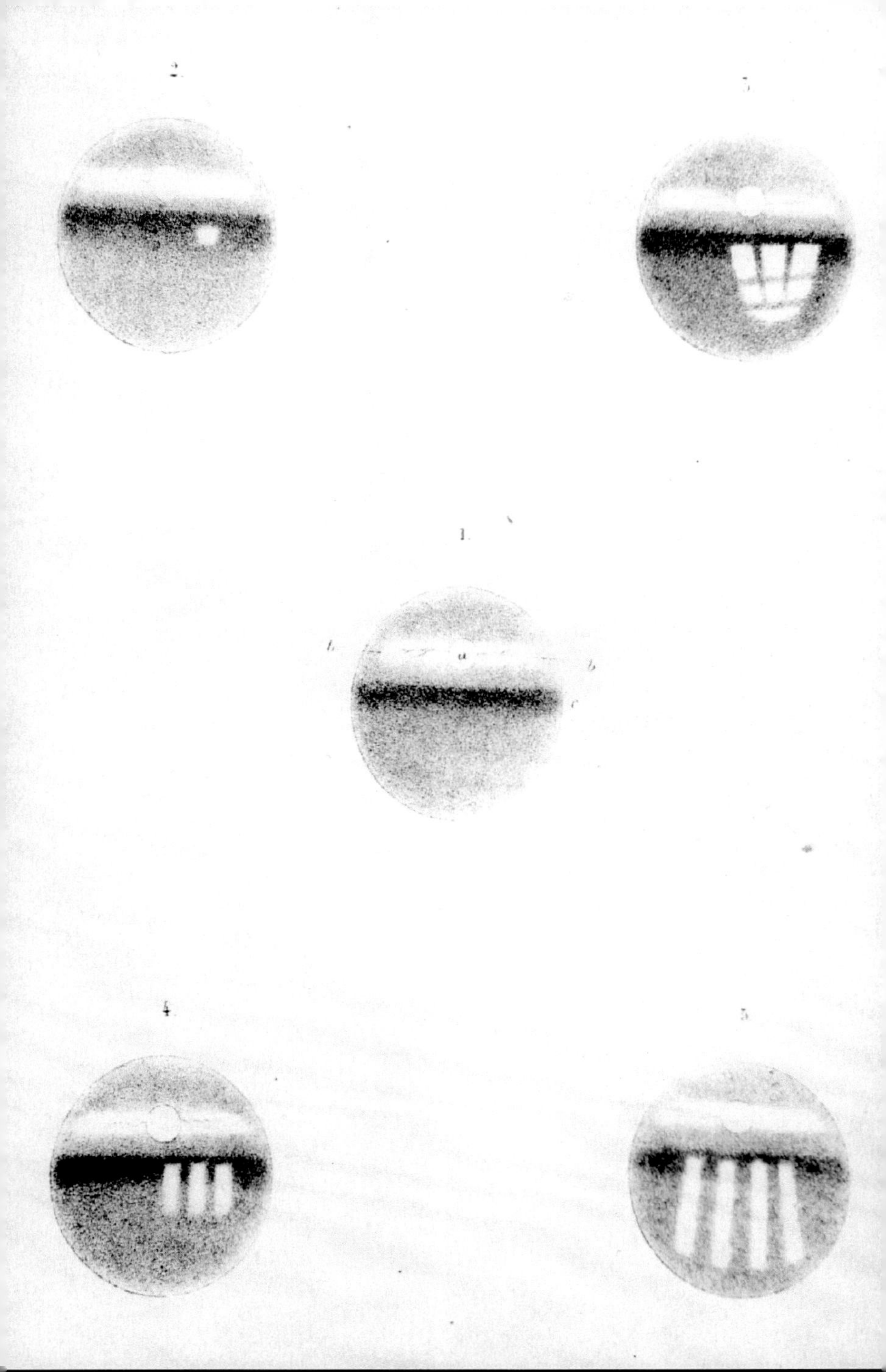

Fig. 2: Kühne's first published optograms. Reprinted from Kühne, 1878b (fn. 23), Pl. 1.

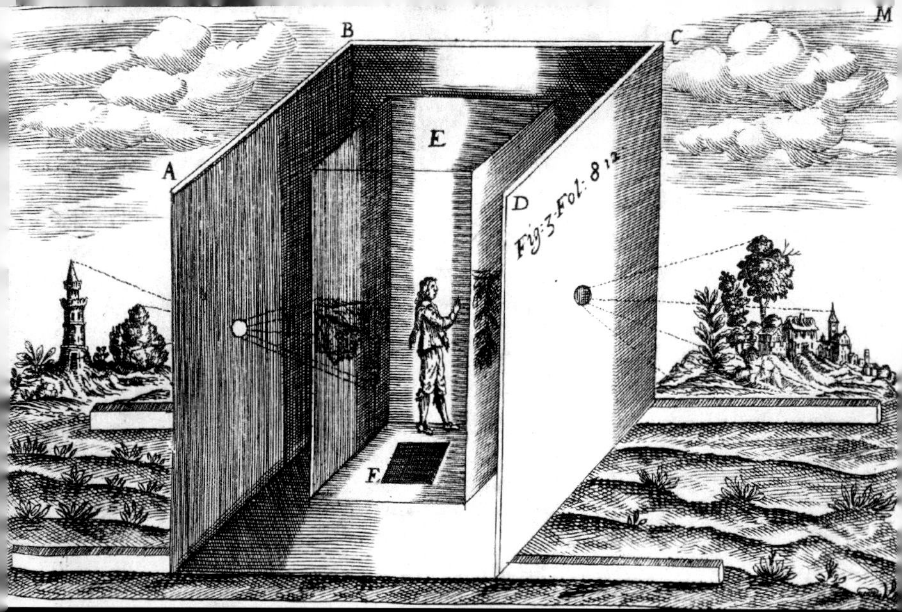

Fig. 3: Camera obscura. Reprinted from Athanasius Kircher: Ars magna lucis et umbrae in mundo, 2d ed. (Amsterdam 1671), p. 709.

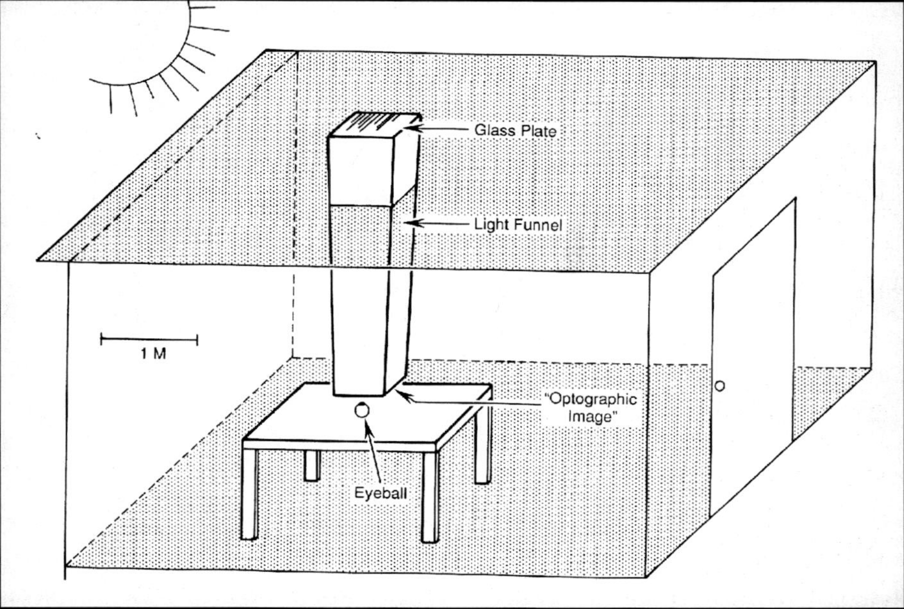

Fig. 4: Kühne's optographic chamber, as described in Kühne, 1878 (fn. 21), pp. 232-33; Ewald/Kühne (fn. 28), pp. 374-75.

FROG'S EYE AS A CAMERA

The smallest camera in the world which has actually taken pictures is doubtless the eye of the frog. It has been found that if a frog is kept in the dark for some time the retina of the eye on being dissected is found to have a purple reddish colour which fades away or becomes bleached on exposure to day light. If the eye is placed in front of a window and left there "exposed" for some time, and then fixed in a four per cent solution of alum the optogram is partially fixed and retains an inverted picture of the window with its cross bars as pictured on the retina. It is claimed that by a similar photographic process the last picture or image retained by the eye of a dead man or animal may be preserved.

Boys Life, September 1920.

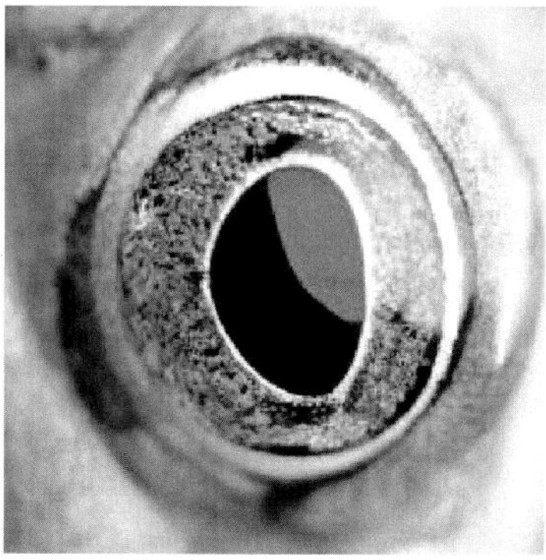

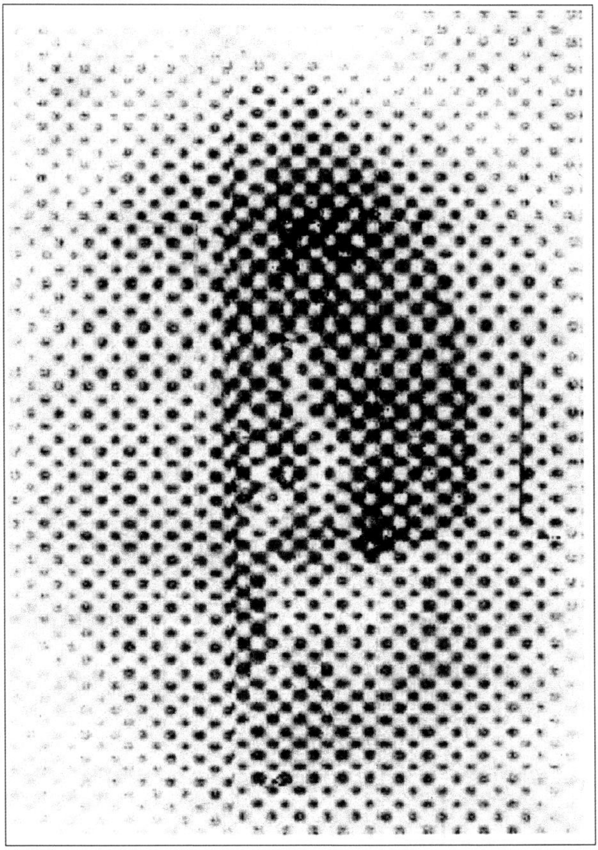

An obviously fake optogram attributed to Dr. Vernois, (An inverted eye and socket) but it is unclear as to whether or not this image was sent to Vernois by a fellow correspondent Dr. Bourion, who claimed it was photographed from the retina of a murdered woman on June 14th 1868. Dr. Vernois apparently attempted many optograms without much success.

IN THE CORONER'S EYE

Was the Picture of the Murderer at Jamestown.

WERE HYPNOTIZED.

Story Comes From a Myth Which Science Has Proven Untrue.

Experiment on a Murderer

The Warren Ledger, Feb 01, 1895

LITTLE CHANCE OF RIGHT CLEW IN GIRL'S EYES

The Evening Gazette, August 23rd 1912, Iowa

THE PICTURE IN A DEAD MAN'S EYE.

CURIOUS RESUSCITATION OF AN OLD SUPERSTITION BY MODERN SCIENTIFIC EXPERIMENTS—A NEW POSSIBILITY IN THE DETECTION OF CRIME—ACTION OF LIGHT ON THE RETINAL RED OF THE ANIMAL EYE.

The New York Times, March 18, 1878

Secrets of Health and Happiness

Murderer's Image Not Held By Retina of Victim's Ey

The Bridgeport Telegram, Wednesday, September 8, 1920

Science Says Eye Won't Photograph Faces Perfectly

The Greeley Daily Tribune, Colarado, June 14th 1932

SELECTED AMERICAN PRESS CUTTINGS FROM 1878 TO 1932

Much was expected from the discovery made by Prof. Boll that the images of objects remained on the retina of animals after death. It was thought, for example, that the last scene of a mysterious murder would be found by properly examining the eyes of the victim. Actual tests have shown that the optogram can be of no use in detecting crime. Dr Ayres made more than a thousand experiments in the laboratory of Prof. Kuhne, at Heidelberg, and met with but poor success. The best result was obtained by exposing the eye of a living rabbit, which had been dosed with atropine, to a photographic negative, and even in this case the optogram was imperfect, indistinct, and evanescent.

The Indiana Democrat, July 28th 1881, Pennsylvania

Science Says Eye Won't 'Photograph' Faces, But It Will Retain Crude Images After Death

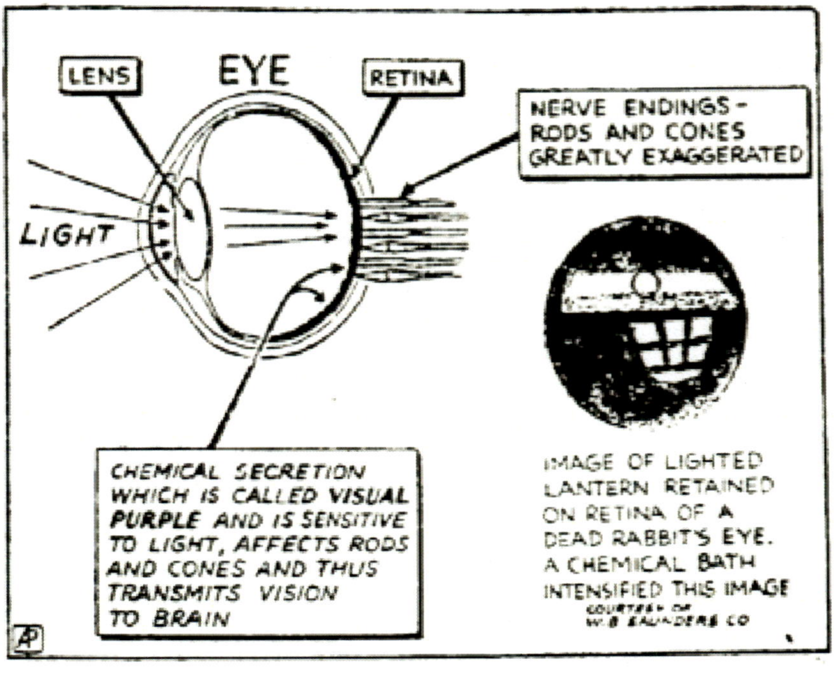

The Dothan Eagle, Thursday, May 19, 1932, Alabama

Me

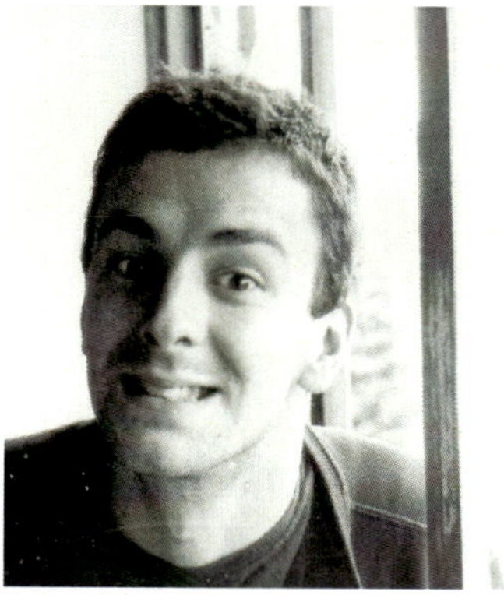

e-mail conversation

21st March 2006

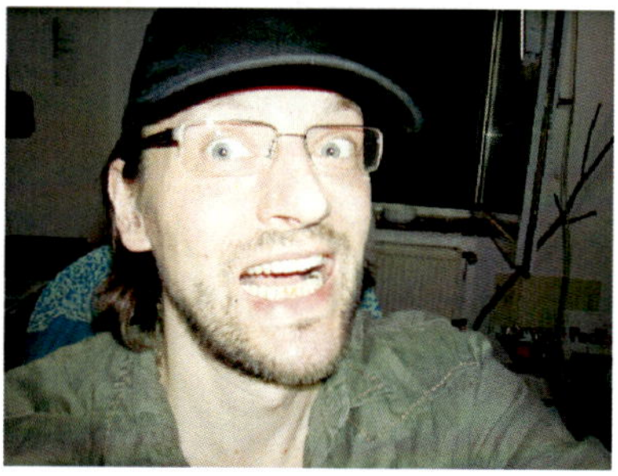

Thom Kubli

Hello Thom
How are you? Hope you remember me from Brigitte's show last year!
I might be coming to Cologne sometime in Easter after I have visited Heidelberg for research for my new project. (see attachment).
I need to find somebody who knows the Heidelberg area who can help me gain access to the University Libraries. I am trying at this end via my University but it's difficult and mainly slow.
I also want to visit a place called Bruchsal and its Prison. This is the place where the only know human optogram was obtained from a beheaded convict. I have the image!
If you e-mail me your phone number I can ring you
All the best
Derek Ogbourne

Hey Derek,
Surely I remember you, good to hear from you.
About Heidelberg I could try to ask someone there.
What I probably would need is the exact date when
you want to work there and a biography saying you're
a famous artist and dearly respected professor.
What I can do is forward the material and try
to make a connection as soon as possible -no guarantee.
Anyway if you'll come by Cologne lets go for a beer.
Looking forward to see you.
How's Susana doing?
Best wishes
Thom

(second answer)
Hello Derek,
I just made it to really read your paper, that's amazing.
It sounds like a forensic print matrix. Also one could imagine
how criminologic literature could be rewritten by a last
picture of your executioner.
As mentioned a bio would be helpful, but I forwarded it
and hope for the best.
Best wishes
Thom

Thom
Any luck with contacts in Heidelberg?
Derek

Dear Derek,
You mentioned Mr. Alexandridis. If it is the right person, he lives in Heidelberg and my mother knows him (not very well but they met before). He might be the one who could know where to find what you're looking for and he might be able to give you access to the library.
You just can say you have the telephone from "frau kubli" and maybe he's very much interested in the project.
What you think?
My mother is sending me the address later and I'll forward it to you.
You probably have to act soon to make sure he'll be around when you'll visit Heidelberg.
best
Thom

Derek,
Here's the address/number. It might make sense to try to call him tomorrow morning around ten/eleven and explain him your project. you're not announced so far, so you might have to talk him into your work. Just be charming as you are so it won't be a problem.
As I said before you can say you have the number from my mother.
He possibly might remember the name.
Anyway he seems to be a person with wide knowledge that has interests in many things so it could be interesting to meet him anyway.
If for some reason it doesn't work with Alexandridis let me know soon.
Then it would be good to know at what date you definitely will be in Heidelberg so my mother will try to talk to the director of the libraries to find an agreement. (no guarantee).
Best wishes
Thom

Dear Thom
Wow brilliant!!! It would be amazing if it were the same guy - although I did a web search on the name and there were many entries under this name but mainly in the US. I think it is an eastern bloc name or even Greek? Have you any idea? Is he an academic? Maybe we are destined to meet just because of the name.
Best Derek

Derek
I hope he is the one. As I just googled he worked in the opthalmic hospital in Heidelberg and he wrote books about ophthalmology. He's emeritus now. My mother just told me she got to know him as he had a crash in the snow with some friends right in front of our house. They came in to wait for the police and had some coffee at our place. My father was scientist too and Heidelberg is not a big place, so he might remember.
Hey, I hope this works out!!
Thom

Thom
It could well be him!!!! Is he old?
Best
Derek

Derek
It is him!
Thom

Thom
How can you be sure?
Derek

Derek
Actually I have no clue, I just have the feeling he´s the person you´re looking for, if not, pretend you want to meet him for some other reason and record it.
you can sell it as a parallel universe documentary drama.
Thom

Derek
Great at least we know its him.
Thom

Powered by NetMail

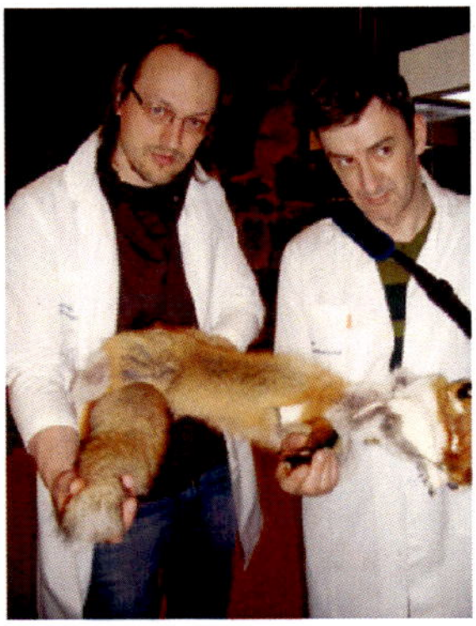

Medina, Susana

SUSANA MEDINA is the author of *Philosophical Toys*, an offspring from which is the short film *Buñuel's Philosophical Toys*, shown across the UK. She is also the author of *Cuentos Rojos* (*Red Tales*), *Souvenirs del Accidente* (*Souvenirs from the Accident*) and *Borgesland: A voyage through the infinite, imaginary places, labyrinths, Buenos Aires and other psychogeographies and figments of space.* Amongst other honours, she has been winner of the Max Aub International Short Story Prize and an Arts Council Writing Grant for her novel *Spinning Days of Night*, which she is currently immersed in.

A RETINAL TATTOO OF LIGHT by Susana Medina

A millisecond divides life from death. Or is it an attosecond? Or a femtosecond? The beheaded lose consciousness in two seconds, if the blade cuts through the neck in one go. The brain has enough oxygen stored for the metabolism to persist for seven seconds after the head is cut off: the eyes flicker, the mouth might still move. On the 16th November 1880, Erhard Gustav Reif was decapitated in Heidelberg. His wife had died and he had killed his two sons, perhaps an act of desperation. If the future didn't exist for him, it didn't exist for his children either.

A physiologist received on execution the warm head. He had come across a phenomenon that he termed optography. Under a cluster of special circumstances, the retina recorded the last image seen before death. By chance, he had first discovered this phenomenon on the retina of a frog. He then experimented on rabbits. He now had a human specimen to experiment with. He went to his laboratory and prepared the dead man's retina with light sensitive chemicals. An image emerged. It was a geometrical, asymmetrical and abstract image. It looked like some steps. With all probability, it was the steps that went up to the guillotine. He drew the image. This drawing became the only human optogram available.

A hundred and twenty years later, an English artist in London becomes fascinated with optography. He likes the idea as an idea. He finds a poetic dimension to it. He closes his eyes and imagines a tattoo made out of light imprinted on the flesh of the retina. The eye as a camera that actually records the last image before death. The retina as a film where the image that separates life from death is imprinted, not in negative form, but in positive form. He finds that very little has been written about the subject. He finds out about the beheaded man, Erhard Gustav Reif. Is an optogram really a scientific fallacy? Is it possible to produce them?

He then becomes involved in other ideas. Optography fades away.

Four years later, he goes to an art show in Cologne with his wife, a writer. He is part of this art show. He talks to another artist from there about this and that, and keeps in touch with him. In an email, he mentions that a doctor in Heidelberg produced some optograms in the 1970s. He mentions the name of the doctor. The German artist says the name rings a bell. A flurry of emails, ensues. The German artist knows him. He crashed his car in the snow outside his mother's countryside home, in Heidelberg.

Coincidences. Chance pressing against the English artist's temples. He goes to Heidelberg, the place where all this happened. It is a university town. He investigates. He walks along the river taking pictures and goes to a disco at night-time with some kids from the hotel. He visits the man who produced optograms from a couple of rabbits in the 1970s.

The English artist becomes fascinated with the idea of producing optograms. It is the scientist in him that wonders about it. He thinks of science with its scientific fads and fallacies, as a branch of the arts. He could get a rabbit and fake an optogram. Faking an optogram becomes a more interesting option. Violent images of a chase after a rabbit run through his head. Fur, grass, speed, fear. The images are disjointed, they're visually haunting, they transmit a disturbing chaos of textures and give the video-piece the right edge: tension, a sense of menace.

Back in London, he finds one day a big rabbit's cage in the street. It is another sign seducing him in the right direction. He should get a couple of rabbits. He disinfects the cage. He goes to a pet-shop and gets a couple of white rabbits with grey blotches here and there. He buys them plenty of treats. He finds out what they like to eat. He feeds them greens, fresh grass, fennel, dandelions, pears, they love pears and raisins, but you're supposed to give them sweets with moderation. He visits the rabbits three or four times a day in the garden. At night time, he makes a hot-water bottle so they keep warm. His wife also visits them and indulges them with sweet fruit. Sometimes they visit them together, especially at night-time, nocturnal visits.

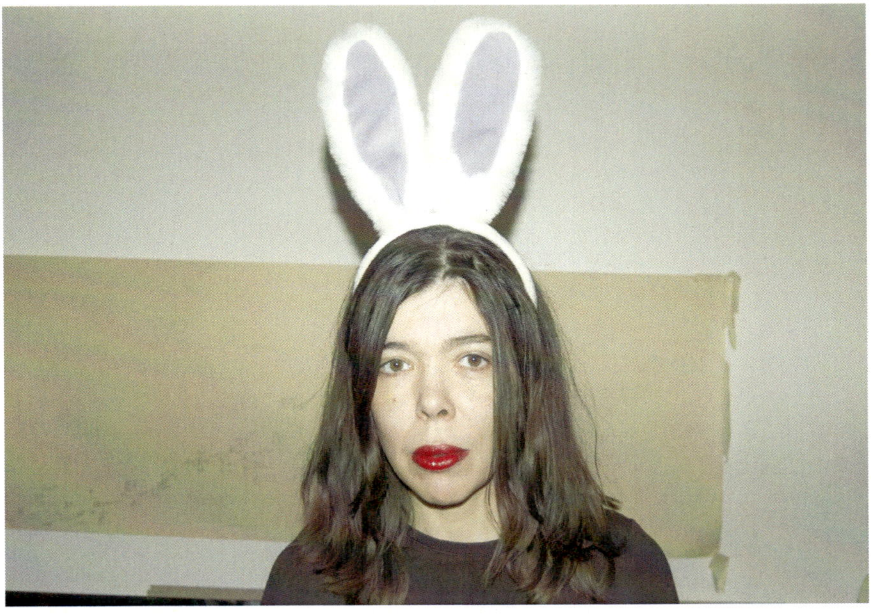

His wife is a writing machine. She sits at her desk and writes. She sways between various writing pieces, her own obsessions and her husband's obsession about optography. The living-room has become an embodiment of her husband's obsession. It has become an optography archive, as her husband prepares for his show 'The Museum of Optography'. She likes fleeing to the garden, where her husband's obsession takes on a different hue by putting her in unexpected contact with nature. The rabbits are boisterous, unpredictable, athletic. They are enigmatic ciphers of life. She likes to watch them hopping around, zig-zagging. It is a magical moment. Like entering a gigantic hallucination, where city-life doesn't exist: only vibrant grass, bushes, twigs and hypnotic rabbits.

The man videos them. He looks at them, thinking their eyes can see in every direction. He could actually make an optogram. It is the scientist in him that thinks this. Peeling the retina, finding the ultimate organic image. It is impossible to handle them, to catch them. Survival has made them timid and swift. In the cage, they dig holes, tunnels, eat their own droppings and shred the litter newspapers. When they're let out of the cage, they're in their habitat. They graze, spin around, explore a branch, nibble on unsuspected weeds and make extraordinary leaps where their body hovers horizontal in mid-air, about one metre from the ground.

He is spellbound.

The 6th of February in 2007 the whole garden is thick with snow. They're built for snow, these rabbits. They're both white with grey blotches here and there, the perfect camouflage amidst snow and broken twigs. The woman lets them out of the cage. One of them is scared. The other one merges with the snow. She calls her husband. 'Come down with the video-camera, you must video this, it's idyllic' she yells through the landing.

He comes down and videos the ground covered in snow, the rabbits relishing this strange event. He then videos his wifes eye's wide-open saying to the camera:

'If it wasn't for the drawing of the last image seen on the retina of a beheaded man in 1880, we wouldn't have bunnies, we wouldn't be enjoying this idyllic moment.'

'Optogram and rabbits travelling slowly across time from Heidelberg to London', he says. 'Chaos theory in slow-motion.'

'What was the name of the beheaded man?' the woman asks.

'Erhard Gustav Reif,' he says.

The gaze of the woman is immersed in the splendid snow: 'Somebody told me that the tunnel of light that people who have a near-death experience see, it's just the way the brain shuts off. The brain is designed to switch off with an apotheosis of light.'

'It's a good way to die.'

'Heaven is in the brain.'

They look at each other. Then at the fixed eye of one of the rabbits. Its greyness is immense. Static. And the eyelid is surrounded by minute eyelashes. The rabbit captures the dilated pupil of the English artist surrounded by hazelnut iris, twitches its nose rhythmically and runs away through the snow. Fast.

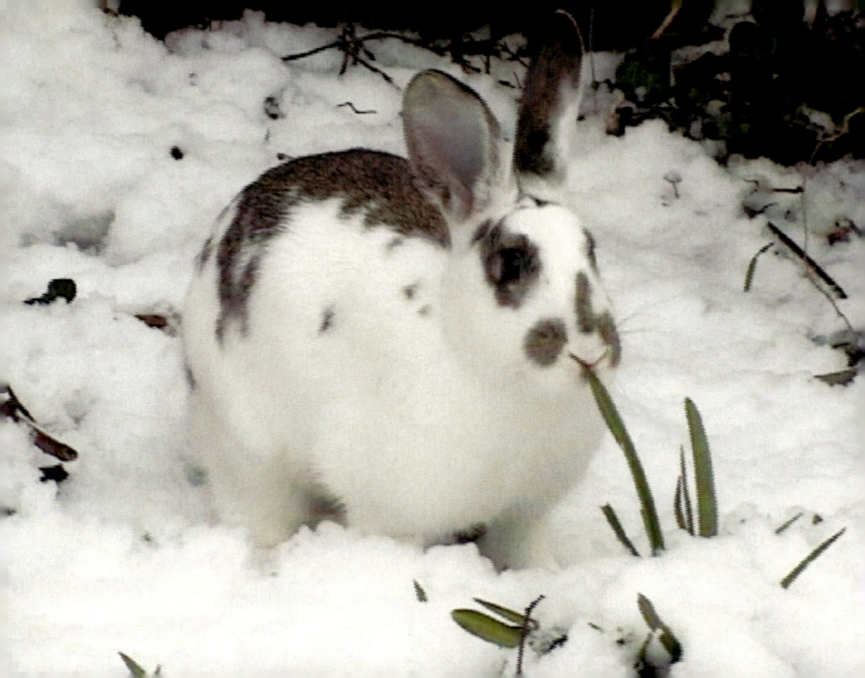

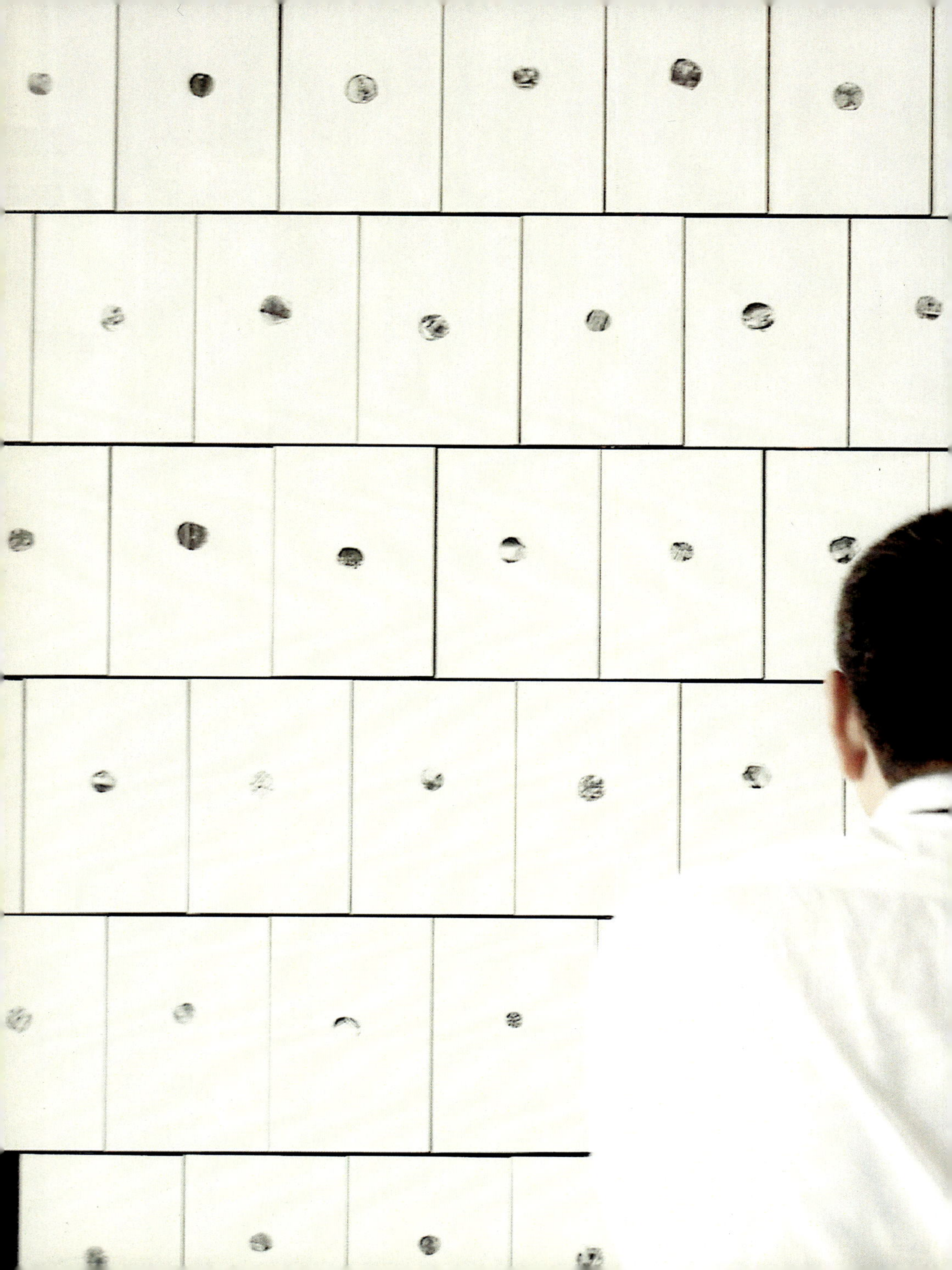

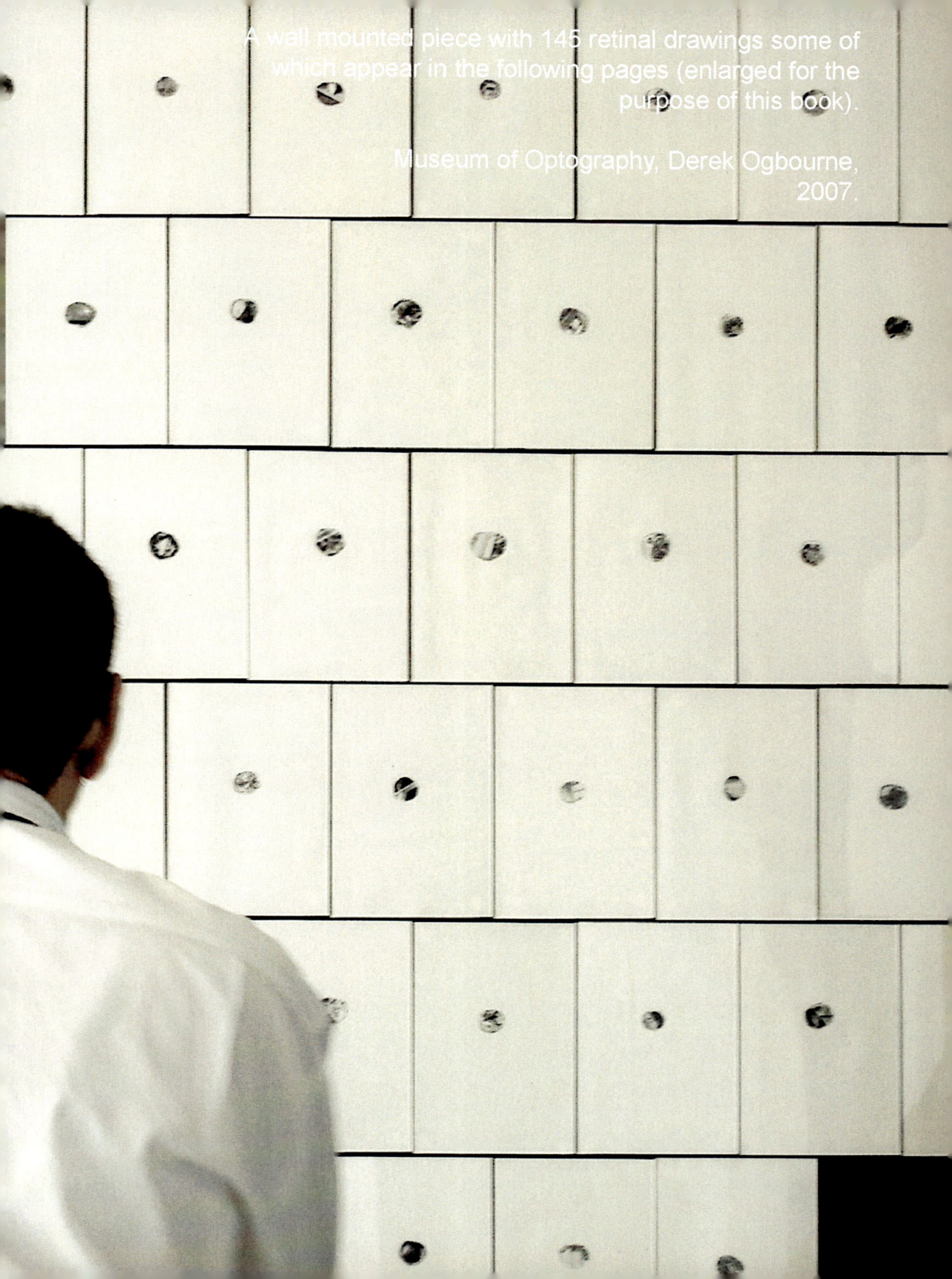

A wall mounted piece with 145 retinal drawings some of which appear in the following pages (enlarged for the purpose of this book).

Museum of Optography, Derek Ogbourne, 2007.

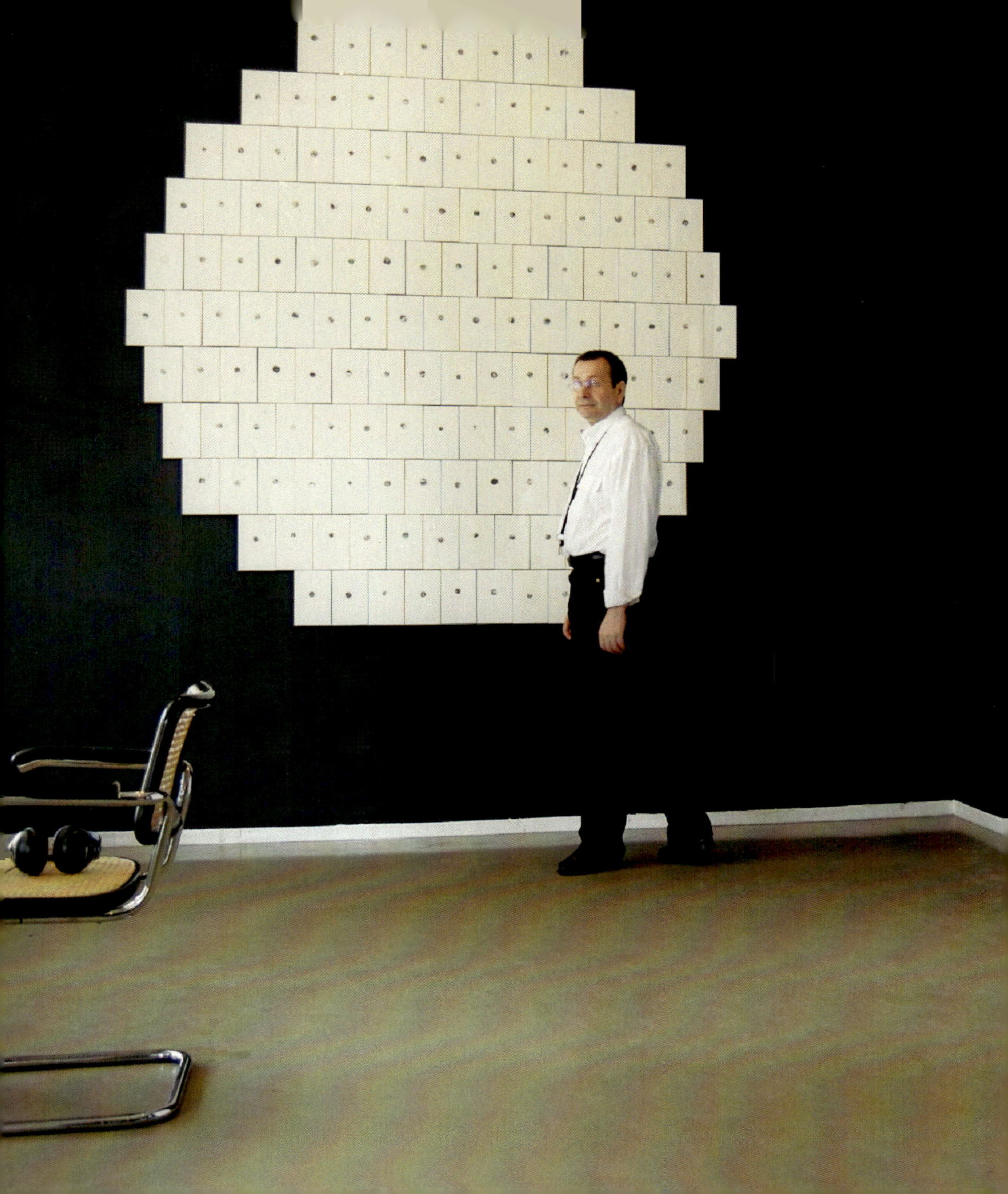

Retinal 145

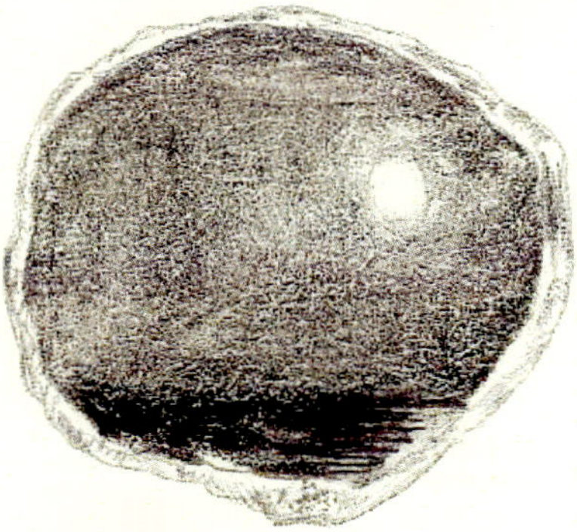

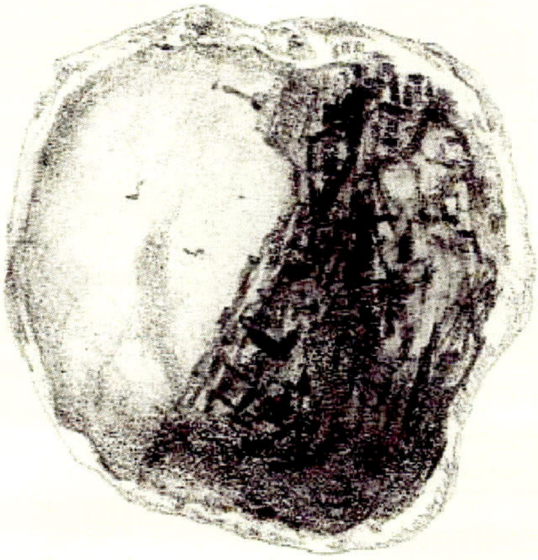

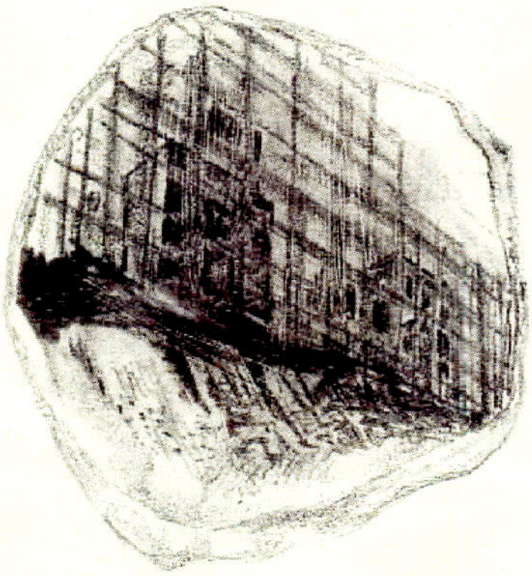

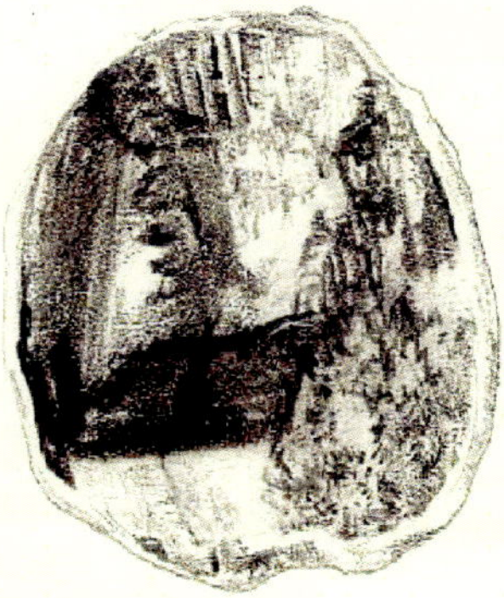

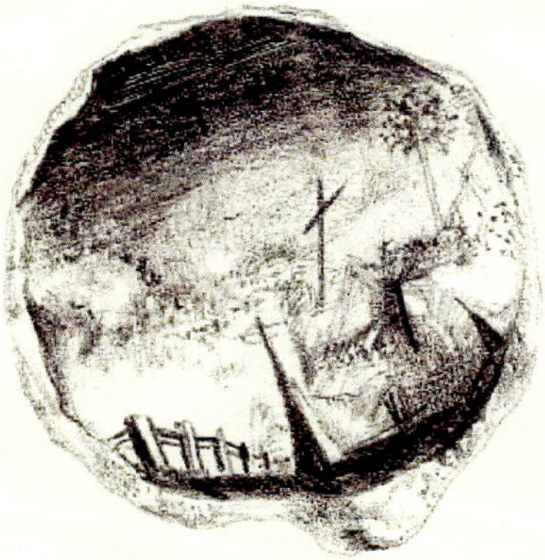

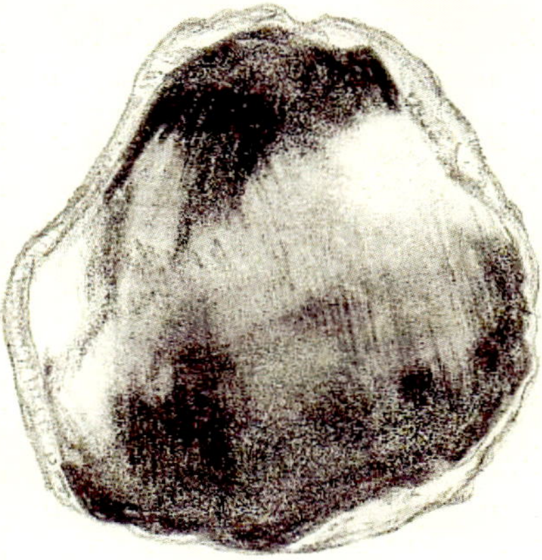

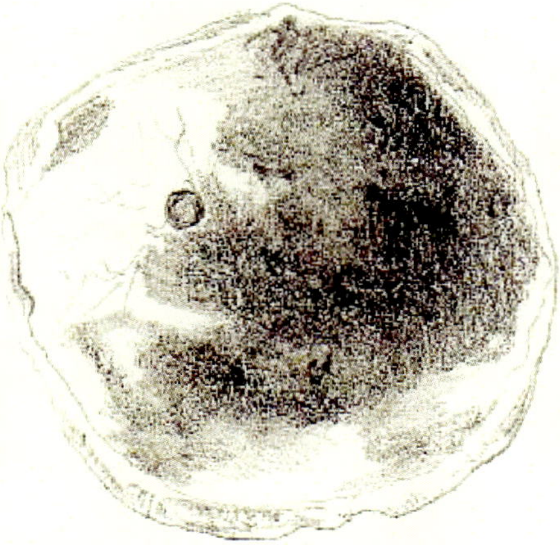

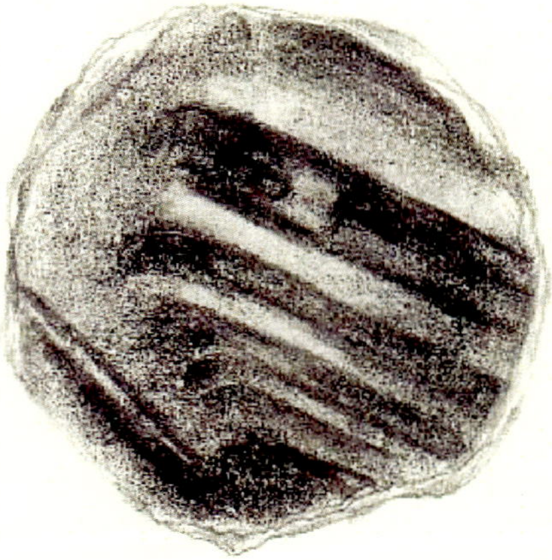

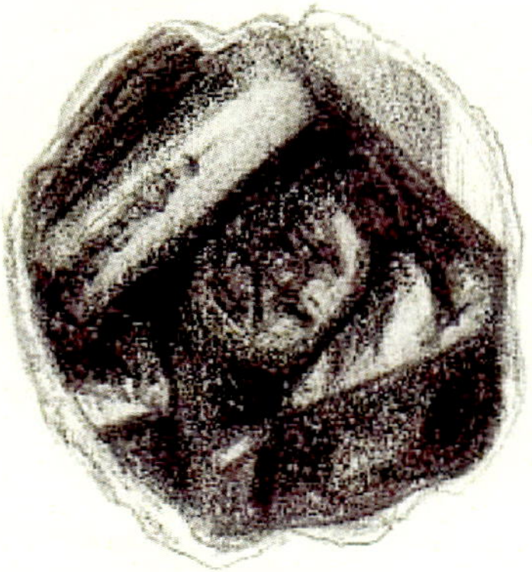

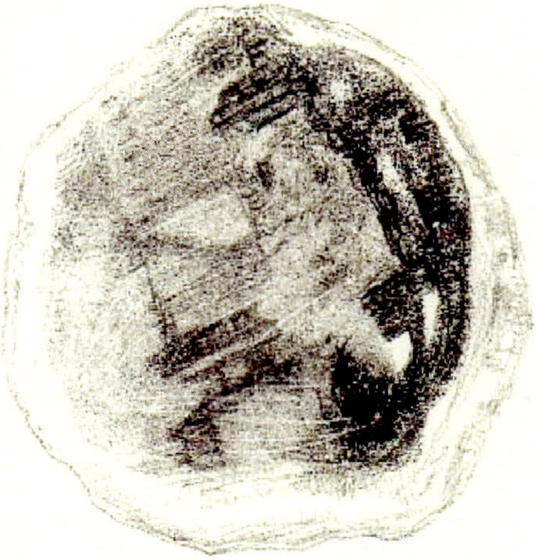

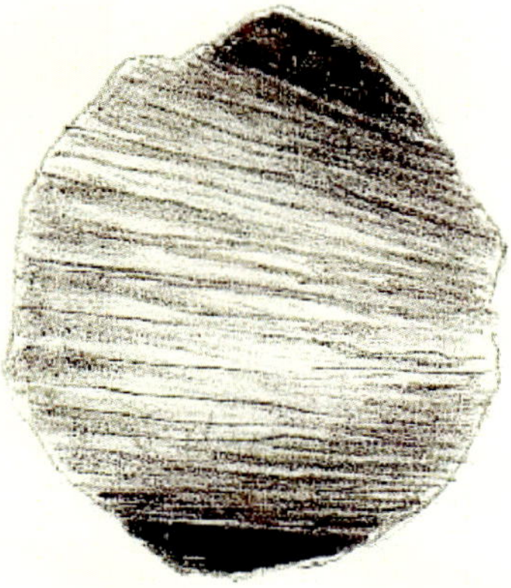

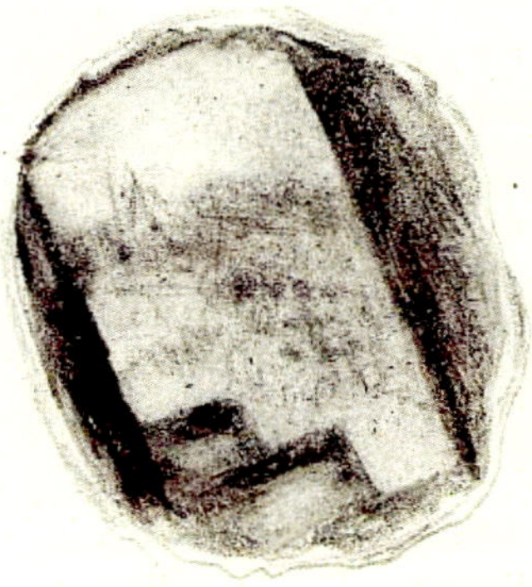

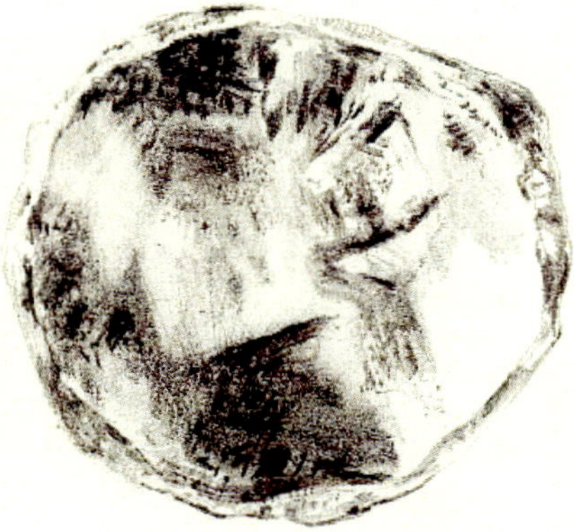

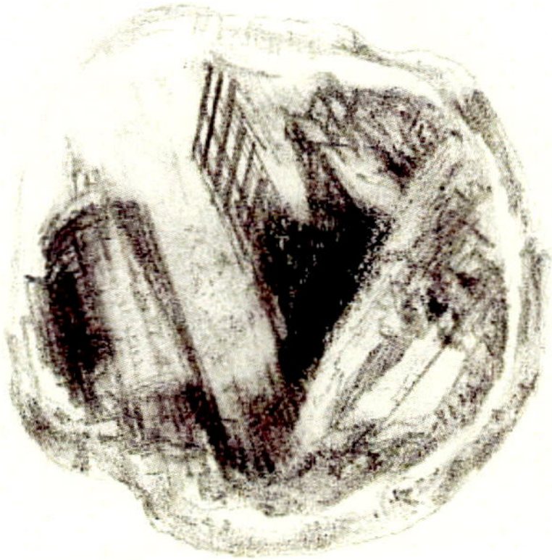

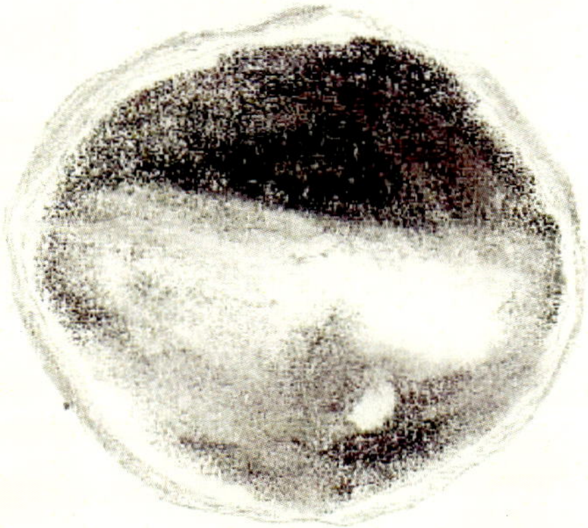

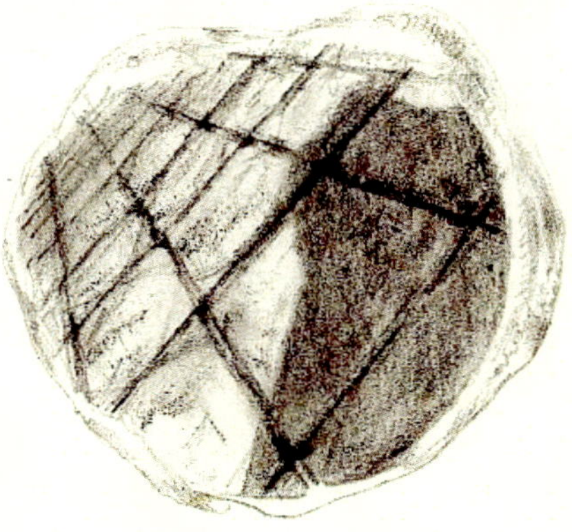

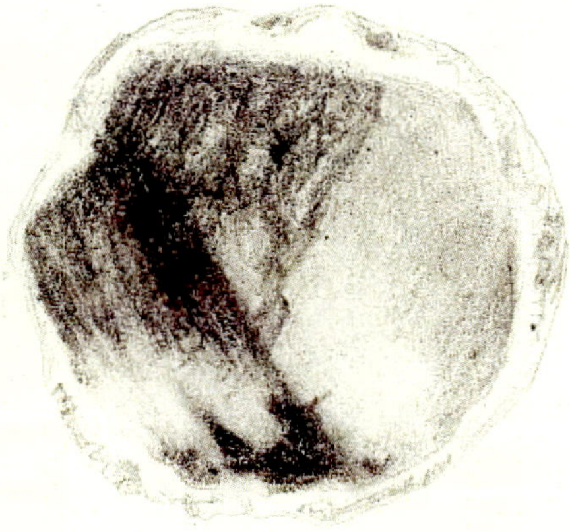

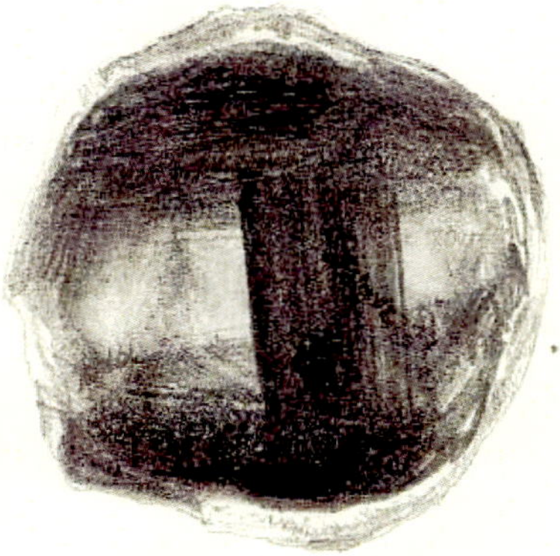

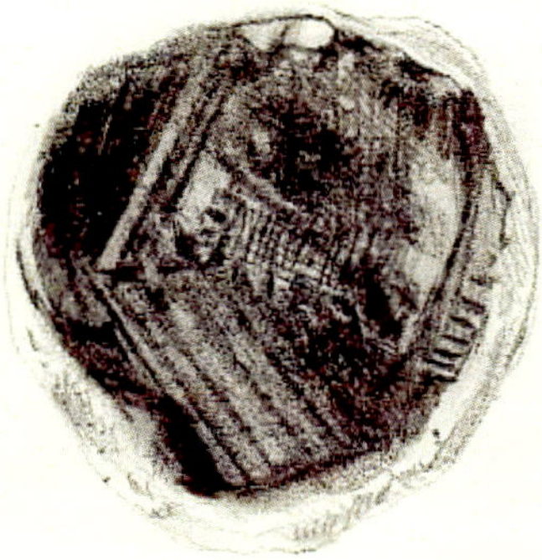

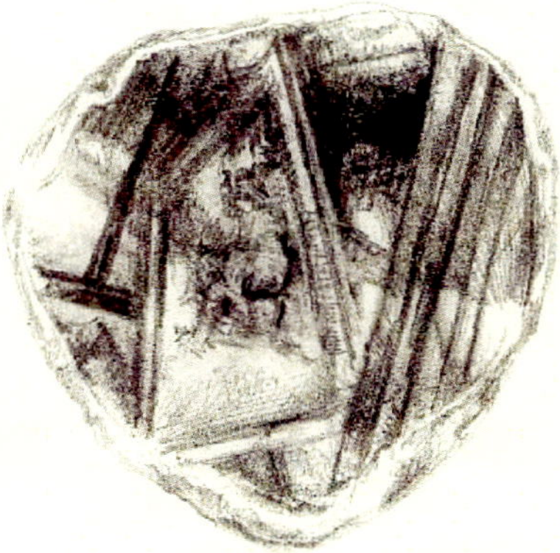

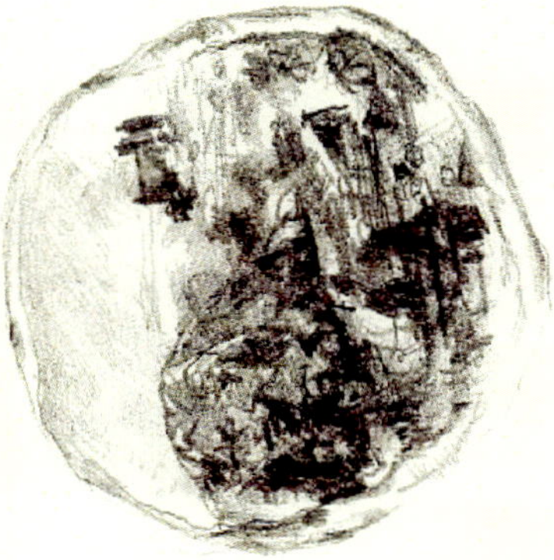

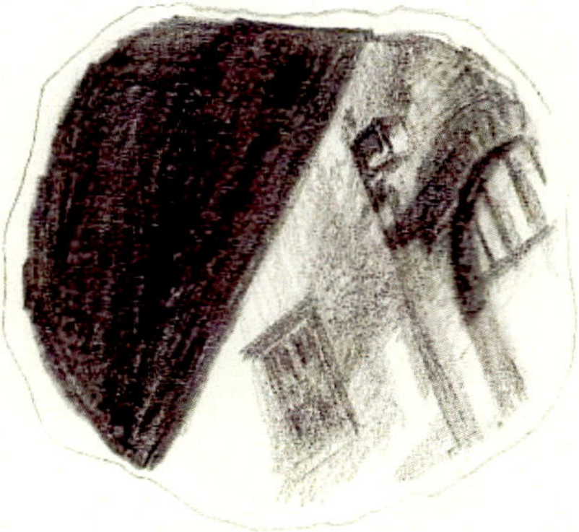

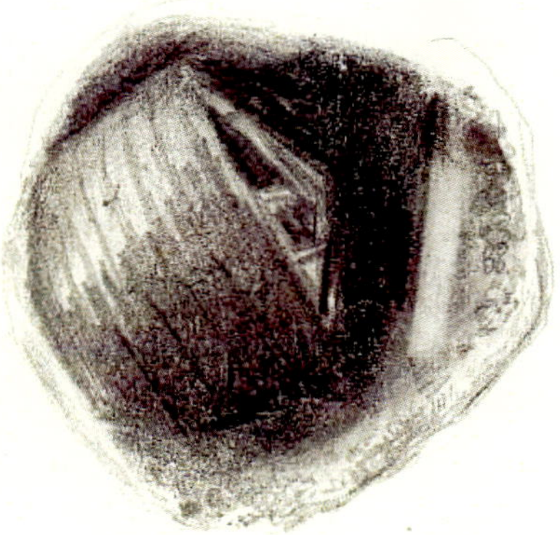

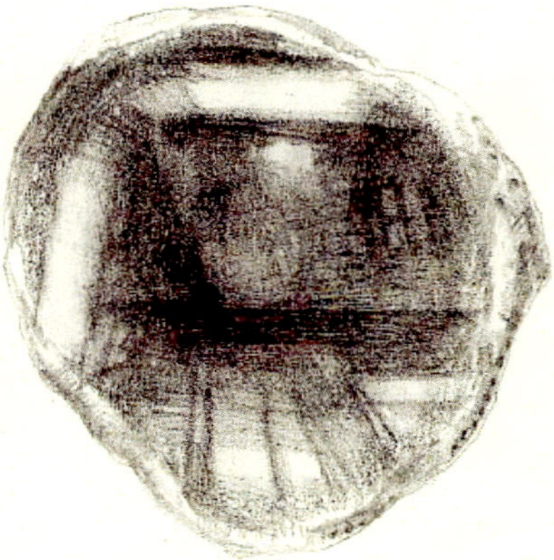

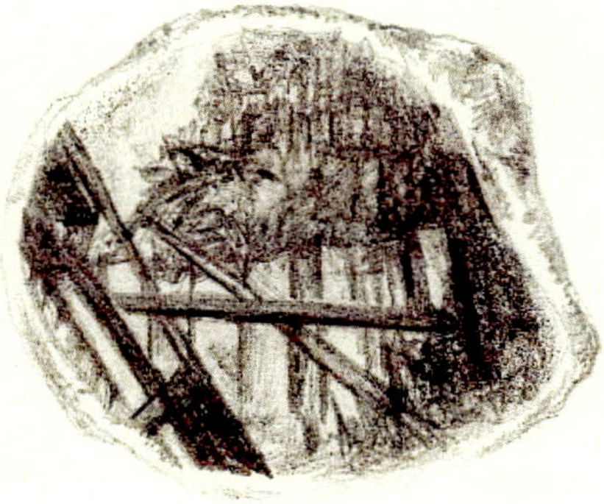

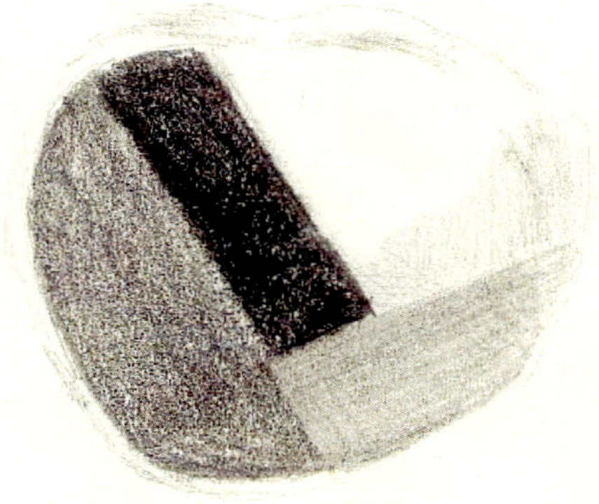

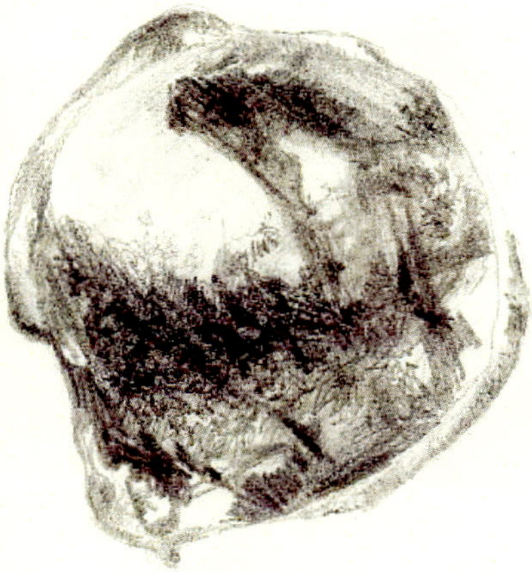

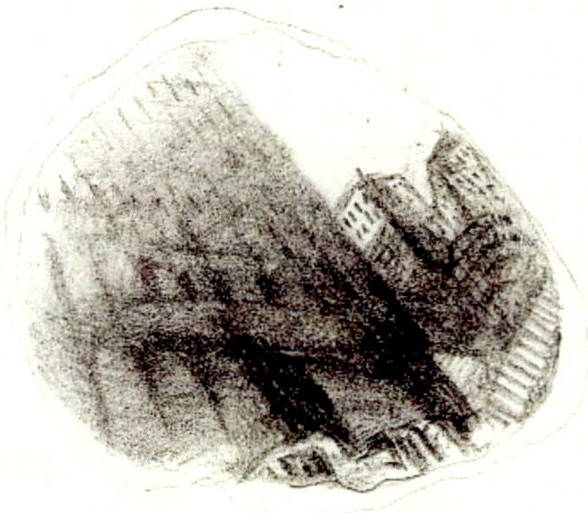

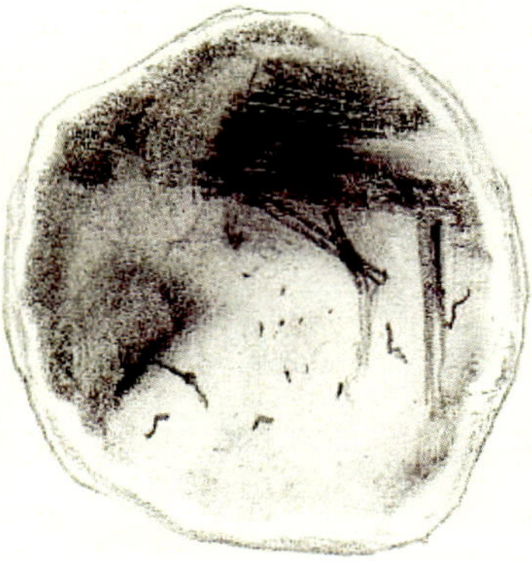

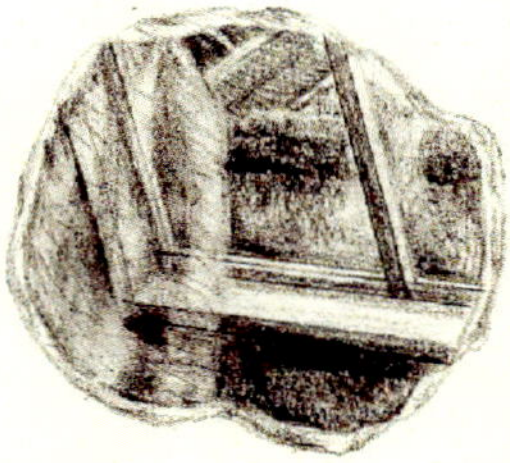

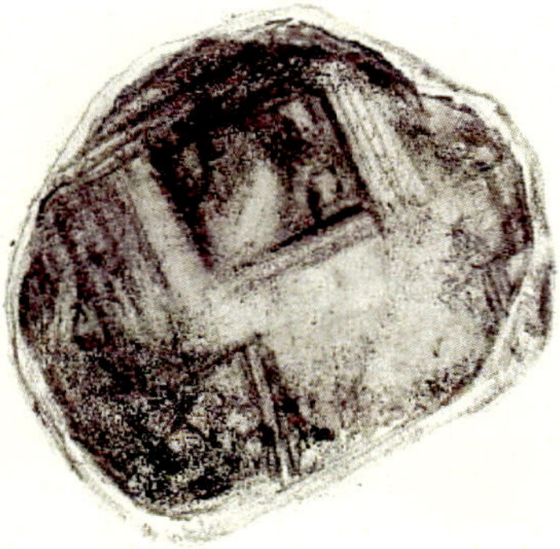

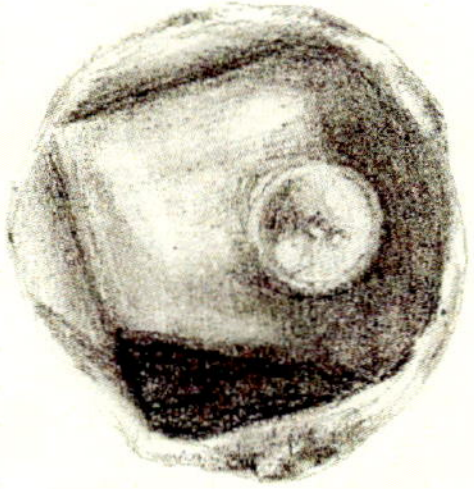

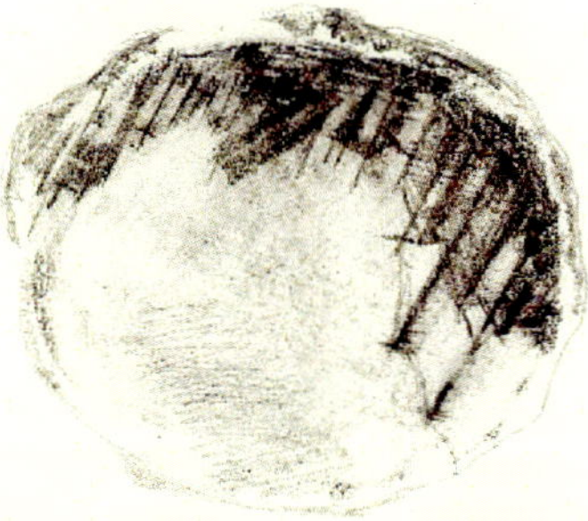

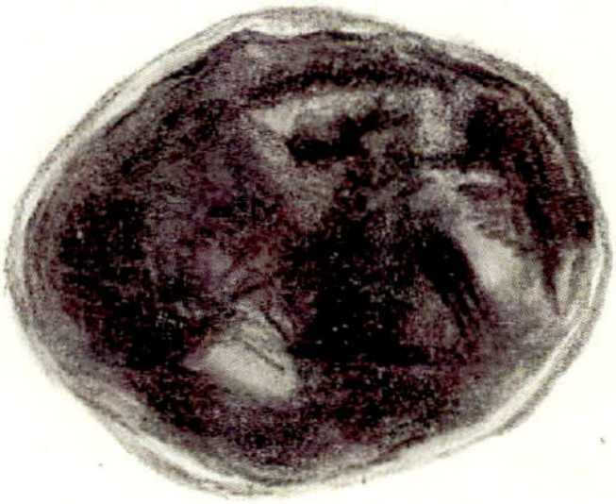

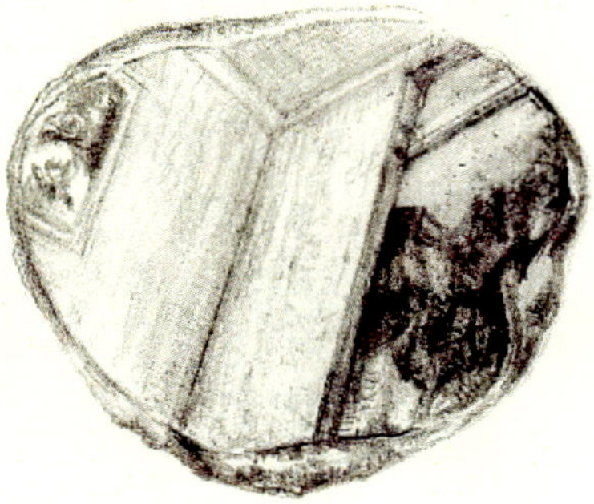

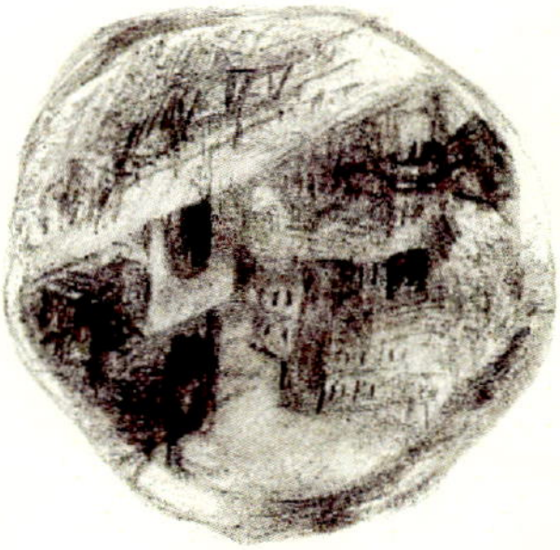

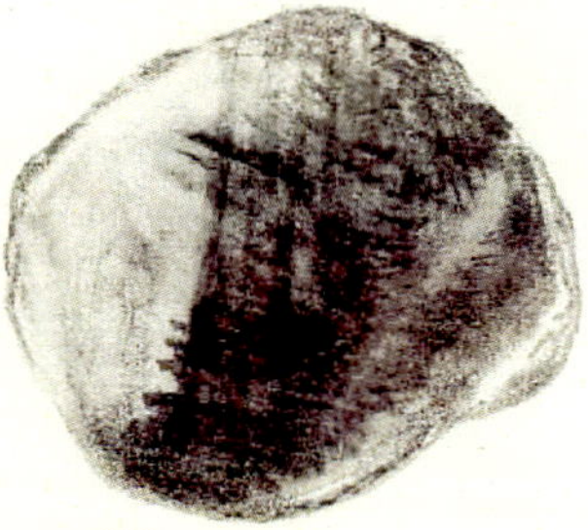

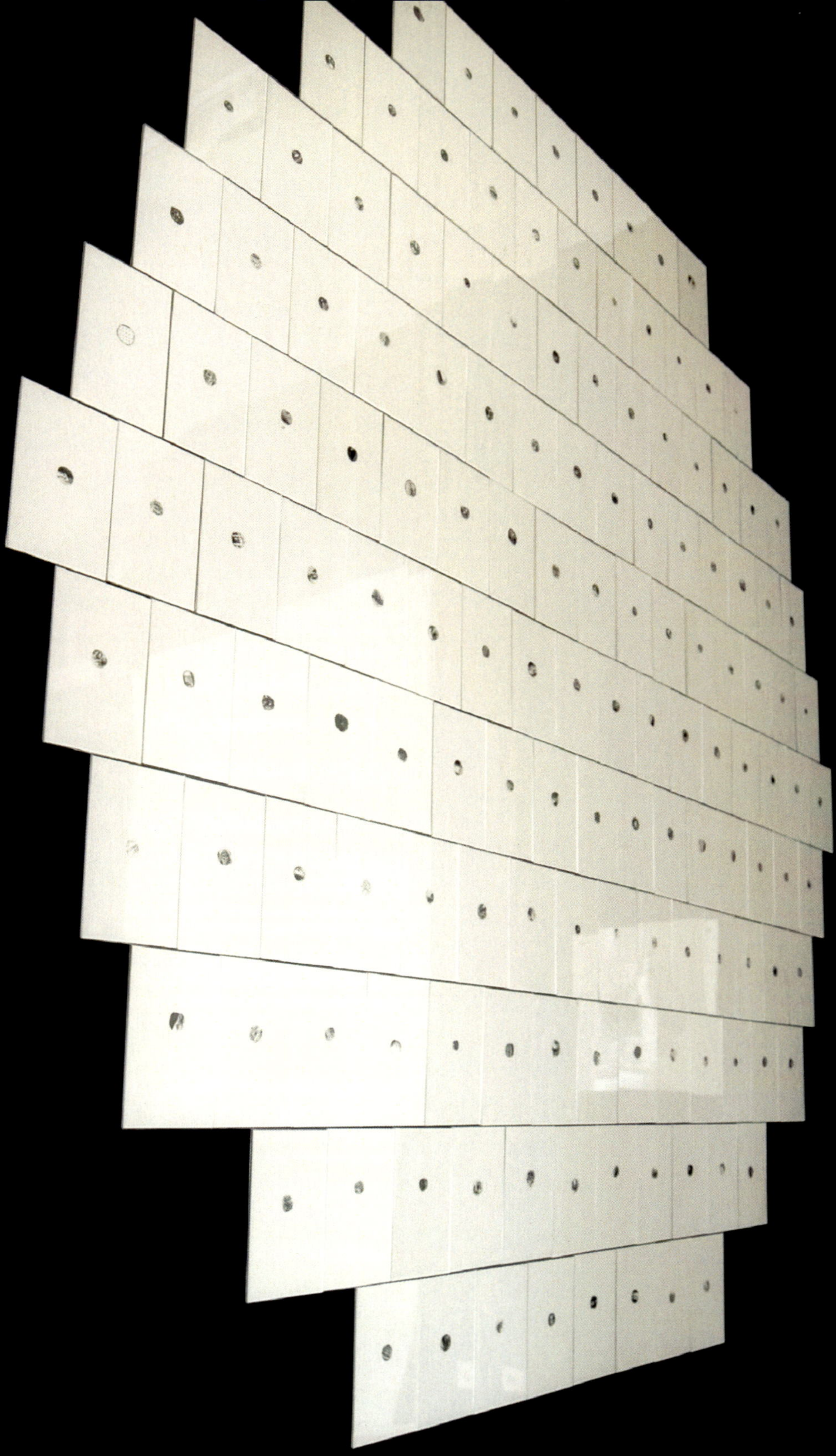

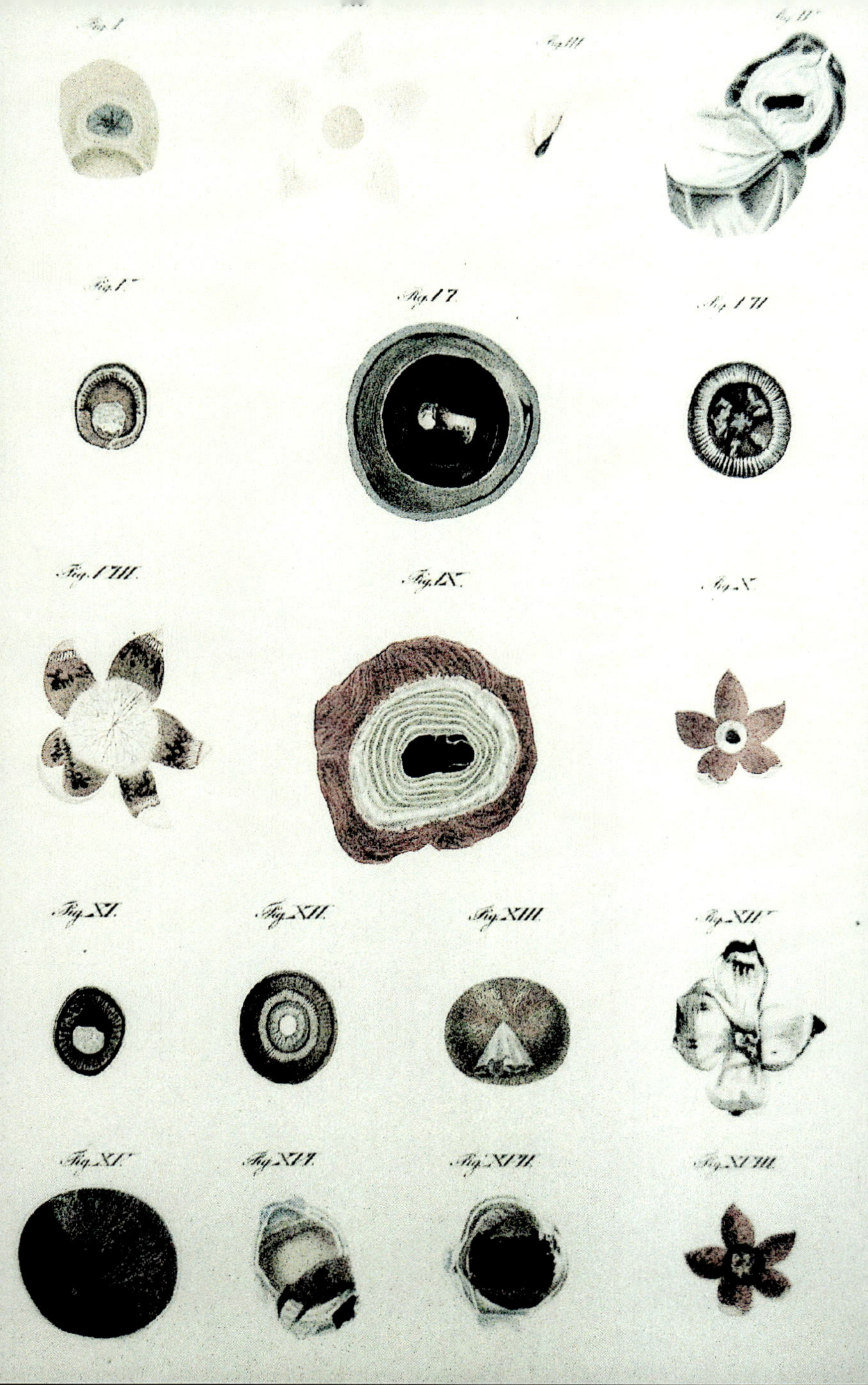

found these watercolours in Heidelberg University Hospital, Ophthalmic Library, the artist was unattributed

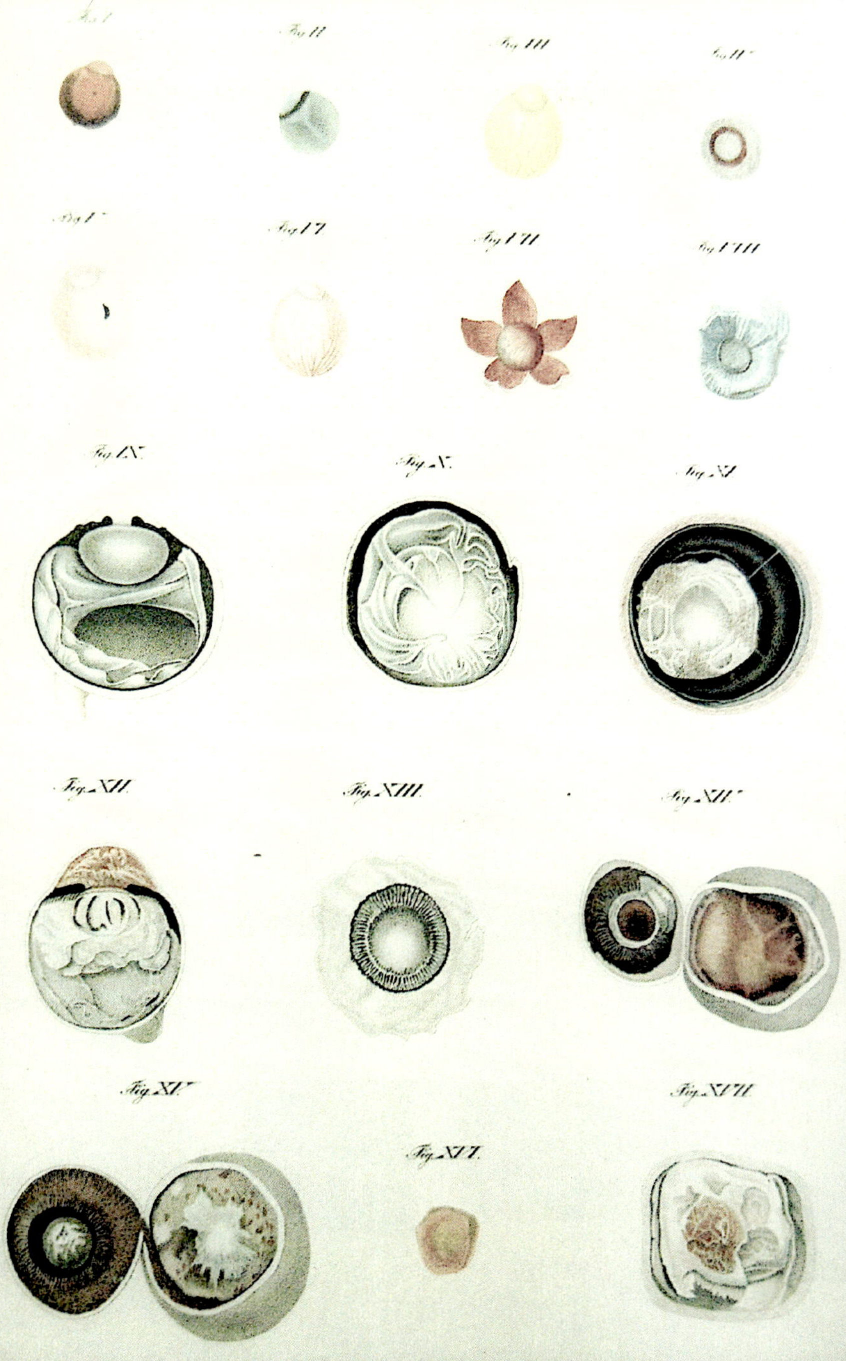
Fig. I
Fig. II
Fig. III
Fig. IV
Fig. V
Fig. VI
Fig. VII
Fig. VIII
Fig. IX
Fig. X
Fig. XI
Fig. XII
Fig. XIII
Fig. XIV
Fig. XV
Fig. XVI
Fig. XVII

THE DALÍ TAPE
September 1975

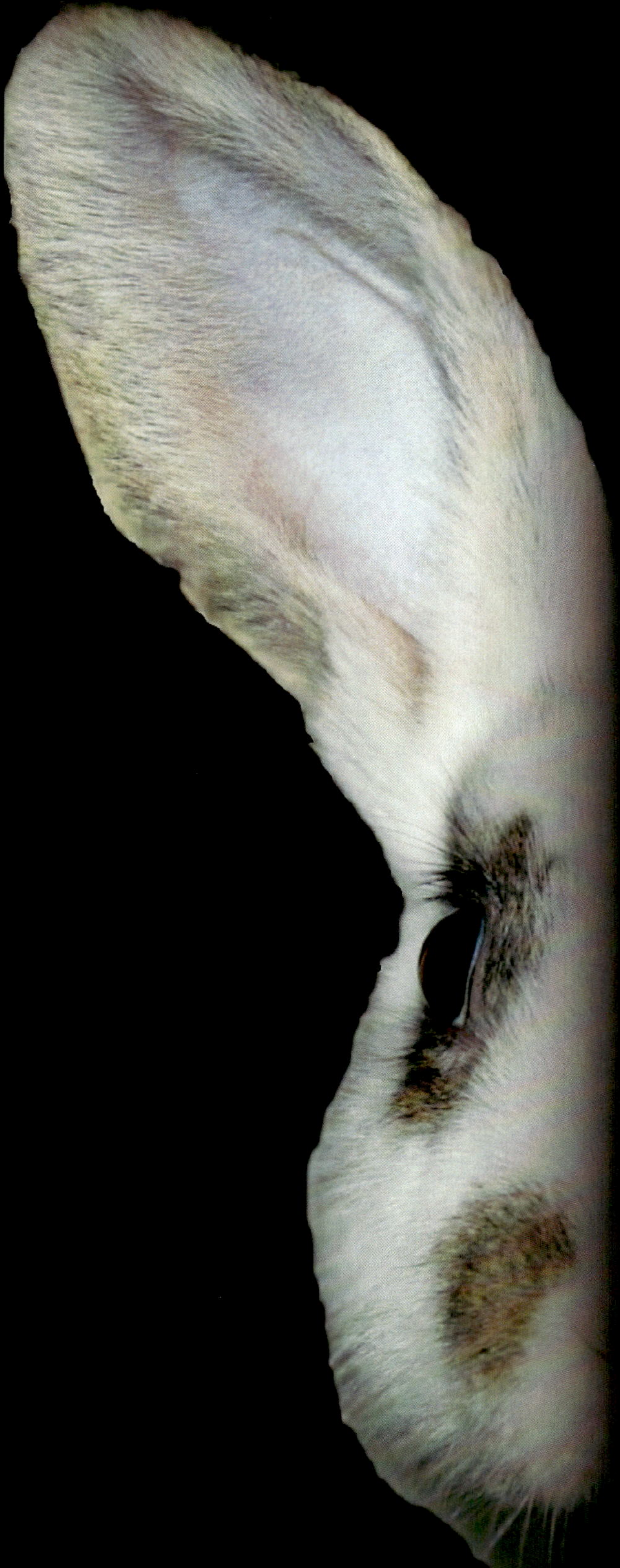

A: Alexandridis, 45
G: Gala, 81
D: Dalí, 77

(Rather chaotic tone on Gala + Dalí's part)

G: Digamé
A: Hello, hello, is that Gala?
G: Yes. Who is this?
A: My Name is Evangelos Alexandridis, I am scientist from Germany. I have a request for Mr Dalí that I think he would be interested in ... Can I talk to him ... is he there?
G: Well can you tell me something more, what's it all about?
A: I'd like to speak with Mr Dalí about optograms, It's kind of experiments I've done to fix the retinal image at the very moment of death.
G: Well, eh, just a minute. Just one second. I'll get him (Gala and Dalí in the background indistinct).

Pause ... background noises
Dalí picks up the phone
D: Quién es. Who is this?
A: Hello, hello, Mr Dalí, this is ...
(Overlapping above)
D: Who is this?
A: Mr Dalí this is a Evangelos Alexandridis,
D: (Interrupting) Yes this is Salvador Dali, Yes, yes.
A: My name is Evangelos Alexandridis I'm a scientist, a physiologist, Mr Dalí I am making experiments that, that I call optograms.
D: I can't, Mr Alexandridis, I can't hear you very well. Can you speak up?
A: Mr...Hello is that (Telephone beep) Mr Dalí can you here me now Mr Dalí?
D: Yes, yes, yes that is fine.
A: Yes, as I said before I want to introduce a kind of experimental process that is called optography this is the very special method to create pictures out from an image that is preserved in the dead animals eyes by the very moment of death.

D + G: Gala speaks to Dalí in the background (Dalí is briefly distracted)
D: Photograms, what are these photograms?
A: No, no, no, no. It's not called photograms, it's called optograms. It's a certain scientific method to preserve the retinal image, post-death. So what it is I can take photos with living eyes!
D: But Mr Alexandris ... Where did you get my number?
A: Oh Mr Dalí, I have to apologise, I currently wrote to you.
D: Did you? Eh, eh, wait a moment. Yes, yes I do remember something like this
(Dalí looks for the letter)
D: Your name again?
A: My name is Alexandridis. I work at the University of Heidelberg.
D: Momento.
(Dalí looks for the letter speaking with Gala).
D: Yes, it is here, we haven't opened it. Mr Alexandridis what do you want of me?
A: Mr Dalí I'm working, I'm working on optograms and I thought you might me very interested in what optograms are because I know your artworks have so many eyes in and I thought would like to see my images and maybe then we could create optograms together.... And it might be a new, new accent of your wonderful works.
D: If this is true, what you say, this does interest me ... er ... a bit but er, I have er, read about this somewhere. But er ... Why are you doing these optograms?
A: Mr Dalí, I can assure you that it is absolutely true what I told you because the police here in Heidelberg asked me to investigate whether the image in a dead man's eyes could reveal the murderer after a crime. So, my experiment was with an animal. My experiment was with rabbit. I want you Mr Dalí to choose an image as the last picture in a rabbit's eye, in a condemned rabbit's eye.
D: Eh, I see eh... Mr Alexandridis, can you wait a minute?
A: Yes, yes Mr Dalí.
D: Wait five minutes, and you ring me back in five minutes.

D: Can you do this?
D: OK, yes, five minutes. Thank you Mr Dalí, five minutes.

D + A put the receiver down. A calls D.
Phone rings.
D: Dígame?
A: Hello Mr Dalí, it's Mr Alexandridis again.
D: Ah yes, now, now um Mr Alexandridis. Carrying on from what we were talking about a minute ago, I think um I would like you to write down, I have here an image but you have to write it down. Can you get a pen or something and write what I say ....
A: Yes, Hold on a moment, I get a pen
(Alexandridis looks for a pen)
A: OK ... Mr ...
D: (Interrupts) Do you have a pen?
A: Dalí, I am ready .... I have a pen, yes ...... OK
Pause

Dalí Plays God
God plays Dalí
No, I tell you what, this is better:

Dalí is God
God is Dalí
Dalí is Dog
Dalí is God
Is Dalí God
Is Dalí Dog

D: Have you written this down?
A: Yes, Mr Dalí I think I've got it.
D: Then you have my image.
Thank you Mr Alexandridis, good bye.

A: But Mr Dalí, Mr Dalí you can't hang up the phone. What am I supposed to do now?

D: Puts receiver down......

Rabbit machine MK.1, Derek Ogbourne, 2006 ☞

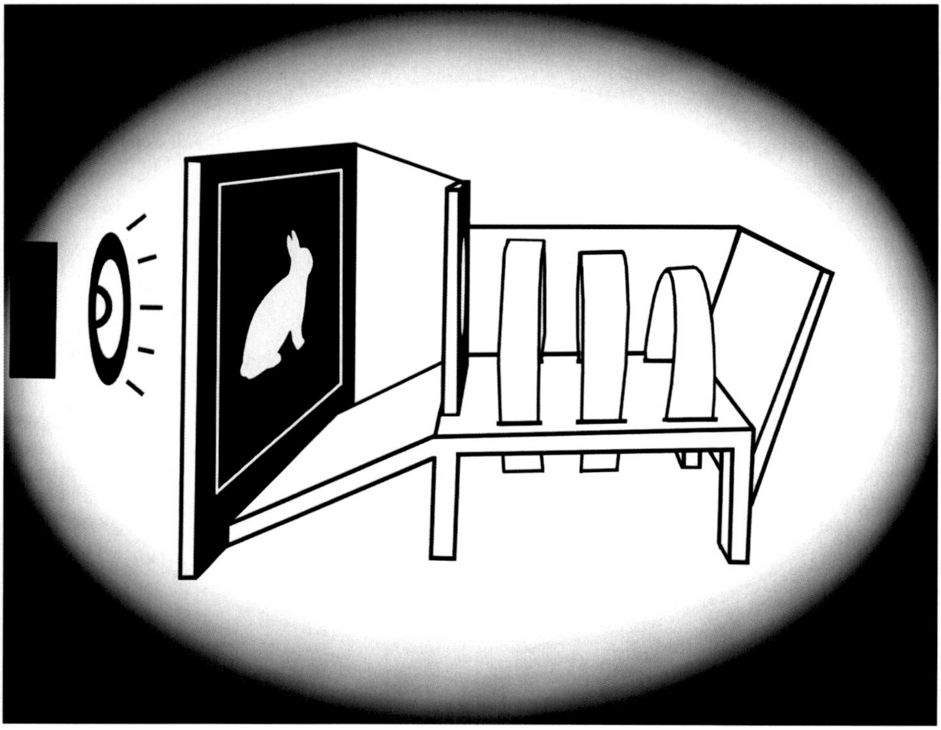

☝ *Rabbit machine MK.2*, Derek Ogbourne, 2006

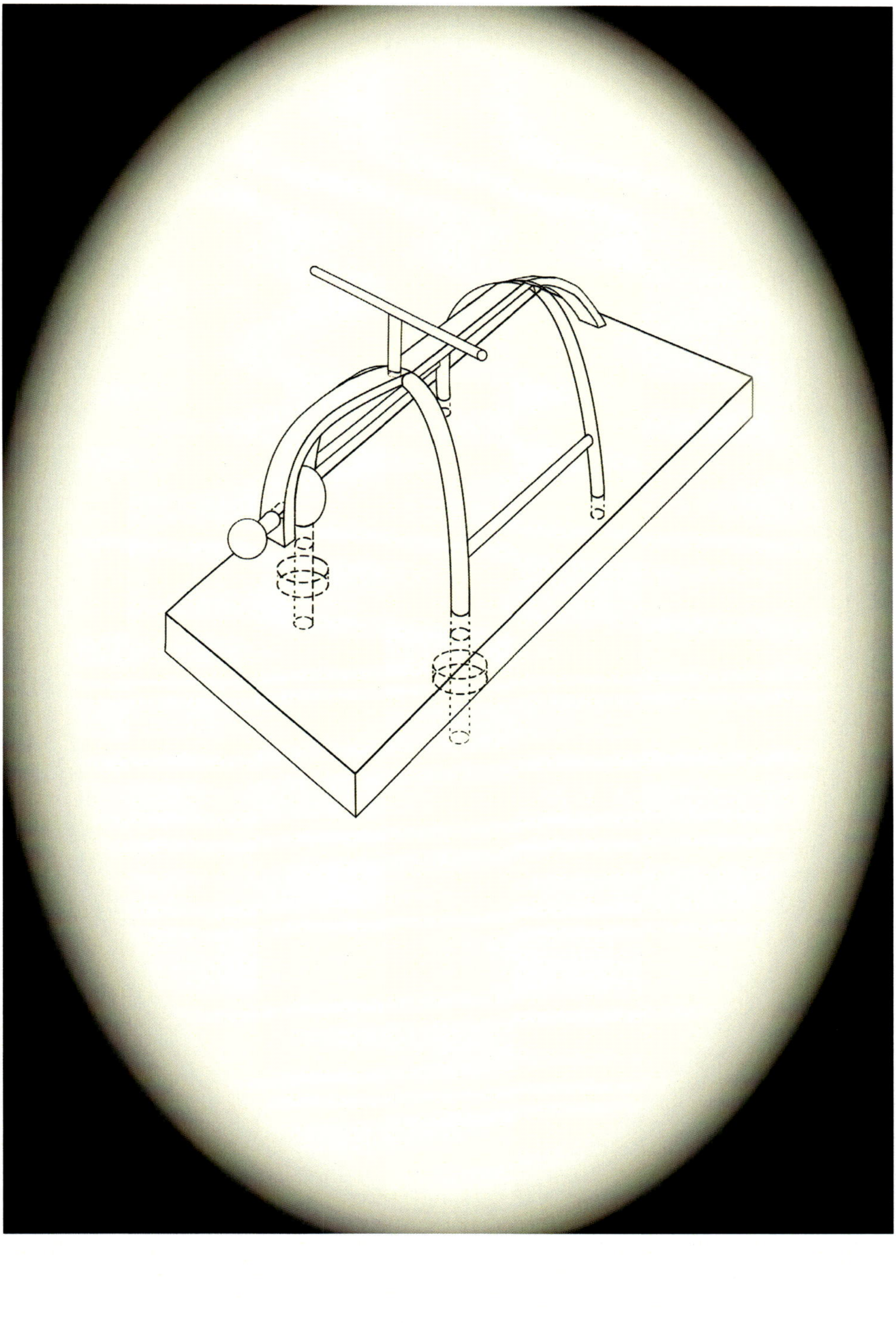

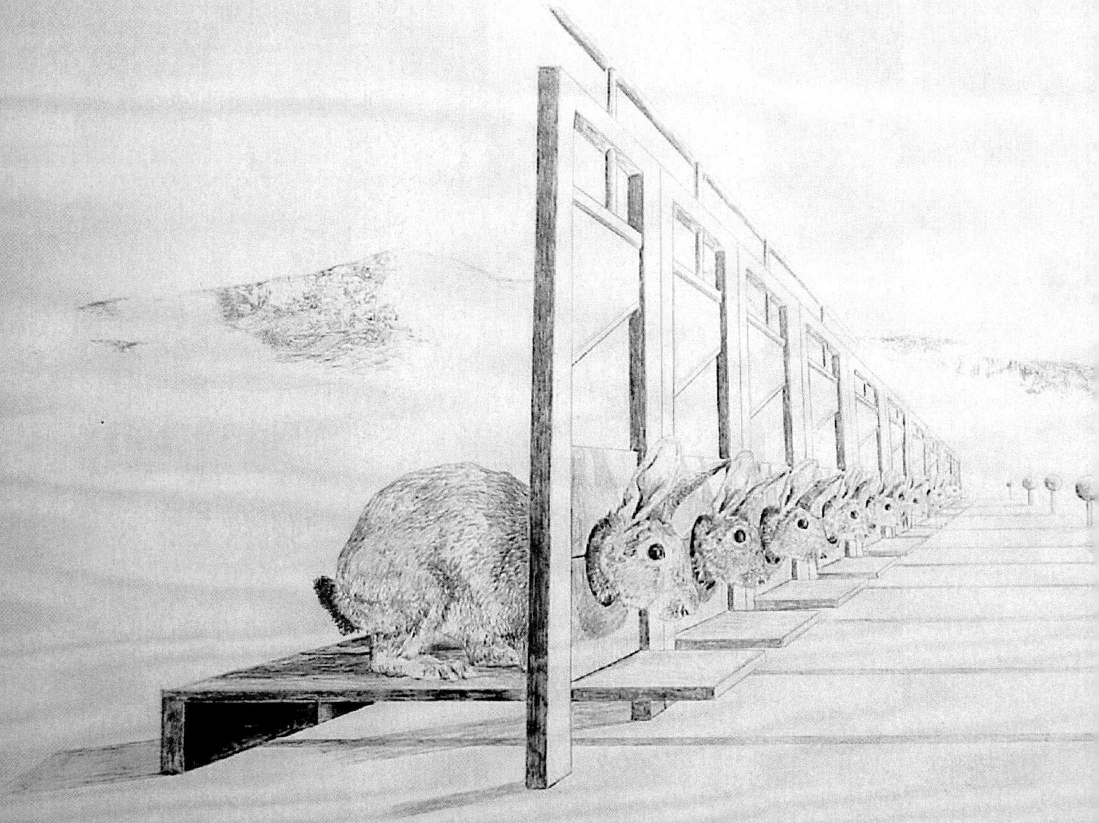

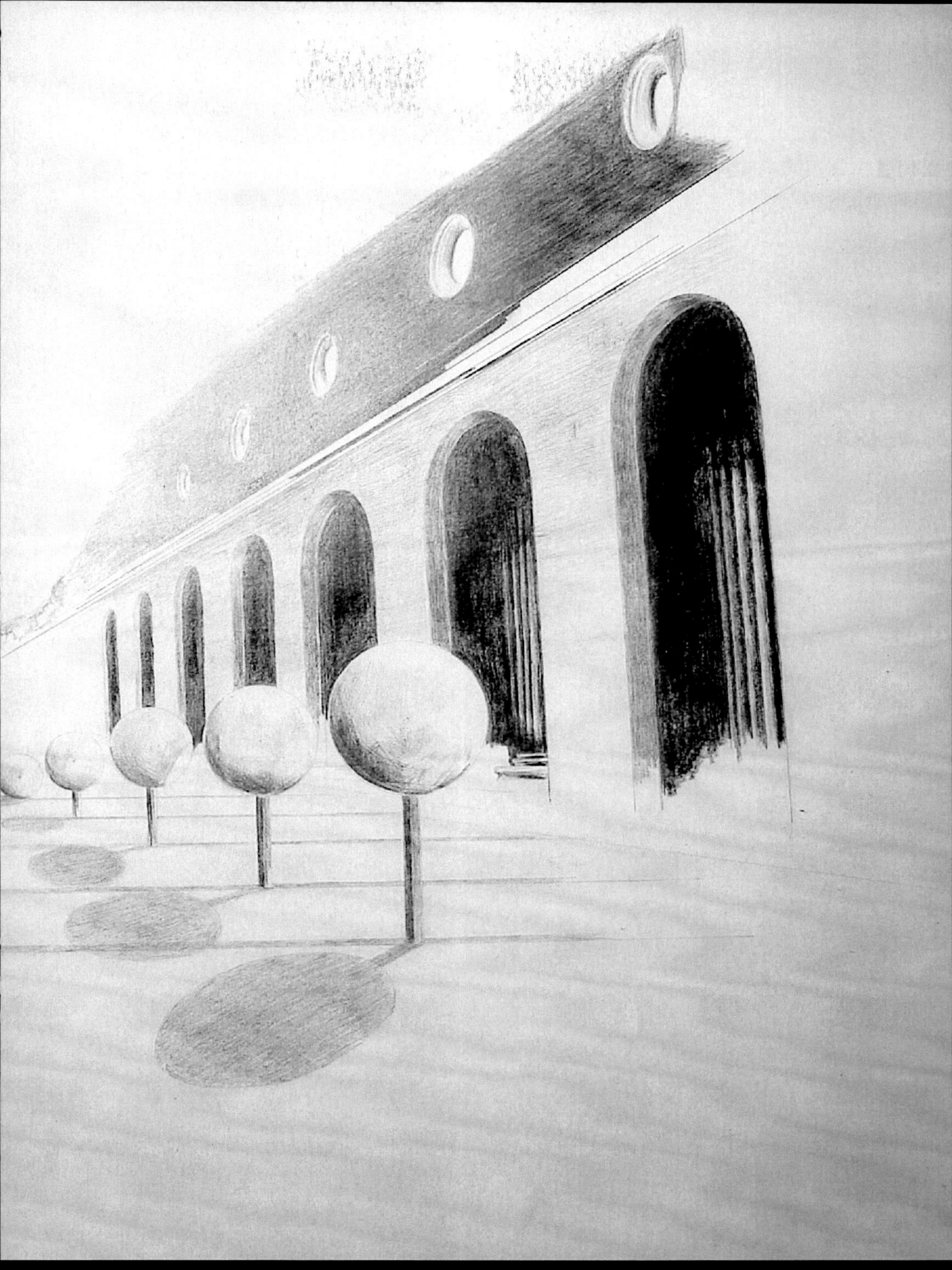

Homage to Eadweard Muybridge, Derek Ogbourne, 2006

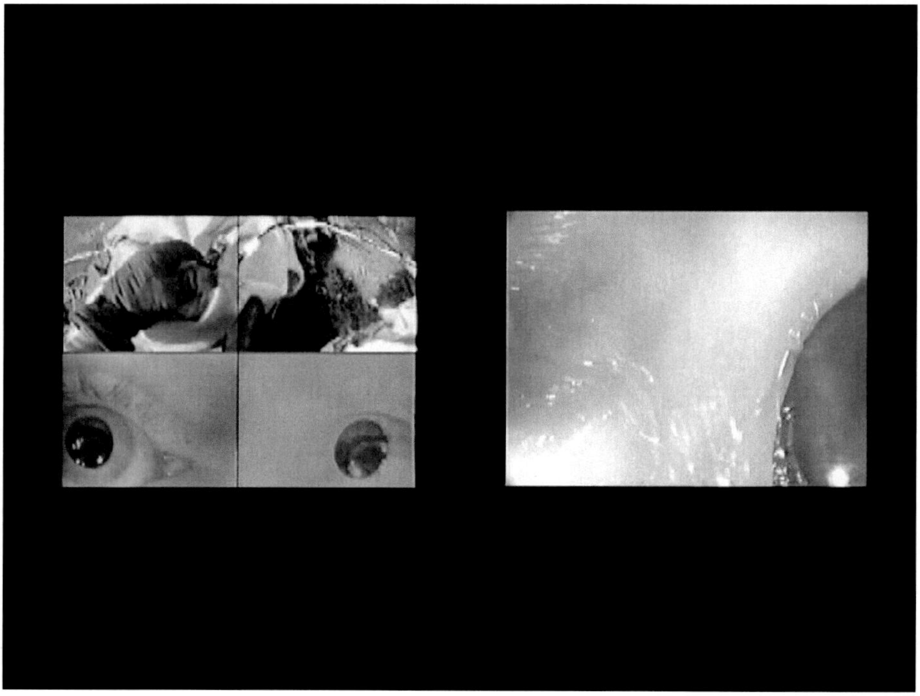

Gift, video still (9 mins) Derek Ogbourne 1999

Here we have a single monitor with two viewpoints. One shows us our protagonist's eyes (bottom left) caught in an act of exploratory attack and its object of offence (above right). The other viewpoint (right, not shown here) shows the concealed object of attack, the inner eye. Layers of insulation (metal, latex rubber, water and concrete) that surround the attacked are broken down by the external force eventually to expose the inner viewpoint (A tiny CCD camera) peering back at its attacker. Finally the inner 'being' is destroyed, leaving the attacker to ponder the deed.

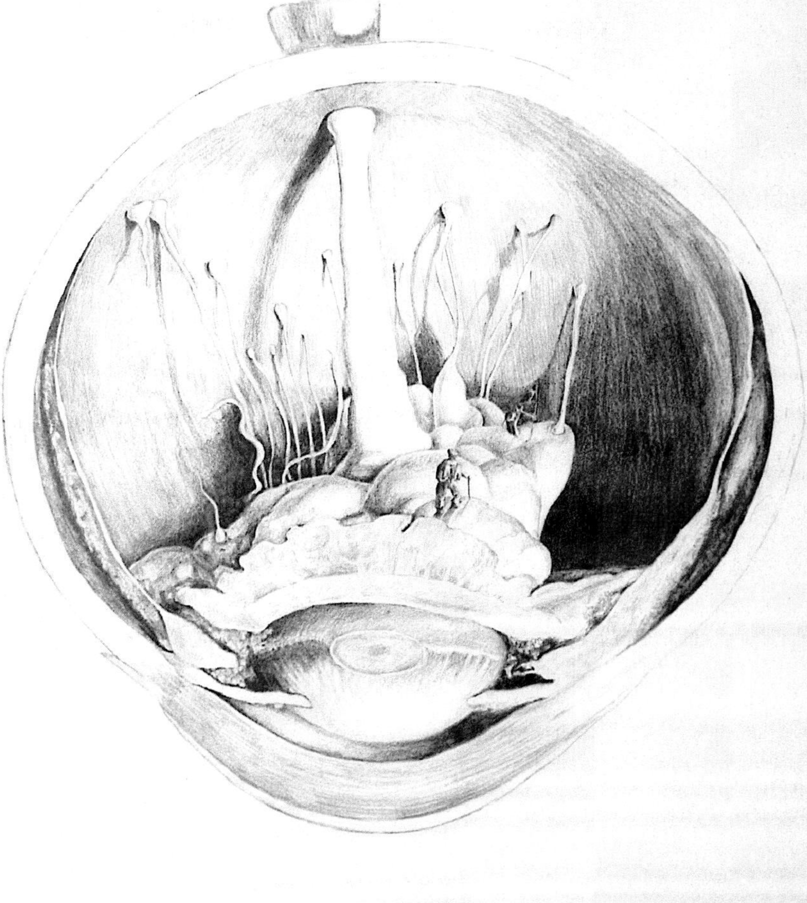

Beck, Olly

Olly Beck is an artist, writer and co-director of the independent artists run space Francis Hair Fashions Gallery in South London. He is widely published and is a regular contributor to the art periodical Garageland Magazine, and he co-edits the art zine The Critical Friend. His paintings are in collections around the world including Italy, Chile, Ireland, Mexico and the United Kingdom.

Memoirs of the Ocular

'If we describe the notion of the sun in the mind of one whose weak eyes compel him to emasculate it, that sun must be said to have the poetic meaning of mathematical serenity and spiritual elevation. If on the other hand one obstinately focuses on it, a certain madness is implied, and the notion changes meaning because it is no longer production that appears in light, but refuse or combustion, adequately expressed by the horror emanating from a brilliant arc lamp.' Georges Bataille

Contemplating the optogram, the final inscription, etched, as it is, onto the life of an eye that has endlessly consumed images during its lifetime; there is at once a sense of excitement mixed with disappointment. And later a feeling of sadness thrust up with church-like vaultings of guilt. How perfectly pathetic and horrific are these slithering templates that appear to testify that the final vista we experience (as is confessed in the eyes of the laboratory animals reproduced in this volume) will be as mundane and local as a checkerboard pattern, the number 75, the light through the cross hatch of a window frame, even a portrait of Salvador Dali, but ultimately whatever happens to be in our immediate vicinity in our final moment. For most then it will be the hospital room and its attendant equipment: the drip feed, the white linen sheets of the bed, a nurses tired brow, the double doors to the ward, the fluorescent ceiling, or perhaps the optogram of expectant and bewildered and mourning relatives. This latter image like a strange unwitting family portrait shooting back through time at the professional photographer who framed them at more mundane moment far from the ultimatum of death.

The eye as an organ of 'truth'. The sublime device that so far, no mechanical reproduction machine has been able to imitate. All the high definition and swarming pixelation in the world cannot compete with the palimpsestual longing that constitutes the eye and its cerebral receiver. Our machines are neither fast enough nor deviant enough to understand the roamings of the ocular drive, its rampant narrative reasoning, its endless desires and figurations. The eye refuses to be epitomized. It is too wayward, too promiscuous, too blind in its frenzy to see all that is before it. Indeed it is a wonder that optograms have any definition at all when considering this hysterical pivoting. One might expect then that an optogram would be more like a blurry triple exposure than a faded still life.

What is also apparent from these eye bulb portraits is that we are always looking out, from a fixed point, at the universe through the star lights in our skulls. These helpless globes of gel, salt, muscle, nerves: fix and then transmit what we purvey in a constant wide-angle stream to the soft pulpy grey-matter circuit boards of our minds. The eyes are like basements, black chambers, dark rooms, that squint at that most bright and burning incandescent star. Shards of light enter the skull piercing these twin cellars, flooding the cross that is the optic chiasm. The eyes are solar fuelled orb shaped lamps, twitching spherical lanterns swaying in the night of our thoughts. The eye consumes. The eye receives. The eye selects. The eye recalls the eye of another. The eye slips. But the eye is always looking out, stuck as it is, in the fortress of its socket, searching like a light house, the meaning and meaningless, the knowledge and non-knowledge of the celestial processions.

Perhaps it is here that we can ponder that the eye is like the universe in its hopeless pretensions to be a refined and eloquent system that will eventually reveal its reason and its limits. For it is the very violence and its attendant meaninglessness that stalks the universe and mankind's existence that makes the eye recoil in horror and then gawp in a frenzy within the same shallow breathe. To gorge ones own eye out would to be to realize with beatific passion that the organ of truth is also no more than offal slithering through bloody fingers.

The philosopher Georges Bataille notes that civilized man's anxiety over the eye means that we would never bite into it, whereas for the cannibal it is a fine delicacy. The eye is so much the object of horror when it is converted into a base material, when it is ripped from the sky and discarded to the earth amongst the dirt. Bataille is operating in his system of 'non-knowledge', knowledge that caves in on itself, upturning musty academic steeples, subverting and belching in the face of 'blind' truths.

In the making of Wilhelm Kühnes human optogram there is much ripping and slicing and discarding going on. The process is full of violence. Kuhnes' guinea pig, the iron founder Erhard Reif is a condemned murderer after brutally drowning his own children. He is to be guillotined and then immediately afterwards both eyes extracted. This all went ahead as planned and it was noted that as the eyes were being removed from the spouting severed head 'violent and disturbing movements around the eye still could be seen.' The squirming eye is then 'drilled' and emptied of all superfluous matter so that the retina maybe extracted and the optogram revealed in the optographic chamber.

After all this bloody dicing, after all this mess, the simplicity of the resulting image, the only known optogram from a human eye is astonishingly and reassuringly tabular, schematic and ultimately an abstract figure. The lab' animals had been more reliable delivering accurate portraits of their surroundings, but in the condemned murderer his last testament is this haunting abstract figuration, a figure of non-knowledge. It is as if Reif was thinking in that final moment, that slip from consciousness into the unknowable abyss of death, 'I know nothing of this life and yet I know everything and I realise it now as I hear the blade screeching over my neck... It is here in this figuration of nothing that fills my bulging, racing orbs...'

Olly Beck
London, June 2008

Georges Bataille, Visions of Excess, University of Minnesota Press, 1985, p.57

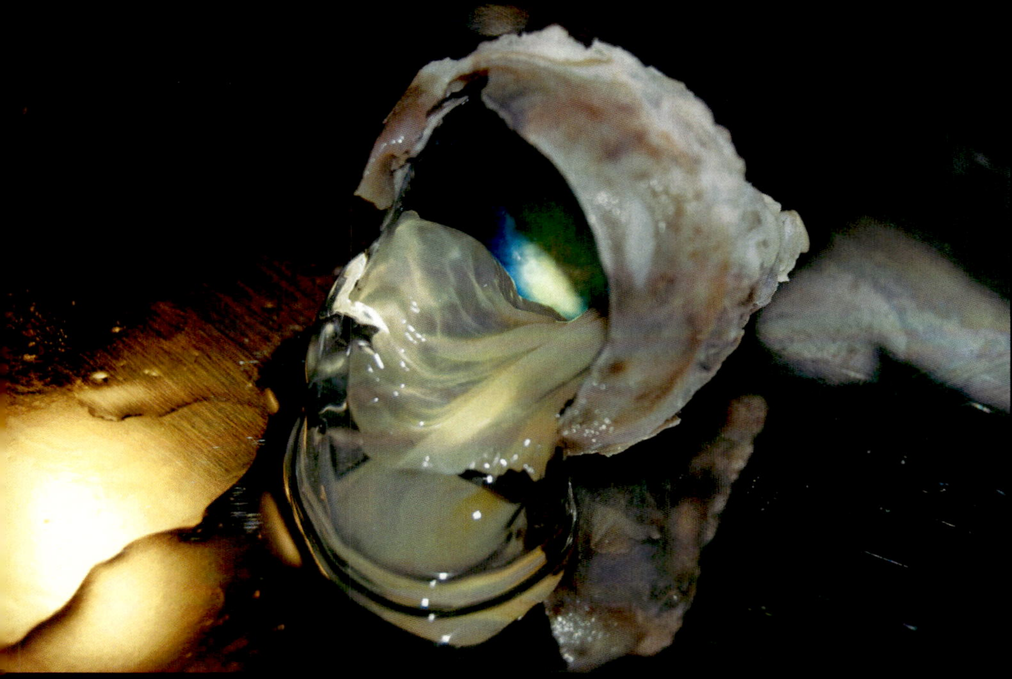

Still from cow's *eye dissection series*, Derek Ogbourne, June 2008

Trauma and the Creative Act.

Derek Ogbourne

Recently I discovered where my fascination with optography, to the degree that my need to do an exhibition and book, became imperative. It is rooted in the fears and anxieties associated with trauma, A trauma that has spurned at least 10 years of artwork. Trauma that began one night after a party nearby to my house.

I was with a friend that had gotten into an argument over a whisky bottle she was supposed to have stolen. We were thrown out of the party and she proceeded to empty the contents of a dustbin on to the front door of the house.

A short time after, both of us were sitting on a low wall facing the road nearby the party when out of the blue a punch flew to my right eye from the left hand side. I was looking straight ahead completely unawares when it happened, I was dressed totally in white, the aggressor I neither saw or heard, the blood glugged out covering my clothing in red.

For the next week or two I had a strange fear of crossing the road. All vehicles became the potential of an unforeseen blow to the eye or worse, never to see again or never to be again. Still now I have what I believe everybody has, a blink of mortality that occurs when a bus passes within a centimetre of the nose. This trauma, a fear of a sudden death, is akin to the photographic moment, although it is understood that we are blind for 10 per cent of our waking lives due to the fact that, in order to avoid disorientation, our optic nerves fall silent while our eyes are moving between stills[1]. Therefore under certain conditions the afterimage remains imprinted moments after the near death moment in a confusion of the senses; yes, no, that could have been it.

Some of us would like to choose that last thing we see. I made a series of drawings after asking people what they would choose as their last image, interestingly males were more egocentric in their choice. Jesus Christ, myself in the mirror, my car, as examples. Whereas women replied with: my children, my husband, a sunset.

1.The Eye: A Natural History. Simon Ings

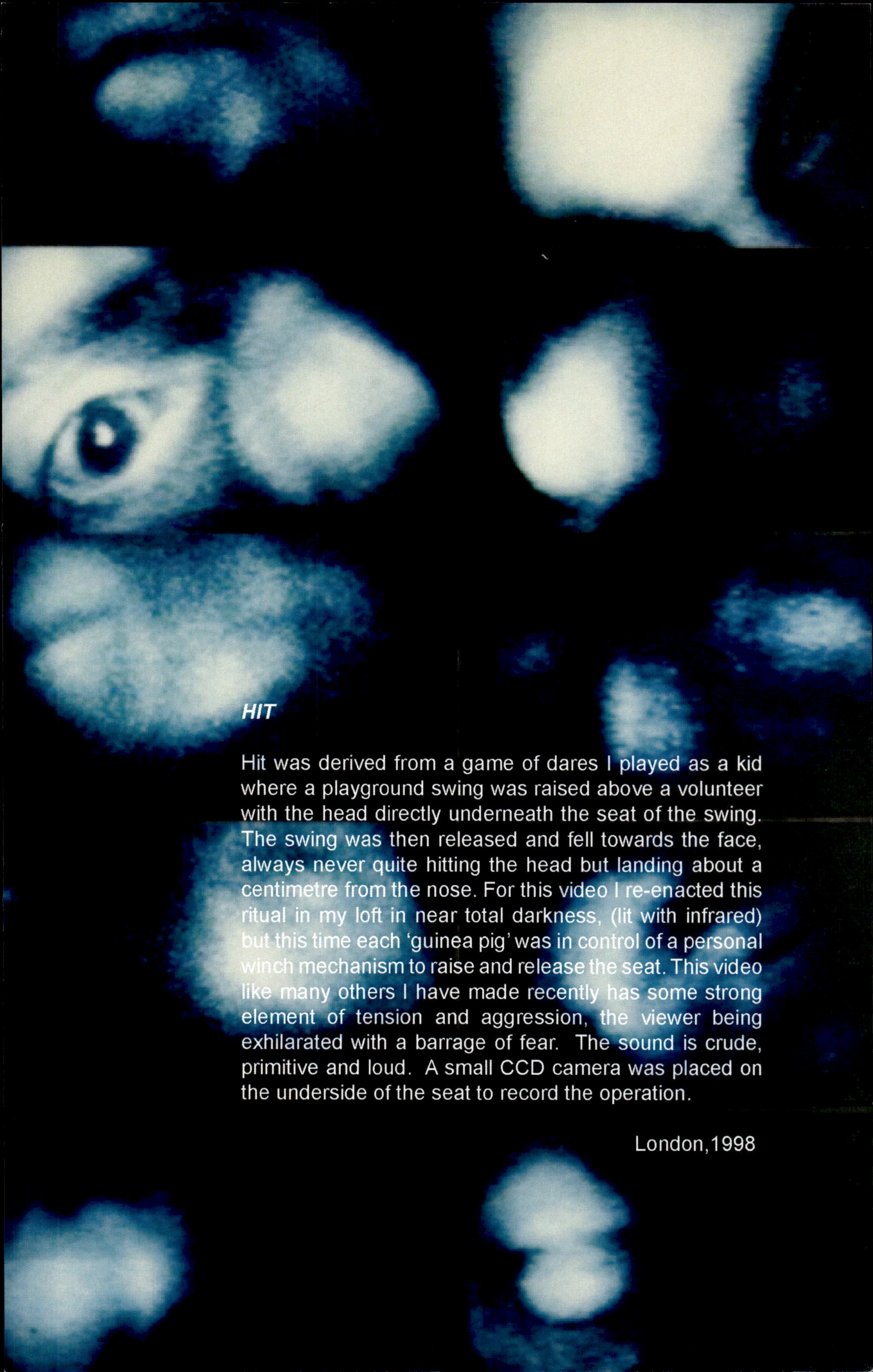

HIT

Hit was derived from a game of dares I played as a kid where a playground swing was raised above a volunteer with the head directly underneath the seat of the swing. The swing was then released and fell towards the face, always never quite hitting the head but landing about a centimetre from the nose. For this video I re-enacted this ritual in my loft in near total darkness, (lit with infrared) but this time each 'guinea pig' was in control of a personal winch mechanism to raise and release the seat. This video like many others I have made recently has some strong element of tension and aggression, the viewer being exhilarated with a barrage of fear. The sound is crude, primitive and loud. A small CCD camera was placed on the underside of the seat to record the operation.

London, 1998

Dario Argento's obscure 1971 film 'Four Flies on Grey Velvet'

The third and final part of the 'Animals Trilogy' sees master director Dario Argento in familiar Giallo territory. Michael Brandon plays a rock musician who is photographed by a masked assailant stabbing and killing a man that has been stalking him. Later, the masked assailant starts to send Michael Brandon photos of him in the act, and that's where the fun starts.

Dead Man's Eyes/Pillow of Death, 1945

An artist (Lon Chaney Jr) is blinded by a jealous assistant/model. His fiance's father generously offers his eyes for a sight restoring operation. There's only one hitch, Chaney has to wait until after the man dies. Not surprisingly, when the benefactor dies a very premature death, suspicion falls on the artist.

mdb.com, summary written by danno@nji.com

The Twilight Zone
Dead Man's Eyes October 9, 2002

A distraught widow and former rehab patient on the verge of a total mental collapse, heavily invested in finding her husband's killer, discovers that her murdered husband's eyeglasses reveal the last moments of his life and possibly the identity of his killer. Step by step she goes through the last minutes of his life, seeing her husband argue with his partner, the prime suspect. But she sees the suspect leave and her best friend come in - the two were having an affair. But in the end she sees who really killed her husband - herself, and she then blanked it out due to her alcohol problems. Forced to confront the truth, she is put away for good.

TV.com

Dreams That Money Can Buy
1947

American experimental feature colour film written, produced, and directed by surrealist artist and dada film-theorist Hans Richter. Collaborators included Max Ernst, Marcel Duchamp, Man Ray, Alexander Calder, Darius Milhaud and Fernand Léger. The film won the Award for the Best Original Contribution to the Progress of Cinematography at the 1947 Venice Film Festival.

"After all the artist has to suffer. It must be a grain of Italian dust (wipes eye) left over from your last campaign or put it down to eye strain. Look at your self (looks in mirror). A real mess, your'e all mixed up, snap out of it, get yourself fixed up. Even if poets misbehave they always remember to shave. Say, What's the matter Joe is some thing gone wrong? Is your head on wrong? No, it's terrific. Here's something you can really pride yourself. You've discovered that you can look inside yourself. You know what that means. Your'e promoted. Your no longer a bum, your'e an artist"

"Remember a poem you once read. The eye is a camera it said. Suppose like a film it could retain the images that glide so secretly through your brain. Have you ever tried to see the shadow word inside photographed by the retina and held suspended in its memory? This is one of the more unusual talents and it's yours it seems Joe. Maybe this will revive your bank balance.Remember everybody dreams Joe. If you can look inside yourself you can look inside anyone"

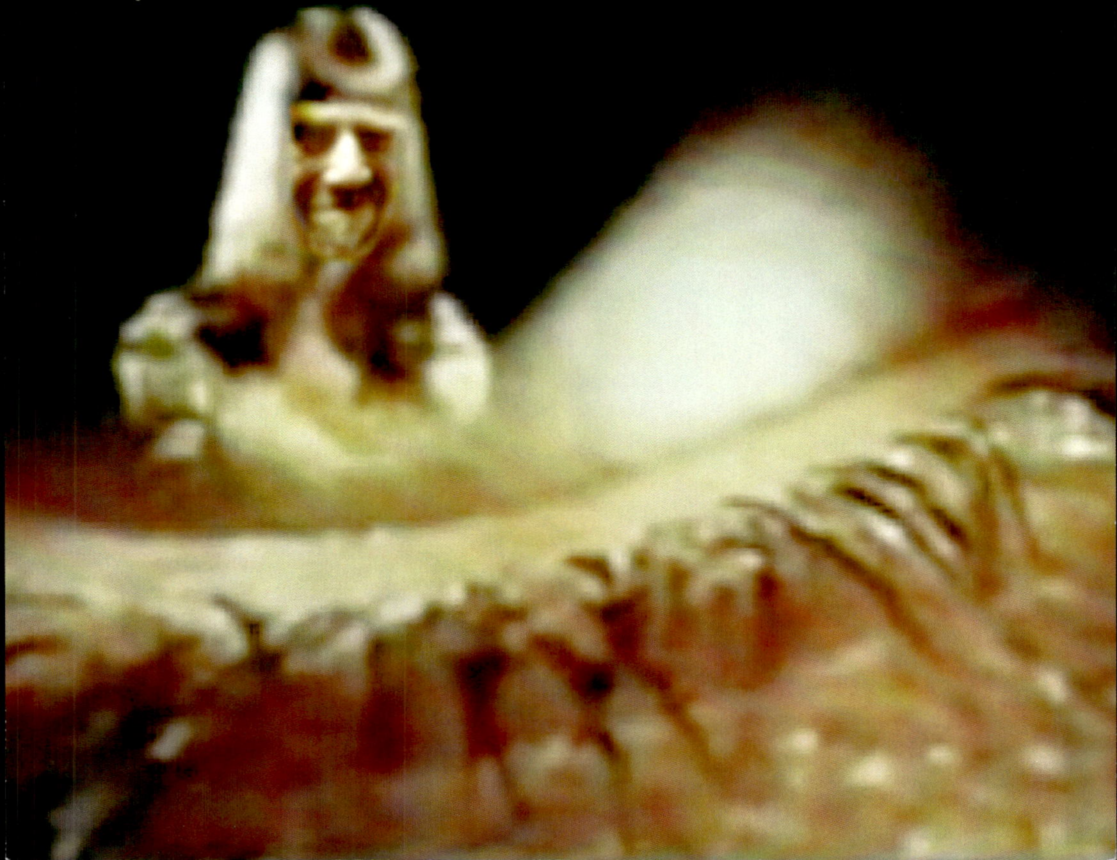

Jay, Bill

Bill Jay began his career in England where he was the first Director of Photography at the Institute of Contemporary Arts. In addition, he was first Editor/Director of Creative Camera and Album magazines. During this time, he earned a living picture editor of a large circulation news/feature magazine and as the European manager of an international picture agency.

After studying with Beaumont Newhall and Van Deren Coke at the University of New Mexico, he founded the program of photographic studies at Arizona State University, where he taught history and criticism classes for 25 years.

Bill Jay has published over 400 articles and is the author of more than 20 books on the history and criticism of photography. Some of his recent titles include: Cyanide and Spirits: an inside-out view of early photography; Occam's razor: an outside-in view of contemporary photography; USA Photography Guide; Bernard Shaw: On Photography; Negative/Positive: a philosophy of photography; 61 Pimlico; Sun in the Blood of the Cat; Men Like Me, etc. He is frequently asked to contribute essays to monographs by well-known photographers, such as Jerry Uelsmann, Bill Brandt, Michael Kenna, and Bruce Barnbaum. He continues to write a regular column for the journal LensWork.

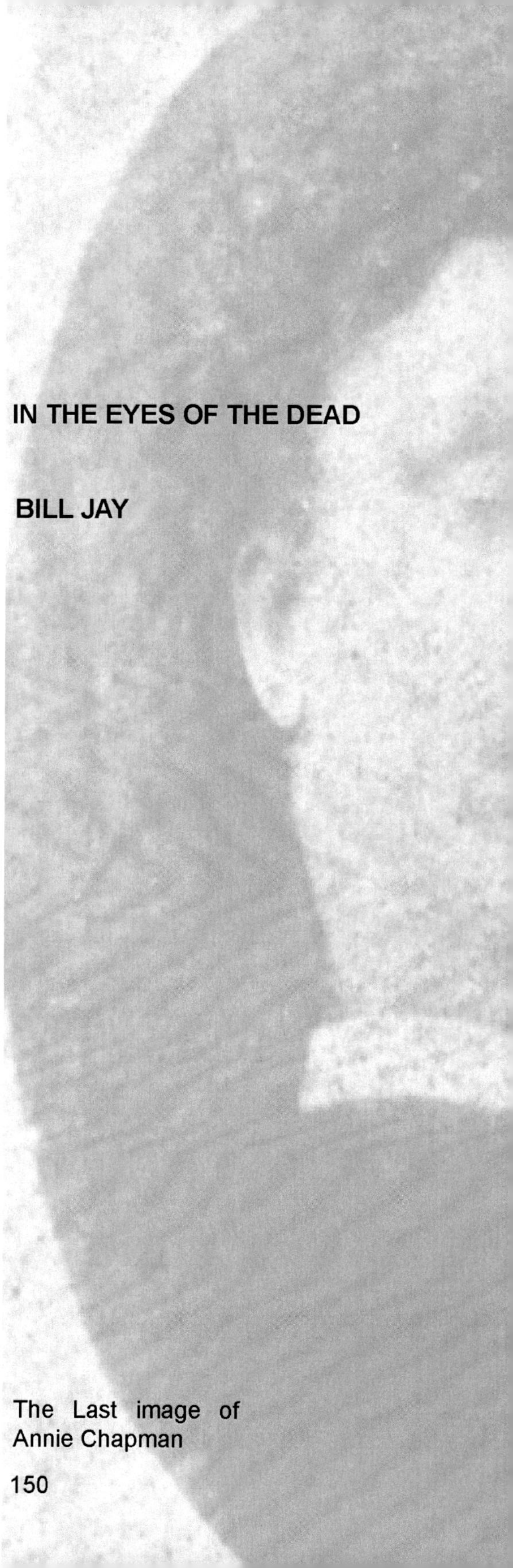

IN THE EYES OF THE DEAD

BILL JAY

The Last image of Annie Chapman

It was a commonly held belief throughout the latter half of the nineteenth century that the last image seen by the eyes of a dying person would be "fixed" on the retina for a considerable period of time. Therefore, if a murdered person's eyes could be reached without delay, the culprit could be identified from the retinal image. This seems to have been a popular belief which resurfaced occasionally throughout man's history, but the earliest specific suggestion that such images could be photographed[1] for criminal investigations was made by William H. Warner, a prominent British photographer of the 1860s.

In April, 1863, a young woman, Emma Jackson, was murdered in St Giles, London. Warner immediately sent a letter to Detective-Officer James F. Thomson at the Metropolitan Police Office, Scotland Yard, informing him that "if the eyes of a murdered person be photographed within a certain time of death, upon the retina will be found depicted the last thing that appeared before them, and that in the present case the features of the murderer would most probably be found thereon."[2]

He based his assertion on the fact that he had, four years previously, taken a negative of the eye of a calf a few hours after death and upon microscopic examination of the image found depicted the lines of the pavement on the slaughterhouse floor. Warner stated: "The subject is of too great importance and interest to be passed heedlessly by, because if the fact were known through the length and breadth of the land, it would, in my estimation, end materially to decrease that most horrible of all crimes – Murder."

Scotland Yard took Warner's suggestion seriously. James Thomson replied, on behalf of the Metropolitan Police Office that photographing the eyes of a murdered person "is of the greatest importance." He was obviously conversant with the idea long before Warner's letter, stating that he had conversed with an eminent occultist four years earlier and was assured that unless the eye was photographed within twenty-four hours after death no result would be obtained, "the object transfixed thereon vanishing" in the same manner as undeveloped negative photograph exposed to light.[3] Thomson did not photograph the eye of Emma Jackson, the murdered woman who had instigated this correspondence, because she had been dead forty hours before Thomson saw the body, her eyes were closed, and she was already buried by the time Warner's letter arrived.

If the idea of retinal imagery after death was not new, Warner at least sparked off renewed interest in the subject. The editor of The Photographic News was asked for more details. He replied that he knew nothing personally about the subject "beyond the reports often alluded to." Warner himself was too busy "enlarging, printing, etc., etc., to enable him to give that attention to the subject which it justly demands." The prestigious medical periodical, The Lancet, considered the subject merely demanded burying, along with the corpse. It wrote:

> The multitude of reasons given by the sapient superintendent of detectives for not attempting an absurd impossibility will remind his readers of the forty reasons of the Mayor for the town-gunner not firing a salute, of which the first – namely, the absence of powder – was held to be sufficient. The information derived from the eminent oculist is singularly interesting. But, before attempting the photographic feat which is suggested, Mr Thompson might find useful practice in endeavouring to subtract the sound of a flute from a ton of coals, or to draw out the moonshine from cucumber seeds. Quid vetat ridendeo dicere verum. Mr Warner has hoaxed himself, and the superintendent of detectives takes the name of the oculist In vain. 'Stone walls do not a prison make,' and the bars on Mr Warner's photograph were not akin to the pavement of the slaughterhouse. Mr Thompson may assure Sir Richard Mayne that such a photograph taken more than twenty-four hours after death will succeed as well as if taken two minutes after – and no better.[4]

But the story would not die. Throughout 1864 and 1865 more than a dozen accounts of retinal imagery, particularly in the case of the dead, appeared in the photographic press. Apart from occasional isolated incidents, the subject lay dormant for ten years and then was rejuvenated with fresh vigour in 1877, and this time it didn't die down until the turn of the century. There was an interesting murder case in 1925 which was reportedly solved by photographing the retina of the victim, and as late as 1948 the subject was being treated with respect, at least by some scientists and police organizations. Crime novelists also found in such reports a new twist in their detective plots.

One of the earliest crime stories that represents a murderer as being convicted by a photograph of his victim's eyes, upon the retina of which was pictured the features of the assassin, was published in the New York Ledger of 1863, by Mrs Southworth. This story seemed to have inspired a photographer named Adams, of Evansville, New York, to investigate the phenomenon in person. Adams was also spurred in this direction by various reports from France where "mysterious murders (were) unravelled through the instrumentality of Daguerre's wonderful art":

> On Sunday forenoon Mr Adams, a photographist of this city, at the solicitation of some gentlemen who had read of similar experiments in France, took his instrument and visited the scene of the late murder in German Township. This was some thirty hours after the murdered man had breathed his last. There was a great deal of dust flying and a great crowd collected which materially interfered with the success of the experiment; but notwithstanding these unfavourable circumstances, Mr Adams succeeded in taking a tolerably fair 'negative.' Upon this he has been experimenting, and yesterday we were called on to witness the results of his experiments.

He had taken an ambrotype picture of the eye of the deceased, and then rubbed out everything but a single object apparently in the centre of the eye; this was placed under an ordinary magnifying glass. At the first glance the object appeared blurred and indistinct, but on getting the proper focus the outlines of a human face were at once distinguishable. The image was apparently the face of a man with unusually prominent cheek bones, long nose, and rather broad forehead. A black moustache was plainly seen, and also the direction of the eyes, which seemed to be looking at some object sideways. One of the eyes was as plainly seen as the eyes in a common ambrotype or ferrotype. Some who examined the image thought the man of which it seemed to bear a resemblance had a Roman nose and also had on a cap.

Mr Adams is continuing his experiments, but whether he will succeed in making any clearer developments, remains to be seen. His labours thus far are abundantly rewarded by the success which has attended his efforts, as it seems to us he has demonstrated that an object was pictured upon the eye of Mr Herke at the time of his death, and that the object was a human face.[5]

Such reports were now pouring into the newspapers and photographic press from all over the world, particularly from France where the phenomenon was treated with respect. The editors were obliged, from their positions of authority, to comment on the validity of the cases. This posed problems because, although the accounts seemed factual enough and were often supplied by respected photographers, there was no basis in accepted fact for supposing the eye of a dead person retained the image of the last object or person seen. They could believe the idea that the retina received the impression, and that it might indeed be retained for a short while; but how does the retina process the property of fixing the image? As one bemused writer stated: "If, in the living subject, the retina only receives a momentary impression, how and by what physiological process can it, in the dead subject, retain such an impression several hours after death?" [6]

The answer was not forthcoming. By now the editors were ruing Warner's revival of the subject. Within nine months reports which seemingly confirmed the phenomena were being printed from London, Paris, New York and now Moscow. Not only the photographic press was involved; The Times also gave prominence to the following report:

A tale of a murder, perpetrated in a mysterious manner, and of the discovery of the murderers by scientific means, is now the common talk of the inhabitants of the Russian capital. In the so-called old city, on the right shore of the Neva, behind the fortress, is a small house, which enjoys the reputation of having once been the residence of Peter the Great. One of the few rooms in the house is stated to have been used as a sleeping chamber by the celebrated monarch, and this apartment is now visited with feelings of veneration and awe by many thousands of Russians. Although

adorned with gold and precious stones, on which account two soldiers are constantly on duty there. A few evenings since, after the priest had withdrawn to his dwelling, situated on the opposite side of the street, he was summoned to return to the chapel, as two men required his services. The good man soon repaired to the little chamber, and
afterwards returned to his house. On the following morning the two soldiers on guard were found murdered at their posts and the alms-box, which contained 400 roubles, had disappeared from its accustomed place, while the costly articles with which the room was so plentifully adorned were found undisturbed. It was suggested that the eyes of the murdered soldiers should be immediately photographed, in the hope of successfully testing the discovery recently made in England; when, to the surprise of all, the result was the production of the portraits of two soldiers of the private guard at the palace, on whose breasts were the insignia of the Cross of St George. The murderers were at once sought out and apprehended.[7]

The next lengthy report originated in San Francisco, and appeared in Scientific American:

The experiment of photographing the retina of the murdered woman's eye, despite the persiflage and incredulity with which it has been in most quarters received, has either developed a remarkable coincidence or produced a wonderful result. Stamped upon the centre of the retina, and conveyed by the photographic process to the plate upon which the picture was taken, there is plainly to be seen the outline of a human figure, so plainly as at once to arrest the attention of the most unimaginative eye. The figure is that of a tall dark man, the lower part of the face muffled in a heavy black moustache and beard, the left arm extended, and the whole body thrown into the position of a man doing some violent deed. The face has enough of outline to suggest the possibility of filling it up so as to recognize the man were he met in a crowded street. The bushy hair surmounting a low forehead, heavy eyebrows arching over the cavernous depths where the eyes be, the shadowy suggestions of the whole face, which cannot be described, but which impress the observer with a strange weird horror, causing one to start back as though with profane hand he had rent the veil and caught a glimpse of that world that lies beyond the confines of the grave. It is idle to laugh at such things. A fool can deny everything, but it is only a wise man who can seriously make up his mind to believe anything.

The writer is not at all an imaginative man (?) and took no stock in the unauthenticated accounts of marvellous successes, which had attended similar experiments in France. Physiology and philosophy both seemed to laugh at such a theory, and the writer was prepared to treat the thing lightly. But seeing is believing; plainly from the photographic plate the figure of a man looks out, the last object the murdered woman saw on earth, as when she turned her piteous eyes to heaven for help, and saw only the cruel face of the murderer bending over her, while his remorseless hand held the sharp knife quivering to her throat.

To suppose that the photographic figure to which we refer is the result of an accidental grouping of shadows, is simply to seek a miraculous explanation for a very simple natural fact. For it is much easier to suppose that the outline of the murderer was caught on the sensitive retina than to believe that in the only instance in which the experiment has been attempted in this country, a combination of light and shade should have occurred to produce a shape so exactly like a human figure as to deceive many sensible and unimpressionable men. In any event, the experiment is worthy of further trial and demonstration is easy. Oxen are killed daily. Experiment's by photographing their eyes would soon determine whether there is anything in this theory or not.

Whether or not, granting that the experiment proves successful, it will ever prove of any actual use, is a matter of question. For, once establish this fact, and murderers will punch out their victims' eyes before leaving them. And the dead retina might in some instances mislead the living judges. For supposing that a man were talking to and facing you, and that another, suddenly coming up behind, dealt a blow which finished him. Your image would be the one impressed upon his retina, and an innocent man might hang were the eye taken as conclusive evidence. The coroner in this case mentioned to the jury that he had had a photograph made of the retina of the eyes of the murdered woman. It was imperfect, and showed nothing. He did not have any faith in the thing, but for curiosity's sake he would have another ambrotype taken immediately.[8]

As one editor remarked: "The long-lived travelled canard, started in a daily paper by Mr Warner, is still moving."[9] And move it did, this time to Florence. This case initiated a flurry of investigation and is therefore worth quoting at some length. By now, the press had had enough of these strange reports and was anxious to lay the matter to rest, once and for all. The following information has been pieced together from reports in Harper's Weekly, The Photographic News, Morning Post, Daily Telegraph, The British Journal of Photography, and the Morning Star.

On 13 April, 1864, a humble but respectable woman, Luisa Carducci, who let lodgings, was found murdered in her house in Florence. The corpse was found lying on the floor, with her throat cut from ear to ear. There was a pool of blood below her head but no blood marks in any other part of the house. Close to her body was a handkerchief, presumably dropped by her assailant. The house was also robbed of various objects, trinkets and cash. As no screams or cries of help had been heard by the neighbours it was assumed, by the Florence police, that the murder had been committed by two men, who had obtained entry on the pretext of viewing and hiring one of her rooms. While one man placed a handkerchief over her mouth, stifling her screams, the other had slit her throat.

At this point the police officer in charge of the investigation, Leopoldo Viti, applied to the higher-administrative and legal authorities for permission to have the eyes of the murdered woman photographed on the possibility that the retina would depict an image of the murderer. Permission was refused.

Two months later, on 2 June, another lodging house keeper, Ester Cellai, was found murdered in her house. All the details were identical. The body was stretched out on the floor of a room, the throat cut from ear to ear, the handkerchief close to the body, and valuables stolen from the house. Also, the woman was alone in the house at the time and there was no sign of a forced entry or struggle. It seemed as if the same murderer had claimed another victim.

Viti again applied for permission to have the victim's eyes photographed; again, permission was refused.

On 22 August, a third murder was committed under almost identical circumstances. A lodging house keeper, Emilia Spagnoli, was found lying on the floor with her throat cut, with a handkerchief by the body. In this case there was a slight difference in that Spagnoli had resisted her attacker, and was stabbed and cut in many other parts of the body. There were seventeen knife wounds in all. Viti again insisted that the eyes of the murdered woman should be photographed. This time his request was granted. Luckily, for Viti, the body was lying on its side, with her right eye turned upward. Immediately after the discovery of the body, the eye was photographed, under the direction of the examining judge, and the negative image greatly enlarged. There on the final print was a two inch high human face, dim and nebulous but none the less recognisable. It depicted a man with "a peculiar dilatation of the nostril, a depression of the upper lip ... an unusual elongation of the mouth, a square but double chin, a certain massiveness about the region of the cheek bone, and the outline of a whisker."

The photograph was made by one of the Alinari brothers, famous nineteenth century photographers, who lived in Florence and specialized in copying art works, selling the prints to Victorians on the Grand Tour. As one writer, who described the murder and its aftermath "of which I was myself an eye-witness," remarked: "When I mention that Alinari, the first photographer of Florence, and indeed possessing a European reputation, was the artist by whom the work was executed, I need say nothing more as a guarantee of the fidelity and care employed on the occasion."[10]

The police already had their suspicions about the murderer's identity. Benjamino dei Cosimi, a native of Velletri, was a suspect in several cases of murder in that town. He travelled to Corsica, then to Leghorn and on to Florence. He was seen close to the location of the first murder but had disappeared before he could be picked up for questioning. He reappeared in Florence at the time of the third murder. When arrested, Cosimi had in his possession articles belonging to all three women and a bloodstained knife.

The photographic image, taken from the retina of the third victim, displayed a remarkable similarity to the appearance of Cosimi. "Whatever there is of marked prominent individuality in that first nebulous profile has an exactly corresponding feature in the likeness of the living prisoner." The photographs, with all the accompanying details, were sent to the Medical College of Florence and to the medical colleges of Naples and Milan. The Prefect of Florence authorised a series of photographic experiments to be instigated on the eyes of the patients in the hospital immediately after their deaths.

The Photographic News summed up the reaction of all commentators: "At length ... we meet with a case which bears unusual evidence of authenticity, and also admits of satisfactory verification ... Nothing can be clearer or more satisfactory."[11]

Unfortunately the magazine's idea of "verification" was to write to the wrong photographer– it contacted Pietro Semplicini rather than Alinari. This was understandable since the Florence newspaper, Gazzetta del Popolo, had also named Semplicini as the photographer by mistake. Semplicini wrote back that he was not the photographer in question, that Alinari had taken the picture, and that he himself had not seen the results but as far as he knew, the accounts of the image on the retina were false. The Photographic News accepted this assumption or speculation as fact, and used Semplicini's testimony as final evidence that the story was false, without bothering to contact Alinari directly.

The seed of doubt had been sown, however, after what had seemed on first encounter to be a convincing proof of retinal imagery. The seed grew into a strange shape when the correspondent of the Daily Telegraph asserted that "the hazy outline which, in the photograph, we are asked to believe represents part of a man's face is on the cornea of the eye, and not on the pupil (sic!) at all."[12]

As a writer remarked, the image "might as well have been on the victim's nose." With doubt piled on doubt, periodicals which began their reports with assertions of the veracity of retinal images at the moment of death, struggled to reverse direction in an untidy confusion. By now, the writers "did not hesitate to avow my entire disbelief" in the phenomenon. The very idea was absurd – as absurd as colour photography and the philosopher's stone, "which will probably be found at the same time." The case of Cosimi, pictured in the eye of his victim, was finally closed by The British Journal of Photography by printing the substance of a letter from Alinari, the photographer:

All that the public papers have related about the discovery effected by means of photograph respecting the eye of the Spagnoli is false as far as regards the result of it. We executed the photograph of it, and the enlargement also, but neither in the one nor in the other did we discover what is presumed it showed ...[13]

That seemed to be the end of the matter. But the idea of

images of the last view seen by a dying person, or animal, was too fascinating not to resurface. The anecdotes became stronger as their basis in fact was removed. A fine example was a fishy story:The mistress of a house was cleaning a large cod fish, when, to her astonishment, she discovered an exact representation of a fisherman in the eye of the fish. It was a very distinct miniature likeness of a fisherman, with his sou'-wester on, and fully equipped, in the act of hauling the fish into the boat.[14]

Wondrous tales of photographs which miraculously appeared in opposition to all known laws of optics and chemistry were told, published and reprinted with variations throughout the world's press. And these images were not restricted to the retina; they could appear anywhere, at any time:

It seems that Mr J. J. Davis, of Findlay, Ohio, went out to feed his cow last year. When he left the house, he had a photograph in his pocket, but when he returned he discovered that it had disappeared. He made a long and anxious search for it, but could not find it. Recently the cow gave birth to a calf, and on the left side of the calf's neck is a hairless spot about six inches square. In the centre of the spot is a capital likeness of Mr Davis, and that gentleman is of opinion that he must have dropped the photograph into the food that he gave the cow on the occasion above mentioned, and she had eaten it. In some way, known only to the mysterious laws of nature, the photograph made an impression on the unborn calf. A number of Mr J.J. Davis's friends have seen the calf in question, and they all corroborate his story.[15]

Photographs could even appear on the inside of an oyster shell at the bottom of the sea:

The following story comes from the Ruckland Herald, and is therefore quite sure to be true. There was once an oyster dealer, who had his stand in the Californian Market. Among his wares one morning he found a bivalve of such superb dimensions that he concluded to open it and make his lunch thereupon. At this point we must digress for one moment to explain that the largest variety of American oyster is proportionately as large as an American lie when compared with the European variety; in fact, Thackeray used to declare that a stewed oyster in the United States resembled nothing so much as a boiled baby! Well, that dealer opened his oyster, and found to his amazement on the surface of the inside shell – a photograph of a lady!

As you may imagine, all thought of lunch was abandoned, and the oyster dealer was shortly surrounded by a curious crowd. Speculation was busy, and conjecture flew madly about. But presently a gentleman stepped up, peeped, gazed, shrieked, and fainted away. It is impossible to faint long in the neighbourhood of an oyster stall. There are too many buckets of dirty salt water lying around. So presently this gentleman recovered consciousness, feeling and smelling for all the world like a decomposed mermaid. He then told the following story.

It was in the broad Pacific, in the equinoctial (or some other kind of) gales, that his fair young wife fell overboard amid the sharks and whales and oysters. This tragical event happened just over the exact spot from which had come this batch of oysters; and the photograph was the photograph of his wife. He presumed that the oyster, opening its shell to air its appetite, placed itself in such a position that the image of the deceased was reflected upon the bright inside shell, and there by some unknown process photographed. It was only a negative, of course.[16]

The close of the Cosimi case in 1865 seemed to have put an end to the plethora of reports about murder and images in the eyes of the victims. In 1877 the whole issue was revived. The spark which set off a blaze of speculation was not a personal anecdote (by Warner), which had instigated the reports ten years earlier, but a series of carefully controlled experiments by two prominent and much-respected scientists.

Late in 1876 a Professor Franz Boll (1849–1879) who occupied the chair of physiology at Rome and was a pupil of Max Schultz and Du Bois Reymond, discovered the fact that the external layer of the retina possesses in all living animals a purple colour. This purple surface, he found, bleached on exposure to light, but regained its original colour in the dark. Like pure silver iodide an image would be impressed upon it by the agency of light and if placed in a dark room the image would disappear, and the surface was again ready to receive a second image. This purple colour, which Boll called seh- purpur (see-purple), vanishes immediately after death. He later modified his views in the light of experiments which showed that the retina remained sensitive, under certain conditions, for up to twenty-four hours after death.

These experiments in the "photographic" sensitivity of the retina were confirmed and extended by Willy Kühne (1837–1900), professor of physiology at the University of Heidelberg, and "a name well-known among microscopic anatomists." In January 1877 Kühne reported his results in a leading German medical journal.[17] He stated that he had been able not only to view the disintegration of the seh-purpur but also render the image permanent. In this way he had obtained 'actual photographic images upon the retina, corresponding with objects which had been looked at during life.' Kühne found that the purple colour did not disappear immediately after death but if kept in a dark room it would remain sensitive for twenty-four hours. In other words it was light, not death, which rendered the retina insensitive. However, the retina was only resensitised after light-bleaching when attached to the back of the eye. Kühne removed a rabbit's eye and lifted a corner of the retina. The colour of this flap rapidly bleached, but as soon as the flap was replaced the purple colour was restored, "so that the eye carries with it a living substance which has the power of resensitising the photographic film whenever such a process becomes necessary." It is the bleaching of this purple, by the action of light, which produces "an actual photograph produced on the retina which can be fixed and preserved."

Kühne called these images "optograms," (now called rhodopsin).

His first optograms were obtained in the following manner. A rabbit was restricted so that one of its eyes (the other was covered) was fixed upon an opening in a window shutter, with an aperture of 30 centimetres square and with the rabbit's eye 11/2 metres distance. The head of the rabbit was covered with a dark cloth for five minutes so that the seh-purpur was as sensitive as possible. And then the rabbit's eye was exposed to the window light for three minutes. His head was instantly cut off and the eye removed in a dark room. The retina was extracted and placed in a five percent solution of alum.

The second eye, which had been kept in the dark throughout the foregoing operation, was then exposed to the window light two minutes after death for the same duration as the living eye. The retina was then extracted and placed in an alum solution. Both retinae were "fixed" in alum for twenty-four hours and then examined. The result, claimed Kühne, was a clear square image with sharply defined edges, the second retina image being more sharply defined than the first living-eye image.[18] The cross- work of the window panes was sharply depicted.

Arthur Gamgee, a physiologist from Manchester, England, quickly duplicated the experiments and "is able to confirm them in every particular." Gamgee's paper, quoting the researches of Boll and Kühne, was published in Nature, 1 February 1877. As might be expected, the photographic press was exceedingly interested in these tests and were quick to point out the analogy between the eye/retina and the camera/emulsion:

That photo-chemical processes take place in the retina is a matter, therefore, beyond all doubt, and photographers to a man cannot but feel deeply interested in the analogy here shown to exist between the eye and the camera he uses everyday.[19]

The photographic writers were equally quick to see the connection between these experiments and "that old canard" of the murderer's image in the eye of his victim. Such a discovery – as the authors of it point out – may lead to the supposition that there may be something, after all, in those stories of which we frequently hear, of images being visible in the eyes of persons after death, of the retina of murdered men, for instance, showing plainly the image of those who slew them.[20]

Again the suggestion was made that the technique be used for the identification and detection of murderers. This time the photographer and correspondent was H. Wilson (The Photographic News, 1 June 1877, pp. 262–263). The editor replied that a) the idea was not new and b) it did not seem to lend itself to any practical application. The editor's opinion seem grounded in fact. Boll, himself, had an opportunity to investigate the idea.

On 5 March 1877, a criminal was executed in Vienna, at 7.15 am in a badly-lit prison yard, surrounded by high walls. Immediately after death, the executioner closed the victim's eyes and kept the light from the retina. Within two hours Boll was on the scene. He made a microscopic examination of the retina. His conclusion was that the visual purple was still present, so that the eye still possessed photographic properties, but that no trace of an image was visible. The conclusion was that even if an image had existed it would have disappeared since the membrane behind the retina would have resensitised the purple; the light in the prison yard was too weak to produce an image; this image would only have remained if the retina was immediately "fixed" in alum. The fresh hopes of the retinal image detectives again diminished if they were not completely dashed.

An interesting article on the experiments of Kühne and their relevance to retinal images of murder was contributed to The Photographic Journal by W. S. Bird, under the title "The Photography of Vision" in 1879.21 Bird states that Kühne also succeeded in fixing the images on the retina of a recently decapitated human head "but the exposure in such case was much longer than when the experiment was conducted with the living animal." As a result, Kühne believed that optography was an established fact and that it would soon be possible to obtain landscapes and portraits photographed on the retina. Bird concluded:

Enough has ... been said to show that it is not exceedingly strange if a ready credence has been given to accounts of images impressed on the living retina with uncommon vividness being found there shortly after a violent death and becoming a damaging witness by the dead victim against the murderer. Fixing the photographic image thrown on a daguerreotype plate was an almost miraculous feat at first, and that nature should be found more wonderful than art is an ordinary experience.

This roller-coaster ride of high hopes and subsequent doubts and fresh possibilities continued until the turn of the century, by which time the astonishing new x-rays so captured everyone's imagination that all other extraordinary topics seemed pale by comparison. Meanwhile, efforts to use retinal photography, or optography, in murder cases proved inconclusive at best. In January 1880, the Manchester police authorities had a photograph taken of the eyes of Sarah Jane Roberts, who was murdered in Harpurhey. The results were not made available. But the attempt did provoke the following remarks by Dr A. Emrys-Jones, honorary surgeon of the Manchester Royal Hospital:

Were Sarah Jane Roberts' eye immediately removed after the murder, and subjected to careful examination, I think it possible that one might trace the outline of the murderer, or the weapon used in the murder, on this visual purple. I am not aware that this has ever been tried... There can be little doubt, however, that optography will yet be brought to a much more perfect-state.

The photographs of Sarah Jane Roberts' eye were probably not satisfactory due to the time delay between death and the photography, and to the fact that she was photographed outdoors in sunlight. When the coffin arrived at the cemetery at Christ Church, Harpurhey, it was taken out into the garden and the body photographed by James Mudd, an eminently respectable photographer of Manchester who was renowned for his highly crafted landscapes. Such conditions, in the haste prior to closing the coffin and burial, would have not been ideal for a satisfactory result. It seems, also, that the test was doomed to failure since Sarah Jane Roberts was killed by blows to the back of the head; she probably did not even see her murderer.

Meanwhile, it was claimed that Kühne had succeeded in obtaining a retinal image of a man, showing the clear outlines of his head, the limits of the hair and the shirt collar. The possibilities of obtaining retinal imagery were given encouragement (that it might be possible under certain extreme conditions) and discouragement (that it was highly unlikely at the present time in the vast majority of murder cases) by Dr Ayres, who made over a thousand experiments in taking optograms of the retina of animals while working in Kühne's laboratory in Heidelberg. Ayres published his report in the New York Medical Journal of 1881.

Kühne suggested that Ayres make an optogram of Hermann Helmholtz and send it to him in acknowledgement of the value of his researches in physiological optics, carried out while he was professor of physiology at Heidelberg. Ayres secured a large negative of Helmholtz and placed it over the eye of an animal which had been doped. The animal had been in the dark for hours. The exposure was made for four minutes in bright sunshine. The retina revealed a dull picture – an image of Helmholtz's shirt collar and the end of his nose. The light transmitted through the negative was not sufficient to bleach the visual purple. As the purple is rapidly regenerated in the living retina, Ayres assumed it had been restored as fast as it was bleached. He tried again. This time he decapitated the rabbit and waited until the regenerative system of the retina had waned. He then exposed the eye to the Helmholtz portrait. The result of the optogram was better – but not good enough. And that seemed to be the end of the experiment. It is difficult to see why Ayres did not continue his tests using a less dense negative, more intense transmitted illumination, longer exposures times and so on. Perhaps this little experiment, no more than a novel idea, interfered with his more serious laboratory work ... for what ever reason, Ayres failed; his conclusion was that, if such images were difficult to obtain even under ideal laboratory conditions, belief that retinal images would be permanently recorded at the moment of sudden death were "utterly idle."

Utterly idle or not, the wish to believe remained strongly entrenched in the public's mind, particularly as regards its use in the detection of murderers. Even the case of Jack the Ripper, who murdered five women in 1880, involved a peripheral mention of retinal photography. Dr G.B. Phillips, Official Police Surgeon at the time of the Whitechapel murders, was called as a witness in reference to the murder of Annie Chapman. He was asked for his views on the possibility of obtaining a clue to the murderer's identity by photographing the eyes of the dead woman. But "as might be expected" he gave no hopes of any useful result. Incidentally, Phillips was "expected" to reject the notion of photography because he had endeavoured to suppress much information on the nature of the mutilations. It was this action on his part which fuelled the notion that the murderer was "some over-wrought experimental physiologist wishful to obtain living tissues from a healthy subject, for experimental use."[24]

In 1891 a photographic exhibition in St Petersburg, Russia, displayed an enlarged photograph of the retina of an eye, which, it was claimed, depicted the image of a man. A young lady was murdered at Samara and a retinal photograph taken immediately after the discovery of the body. There on the optogram was the image of a soldier "so clearly imprinted on the retina of his victim that it was possible to discover the criminal, and bring him to justice."[25] One year later a book appeared in Moscow, the Russian title of which translates: Is it possible to obtain in the eye of a person killed a photograph of the murderer?, by R. Tille. (A copy of this book is in the library of The Royal Photographic Society of Great Britain.)

According to the New York Record of 1896 the answer must be in the affirmative. In an article on "Fin-de-Siècle Vidocquism," the following passages occur:

A startling development was made in the Shearman murder case today. A photograph of the murderer has been discovered. Both of Mrs Shearman's eyes are believed to hold pictures of the man who murdered her. Sheriff Jenner and Coroner Bowers on Wednesday discussed the statement often made that the eyes of the dead retain pictures of the last objects on which they rest before the last breath is drawn. This morning it was decided to proceed on that theory, and taking Fred S. Marsh they visited the Shearman farm. Mr Marsh with his Kodak photographed one eye of Mrs, Shearman, and the form of a man was found there, a big, burly man, wearing a long overcoat, with the cloth of his trousers badly wrinkled. The face of the man was not obtained.

This revelation caused a sensation at the farmhouse. Undertaker Partridge was present and says the photograph of the man's form and clothing on the one eye of Mrs Shearman which was exposed to Mr Marsh's camera was perfectly distinct. It is hoped the other eye will furnish the means of identifying the murderer by giving his face.

Coroner Bowers accompanied Mr Marsh, who is a scientist. They made a microscopic examination of the eyes of Mrs Davis, but on one of those of Mrs Shearman the form of a man was distinctly photographed.

The microscope used enlarged the object viewed 400 times its real size. The picture as revealed did not show the face of the man clearly. The man's position was such, according to those who made the examination, that the body was shown only from the breast down to the feet. After the first surprise of the startling discovery made by Mr Marsh was over, he made a most careful examination which clearly revealed the man's form. He was apparently a big man with a long heavy overcoat unbuttoned, and which reached below the knees. The wrinkles in the trousers could be plainly seen, and one foot was behind the other, with the knee bending as if in a stooping posture about to take a step.

Dr Bowers, the Coroner, then made an examination, and says he saw the picture as distinctly as he could have seen a man standing in front of him. E.G. Partridge, Albert Hazeltine, and the Rev. Mr Stoddard who were at the house when the examination was made, were called into the room and examined the eye, each one of them verifying the statement as describing the man in similar language.

And still the tales kept coming. A London evening newspaper in 1897 claimed that "a certain medicine man" who was also a keen amateur photographer had examined the eyes of "legions" of the dead and had found traces of letters and objects on the iris (sic!) and that these images became more visible by means of photography. In one case a capital letter of peculiar form was revealed, which could be traced to a Testament held in the hand shortly before death.

In another instance a numeral was distinctly pictured, which was traced to a clock face in the room. The Lancet, a medical journal, immediately responded with a restatement of Kühne's experiments and the reasons why these images were improbable, even if on the retina and not on the iris. The Amateur Photographer was more practical:

For those who wish to experiment in this gruesome branch of "photography," the formula presented is as follows: First catch your man, and keep him in the dark for an hour or so. Then expose his eye for a few minutes to an illuminated object, extirpate the organ, open it, and plunge it immediately into a solution of alum. Allow twenty-four hours for development, and dish up any quasi-scientific narrative you please, garnished with sauce a la Grinne!

Such facetiousness did not deter the well-meaning police. When a murder was committed in Yarmouth in 1900, "photographs of the wide-open, staring eyes of the corpse (were) taken in the faint hope that some image of the murderer might be found."[29]

As late as 1925, the police of the village of Haiger in Germany were alleged to have used photographs of the eyes of a victim in order to solve a murder case. A man named Angerstein was charged with several murders. While examining one of the victims in the morgue the coroner noticed an image in the open eyes of the corpse Photographs of the eyes. The report stated, plainly revealed an image of Angerstein with an axe raised to strike. This case is interesting because Professor Bohne, a scientist at Cologne University, suggested that the report might have a basis in fact. He was well aware that the regeneration of visual purple in the retina would tend to obliterate such an image, but considered the possibility that under a mental or physical shock the image might remain. Suppose, said Bohne, the case of a murderer who kills his victim with an ax. The image of the advancing murderer is reflected in the eyes of the victim. Under such 'nerve shocks' the nerve centers of the eyes might lose their power to form new images or obliterate previous ones, "with the result that if the person died at such a moment the reflection might remain fixed in death."[30]

Whatever the merits of the belief that a murderer left behind at the scene of the crime his portrait in the eye of his victim, the idea was avidly appropriated by writers of detective fiction. Reportedly scores of stories, plays and books employed this idea in their plots. Jules Claretie, Member of the Academie Française and Director of the Theatre Français wrote a serial novel entitled L'Oeuil du Mort which "is based on some extraordinary experiments made in this country some years ago with a view to the discovery of a murderer by the impression left on the retina of his dying victim's eye."[31] The experiments referred to, which prompted Claretie's story, were conducted by a Dr Bourion "who was practising in the Department of the Vosges." In 1869 a woman and her child were murdered in broad daylight. Bourion arrived on the scene fifty-six hours later, but had their retinas photographed. The results were communicated by him to the Society of Legal Medicine together with a report by his colleague, Dr Vernois: The mother's eyes revealed nothing. The photograph of the child's eye, when enlarged, "plainly disclosed an uplifted arm, with a dog's head distinctly traced above it." No more is know of Bourion or his experiments; he is presumed to have died suddenly, a short time later.

An evening newspaper in London ran a serial during the winter of 1900 and 1901 in which the villain was identified by means of an enlarged reproduction of the victim's retina, even though the picture was improbably made by flashlight in the street. This would not be noteworthy except for the fact that the review in the photographic press[32] was immediately preceded by an announcement concerning a stage version of Rudyard Kipling's Jungle Book. (Kipling was induced to write the stage version by the photographer H. H. Hay Cameron, son of the Victorian photographer, Julia Margaret Cameron.)

Undoubtedly the best written, if not the most interesting, short story to use the idea of retinal imagery was Rudyard Kipling's At the end of the passage.[33] Four men, lonely, bored and suffocating in the heat of India, would meet once a week from their various Empire postings to play bridge and release their tension in irritable gossip. One of them, Hummil, was particularly cantankerous on the night in question. Surly and ill, he drove his guests away, except the doctor Spurstow, who insisted on staying to try and help him. Later that night, Hummil admitted he had contemplated suicide, that he was driven to sleepless despair by a blind face that chased him down corridors. Hummil was convinced that if he was caught then he would die. He was being driven insane. After Spurstow had dosed him with opium, Hummil slept, and awoke fresher the next day. He was then left alone until the next weekly meeting of the group. When the three guests arrived at Hummil's place they found him dead, "in the staring eyes was written terror beyond the expression of any pen." Spurstow noticed something in those eyes. He photographed them. Later that day, the doctor retreated into the bathroom with his Kodak camera. After a few minutes there was the sound of something being hammered to pieces. He emerged, very white indeed. "Have you got a picture?" he was asked. "What does the thing look like?" The doctor replied: "It was impossible, of course. You needn't look ... I've torn up the films ... It was impossible." "That," said one of the others, watching the shaking hand of the doctor striving to relight his pipe, "is a damned lie."

Footnotes and References

1. Ten years earlier research had been conducted on retinal imagery. See: William Scoresby, "On Pictorial and Photochromatic Impressions on the Retina of the Human Eye," Transactions, The British Association for the Advancement of Science, 1854, pp. 12–13. Scoresby did not photograph these images.

2. Quoted by William H. Warner in the correspondence columns of The Photographic News, 8 May 1863, p. 226. 3. Ibid., pp. 226–227.

4. Quoted in The British Journal of Photography, 15 June 1863, p. 259.

5. From the Evansville Journal, quoted in The Photographic News, 6 November 1863, p. 535.

6. The British Journal of Photography, 1 January l864, p. 14.

7. The Times, quoted in The Photographic News, 29 January 1861, p. 59.

8. Scientific American, (quoted in The Photographic News, 6 May 1864, p. 223.)

9. The British Journal of Photography, 2 May 1864, p. 158.

10. Harper's Weekly, 25 February 1865, p. 123.

11. The Photographic News, 6 January 1865, p. 3.

12. The Daily Telegraph, 22 January 1865, quoted in The Photographic News 27
January 1865, p. 38.

13. The British Journal of Photography, 24 February 1865, p. 100.

14. The Photographic News, 24 October 1869, p. 525.
15. The Photographic Review of Reviews, April 1895, p. 136.
16. The Amateur Photographer, 5 June 1885, p. 126
17. Centralblatt der Medicinischen Wissenschaften, January 1877. Kühne said the retina behaves not merely like a photographic plate but "like an entire photographic workshop."
18. Details of these experiments can be found in several photographic journals of the time, including The Photographic News, 16 February 1877;18 May l877, p. 237.
19. The Photographic News, 16 February 1877, p. 73.
20. Ibid
21. W.S. Bird, "The Photography of Vision," The Photographic Journal, 23 May 1879, pp. 93–96. Bird relied heavily on an article in the Revue de deux mondes, March 1879: "Les Colorations de la Retine et les Photographies dans l'Interieur l'oueil." Bird's paper was read before The Photographic Society of Great Britain and reprinted in The Photographic News, 30 May 1879, pp. 260–262; 6 June 1879, pp. 265–266. Also: The British Journal of Photography, 30 May 1879, pp. 258–259.
22. The British Journal of Photography, 23 January 1880, pp. 47–48.
23. Quoted in The Photographic News, 20 May 1881, p. 240.
24. The Photographic News, 21 September 1888, p. 608.
25. The Photographic News, 12 June 1891, p. 482.
26. New York Record, 21 December 1894; reprinted in The Amateur Photographer, 11 January 1895, p. 19.
27. Quoted in The Amateur Photographer, 4 November 1898, pp. 869–870.
28. Ibid., p. 870.
29. The Amateur Photographer, 19 October 1900, p. 302.
30. Information Roundup, 1948, pp. 357–358.
31. Daily Telegraph, quoted by The British Journal of Photography, 8 January 1897, p. 29.
32. The Amateur Photographer, 18 January 1901, p: 41.
33. See: Maughan's Choice of Kipling's Best. Sixteen stories selected and with an introductory essay by W. Somerset Maughan, New York: Doubleday and Company, Inc., 1953, pp. 65–2. Note: The only full photographic retinal image seen by the author was reproduced in Popular Mechanics, July 1934, p. 79. The retina was taken from a woman killed in an automobile accident. The image, of the wrecked car, is astonishingly detailed and, it is said, "helped police working on the case." First published in The British Journal of Photography, 30 January 1981 and then, in an edited version, in American Photographer, July 1985.

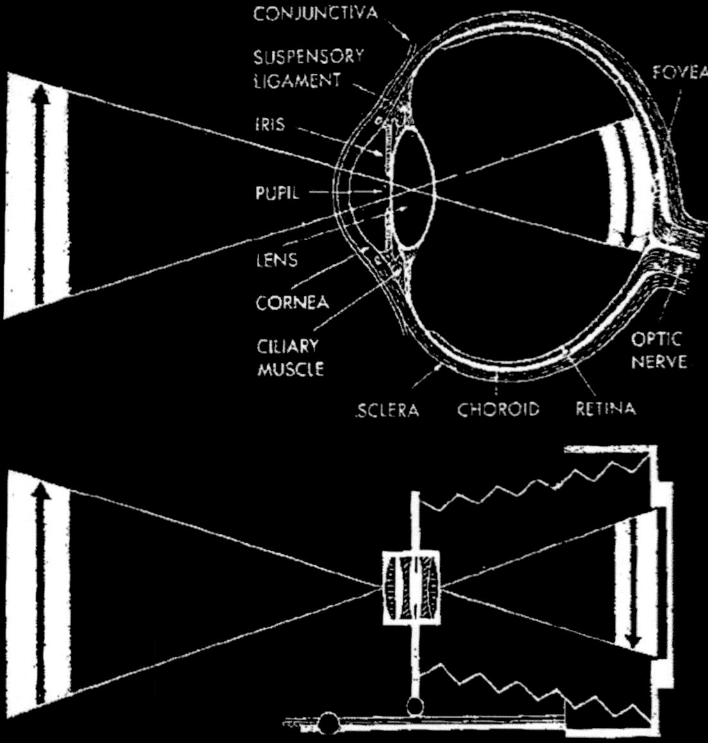

The structure of the eye compared to the camera (Wald, 1953). Courtesy: Ali Hossaini.

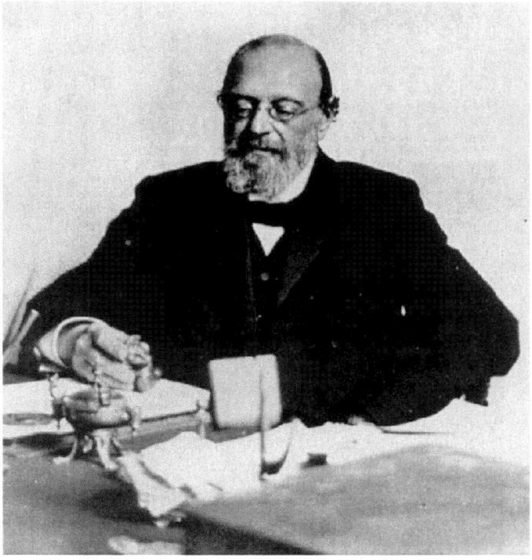

William Kühne,1837-1900

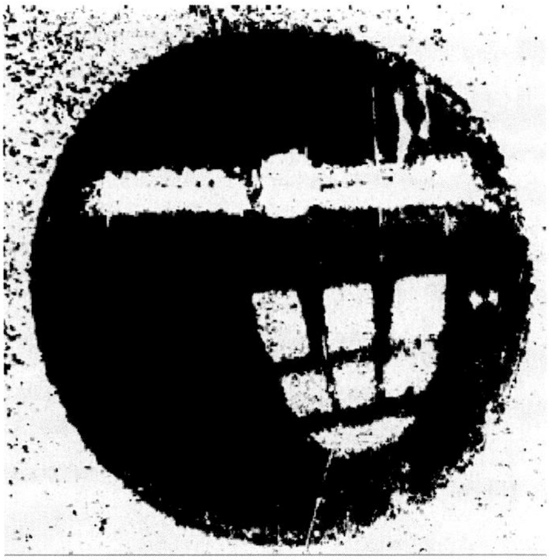

His rabbit optogram,1878

Optography and Technologies of Perception

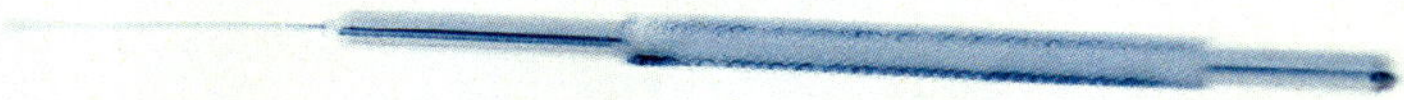

Ali Hossaini

Hossaini, Ali

Executive Producer, Equator HD; Faculty Member, Water Mill Center for the Arts and Humanities

Ali Hossaini is a philosopher who seeks to transform society through media. His publications include essays on the origins of optics, media policy, virtual community and the politics of identity. He applies theory, experimentation and an avant-garde sensibility to popular culture, and he has collaborated with a wide range of artists, including Robert Wilson, Leslie Thornton and Tony Oursler. His productions include performances by Johnny Depp, Brad Pitt, Jeanne Moreau, Princess Caroline of Monaco and numerous other Hollywood celebrities and cultural icons. Exhibitions of his productions have been held at the Lincoln Center, the Metropolitan Opera Gallery, PS1/ MoMA, the Whitney Biennial, the American Museum of the Moving Image, the Borderline Arts Festival in Beijing and other venues. He serves on the Advisory Board of Anthology Film Archives in New York City.

Optography is the art of making photographs with an eye. Or is it the technology of making photographs with an eye? Does anything hinge on this distinction, particularly if the eye in question once belonged to a human? The expressive potential of this gruesome craft, one where eyes replace cameras, has never been fully explored, though it captured the popular imagination after Victorian experiments revealed that it was possible. No one seriously maintained that artists should wield eyes as yet another tool for expression. Yet optography could have forensic value. What if the eye fixed the last instant of a person's life, for instance, the moment when, frozen in terror, they confronted their own murderer? Such an image, called an optogram, might be captured by photographic processes whose goal, justice, overcame the revulsion of dismembering a cadaver. As an art, optography has little to offer, but when we consider the medium as a technology, it leads us down a path that is rich with interest because it touches on some of the deepest issues we confront as a species.

Jules Verne popularized the idea that optograms could solve crimes in "Les Freres Kip." Verne's story was a mystery, but it is not happenstance that optography has the retro-scifi aroma of Mary Shelley about it. Shelley conceived of Dr. Frankenstein, the original mad scientist, at a time when science seemed prepared to reduce organisms to mechanisms. Frankenstein was the logical outcome of Cartesian philosophy, a school of thought that reduced animals to mechanico-physical laws, and that had later inspired the French philosopher de la Mettrie to publish book suggestively named Man a Machine. Shelley's Frankenstein combined these insights with a key lesson of the Industrial revolution: a smart designer ensures that machines have interchangeable parts. If men are machines, then why can't our bodies be cobbled from spare limbs, rebuilt, then, as science fiction authors have speculated, applied to other purposes?

Medical science has largely caught up with fiction. Body parts are traded, implants are common, and machines amplify our senses. Far from being an oddity, optography is instead an early paradigm for progress in cybernetics, the discipline of communication and control, especially as it pertains to the integration of biology and technology. The human optogram straddles three boundaries, and I will use these boundaries to explain how something as intimate as eyes became a tool for solving crimes: self and other, individual and group, person and machine. Each of these boundaries forms a frontier where, from the vantage point of the optogram, which represents the mechanization of bodies, we can explore fundamental issues related to the history, ontology and the ethics of technology.

Dr. Frankenstein's monster was made of spare parts taken from corpses, a practice that is a thriving industry today. Artificial body parts have also become common, reinforcing our treatment of the body as mechanism. These augmentations are not confined to implants—think of mobile phones, music players and other digital assistants. Even a search engine qualifies. My drift is that Shelley's paradigm also applies to our eyes, ears and even our thoughts. That is, there is a cybernetic as well as a mechanical dimension to the medical concept of prosthesis. But mental prosthetics derive from a completely different tradition than organ transplants and artificial limbs. They are not based on mechanics; rather they are technologies of perception, or devices that complement or couple to our senses. Photography is the prime example of a perceptual technology because it reproduces many of the qualities of vision with a device that resembles an eye. What kind of society would invent an artificial eye? Optography raises the question from another approach. By taking an eye, and using it as a camera, it points to the brute physical basis of vision, something that is very close to thought itself.

The similarities between eye and camera are not simply coincidence. Instead they are the product of convergent evolution, which happens when two systems independently arrive at a similar design. Convergent evolution usually occurs in nature, but, as biologist George Wald discusses in "Eye and Camera," published in Scientific American in the 1950s, this example occurred in organic and technical systems related to vision. Unlike titanium joints, plastic hearts, or cochlear implants, which have been based on detailed study of anatomy, cameras were used before scientists understood the physical principles of the eye. Early cameras contained a simple pinhole apparatus and the camera obscura, predecessor to the photographic camera, derived from the study of perspective in the arts.

Wald uses optography as a touchstone for a discussion of physics and chemistry, showing how cameras and eyes process light in analogous ways. Here I am using convergent evolution as the starting point for a discussion of history, specifically the history of visual media based on optics: photography, cinema, television and digital imagery. These technologies of perception fulfil cybernetic goals in contemporary societies across the globe; in other words they circulate perceptions in the body social. Scholars have written a great deal about photography, cinema, television and digital imagery, but they have yet to explore the evolutionary basis of these media. These technologies did not arise spontaneously, nor did they arise recently. Instead they are the product of long-term trends, and they derive from our biological endowment, not in the abstract but when it confronts the reality of specific environments.

We can accept the convergent evolution of the eye and camera, of the brute resemblance of ocular and photographic images, but we have to wonder what forces propelled the evolution of cameras. How did technologies of perception arise? And what do they say about the societies that invented them?

* * * *

Distinct historical conditions gave rise to technologies of perception. We are used to dealing with media from a cultural perspective, but they are also systems that maintain the stability of society. They are control systems, and thus they have a strongly political dimension. Beyond that they are visual prosthetics that generate artificial experiences. We are so acclimated to synthetic perceptions that only a few academics have questioned their implications, even though they today deliver the bulk of information about the world. Why did these technologies emerge? Like other innovations they came from experimentation. Let's not confuse this experimentation with the ideals of individual scientists who seek to perfect knowledge. Once acquired knowledge enters the evolutionary struggle, as societies adapt it to conquer nature, neighbours and anything else that threatens their survival. Like eyes, which orient individual bodies in space, cameras orient the social body, giving societies a means to dominate their environments.

In this essay I abandon the philosophic framework commonly used to explain the origin of photography and other optical media. This is not the place to argue method, but in brief I replace critical theory with an analysis based in biology and history. The emergence of cameras can be explained through material processes if we can find the point where culture, the communication and control system of human society, took on characteristics of biological evolution. I started this inquiry by asking what sort of culture would produce such devices. I considered the functional similarities between eyes and cameras, and related them to their uses, namely the organization of bodies in a representational space. By linking history, technology and biology I discovered a schema that explains how technologies of perception like photography developed. We may call this account a theory, but I resist the idea that humanist inquiry relies on theories. Philosophy long ago passed the mantle of truth to science, and what I am to present here is a story, one that rings true not because it is based on a "theory," but instead because it is story that is reasonable and, most of all, useful.

Boundary One: Self and Other

What are technologies of perception? They are mechanisms designed to enhance human performance. Some technologies, fire making for instance, add new capabilities like cooking, but many others have their origin in natural human faculties. For instance the lever enhances our ability to lift. Like levers, technologies of perception amplify the sensitivity, range and stability of our sensory organs. Sight, hearing, touch, smell and taste have all to some degree been enhanced or replicated by machinery. Here we are solely concerned with vision, a sense that has been studied fruitfully for almost 3,000 years. This long period of study has resulted in an immense array of visual devices, many of which are vital to civilization.

Technologies of perception have done far more than enhance our vision: they have also overturned the ontology of perception. A fundamental problem of philosophy is the paradox of other minds. How do we know other minds exist? While most people assume we resemble each other, philosophers (and a few psychotics) have actively explored the possibility that we do not. The paradox has impeccable logic, but technologies of perception turn the problem inside out. Photographs and motion pictures function as perceptions, but they are easily shared. Optography goes a step further, revealing the inner image, as least before it disappears into the brain—a region now being revealed by neurology. The paradox relies on an essential difference between subjective and objective experience, which in turns defines the difference between thought and communication. Technologies of perception collapse the paradox because they generate thoughts, figments of inner life, that exist as concrete objects.

Other minds are one of life's great mysteries. What is my friend, neighbour or lover thinking? To bridge this gap we use media: words, gestures and pictures that convey meaning. These media are ultimately poetic, since they use one thing to stand for another. Media created by technologies of perception have a different quality—they are much closer to the original because they rely on measurement. They are a kind of science, one that produces objective judgments. This may sound complicated, but objective judgments are part of everyday life. A common example is the ruler. Architects without would have an impossible time erecting a structure of any size—would large, small and arm's length suffice?—but when equipped with technologies of perception, that is, with rulers and other tools of measure, they can direct large projects. In this case the words "long" and "short" are augmented by exact quantities that can be cut with precision. It is useful to bear in mind that rulers were once considered a high technology that required advanced training. Over time most of these tools pass into common use.

Architecture neatly captures the processes that make for a successful technology of perception. It builds on an organic faculty, the capacity to estimate length and surface area, then it applies a system of measure that amplifies the power and precision of that faculty. More importantly for our purposes, it produces judgments that can be shared as objects—as thoughts made concrete. Such judgments are part of a larger scheme, a plan, which organizes a group of individuals. In architecture measurements play the role of vision while the plan functions as imagination. The analogy is closer to our mental faculties than it may appear. Eyes perceive distance in terms of visual rays, rays of light, and rulers mimic these rays. And measurements, like eyesight, are insufficient guides. Rulers and eyes feed into a larger system of organization, the planning or imaginative faculty which is based on geometry, a system that describes our experience of physical space.

Rulers and knotted cords were the first technologies of perception, and they began a chain of development that resulted in satellite based GPS and GIS (Geographic Information Systems) of today. They enabled the rise of shared experience that reduced ambiguous expressions of length and other quantities to clear measures. Most of today's media—photography, television, film—lie within this continuum of measurement, but we rarely hear about it. Too much has been written about the qualitative experience of these media, and not enough about their quantitative underpinnings. Magical as they may seem, photographs are nothing more than measurements presented in a form that appeals to our eyes. The convergence of these forms—the outward form of the photograph and the inner form of our visual sense—parallels the convergence of eye and camera. We can make photographs with our eyes because geometric optics governs both eye and camera.

To get back to my first analogy, technologies of perception, like levers, extend the range of our physical faculties. Levers operate on the mechanical principles of Newtonian physics, and visual technologies exploit geometric or Euclidean optics. It might sound strange to claim that modern media operates on a classical paradigm, particularly when studies ranging from the ecological optics of J. J. Gibson to recent neurology shows how vision involves far more than Euclid's principles. But the photograph, which displays the brute realism of classical and Renaissance representation, seems natural. We might say the classical paradigm ends at the retina, which is a physical boundary between the optical and the neurological. Scientists have crossed the boundary, inducing vision directly into the optic nerve, but for the past century the photograph has been good enough, taking form in cinema, video and digital media.

Technologies of perception have made a distinct contribution to the evolution of culture. Without them our ancestors could not have created civil societies because it is impossible for people to self-organize on a large scale. Civilization, science, property, hierarchy, and the concentration of power in an elite—none of this could have happened without technologies of perception, starting with the simple measuring rod. Objective judgments are essential to forming social hierarchies, and, while these greatly enhance our ability to coordinate our actions, they demand a sacrifice of freedom. Media are systems of control as well as communication, and media systems reduce individuals to mechanisms, to programmed workers and consumers rather than creators. In its reductionism, the optogram captures the essence of bureaucracy: the tendency to treat humans as components of a machine.

Boundary Two: Individual and Group

No less than eyes, cameras developed in response to evolutionary pressure. In biology the evolutionary unit is the species, and for technology it is societies. The first technologies of perception appeared in the city-states of ancient Sumer, what we also call the first civilizations. The city-states formed in response to several conditions, each of which began a self-reinforcing feedback loop: environmental change, technological innovation, social stratification, intensification of agricultural. A similar constellation of forces has been the backdrop for urbanization elsewhere in the world, in places like China, the Indus Valley and Mesoamerica. Each of these civilizations has also possessed technologies of perception, namely instruments that could be used for surveying, though only one, the Mesopotamian society of Sumer, led to the development of cameras.

Sumerian city-states were governed by high priests, then kings, who seemingly dominated their region overtly through military and economic might. What really ensured their power was information-based management skills: they were trained in the measurement, documentation and judgment protocols required to manage large estates. Surveying was the centrepiece of these early bureaucracies—and it remains the mainstay of urban civilization. Even the first cities were well beyond the capacity of an individual to comprehend, so it fell to surveyors to measure productive land, then present leaders with a virtual image of their domains. The first surveyors were priests, and surveying itself was a high technology, a seeming act of magic that was venerated. This is why I count surveying as the first technology of perception. It replaced a subjective exercise of our faculties—the ability to judge surface area—with a far more powerful mechanism of judgment, practical geometry. It resulted in a virtual image, survey cadastres and maps, that replaced natural experience and let its users dominate society. The military, economic and religious dominance of elites has always been underpinned by the control of information.

Surveying developed from the imperatives of architecture and estate management. Conceiving of large buildings, pyramids, ziqqurats and temples, and developing large productive farms is beyond the capacity of human visualization. We can imagine such things, but only in feathery terms. Success requires framing of exact dimensions, along with precise projections on the quantities and types of materials necessary to build them. These figures become the basis for project management: the number of labourers required, and for how many years, along with the food, tools and other resources they need. When the imperatives to build civilizations grew, architects started humanity literally on the path to the moon, as our ancestors invented mechanisms to organize vast projects. These technologies of perception augmented natural faculties, extended the power of imagination and communication. They allowed early civilizations to exercise unprecedented power by creating corporate bodies that subsumed individuals within a mechanism of rules, tools and grand designs.

Examining the difference between collective and corporate entities is worthwhile. Collectives are groups of individuals who in concert under egalitarian rules. Corporate bodies are quite the opposite. They are organized hierarchically, with power flowing from the top to the bottom, and they generally have far more specialization than collectives. Collectives honour egalitarian principles, while corporate bodies honour elites. Both forms of organization exist today, but humanity has been organized on collective principles for most of its existence. Corporate bodies arose at a distinct historical juncture, the beginning of civilization, and since then they have achieved dominance in human affairs through the development of states. This boundary is the point where the convergence between eye and camera began.

Welding corporate states from tribal collectives required new mechanisms for communication and information gathering, that is, technologies of perception. Could this have happened any other way? Imagine running a city without surveyors. Estate management required rulers to comprehend far more resources than our natural mental capacity can support. Surveying reduced these expanses to compact logs that could be reviewed without even visiting the place in question. The first surveying tools were knotted cords followed by graded rods, angle measures and sighting tools used to precisely measure land. Equally important was calculation, the assemblage of measurements into a meaningful whole, and the first written words were actually numbers used for bookkeeping and resource management. Like natural perception, technologies of perception possess physical and cognitive components—they are an ensemble of functional structures coupled to methods of judgment. Thus surveying tools accompanied the development of a new discipline, geometry, that made sense of the numbers gathered by surveyors.

Schoolchildren learn the basics of geometry today, but, at the beginning of civilization, these simple tools were equivalent to supercomputers. They were viewed with awe, and they allowed elites to provide valuable management services that, in the balance, justified their privileged status. The impact of surveying may be greater than that of any other invention—without it we would have no roads, no architecture, no cities. Nor would we have private property and the political edifices that rely on it. Surveying has been elaborated by new technologies like cameras, lasers and satellite, and by advances in mathematics, but it is still practiced for the goals developed in Mesopotamia: the regulation of a class system that efficiently exploits resources. It is the basis of global civilization.

Boundary Three: Person and Machine

Surveying began the mechanization of vision. Archaic geometers had no idea how eyes work. But they created an apparatus that externalized the eye's function into a set of practices, creating a machine that produced objective visual perceptions. We think of automation as a recent phenomenon, a product of the Industrial Revolution, but in essence a machine is a set of processes that can be executed by anything, including a human being. As Lewis Mumford demonstrates, "human megamachines" existed as along ago as ancient Egypt and Mesopotamia—precisely when civilization started. Early surveyors perform substantially the same labours as the surveyors of today, and what they produce is a direct analog to the products of photography. Surveying predates the camera by 4,000 years, an eyeblink in evolutionary terms, and there is an obvious resemblance between survey maps and aerial photographs. (See Figure 1) The similarity we see between these media is not only on the surface. Both emerged from the same geometric laws, the same social imperatives, and the same historical continuum.

If we call the camera “a machine for seeing,” then its evolutionary frame is clear. Surveying, photography and other information systems enhance efficiency, giving competitive advantage to their possessors. Put differently corporate organizations are mechanical systems for managing information and resources, and cultures that possess mechanical paradigms outcompete cultures that do not. Sumerian city-states did not possess autonomous machines, but trained surveyors functioned like a machine, gathering information and assembling it into virtual image of the landscape. Surveying, bookkeeping and other forms of economic management projected natural faculties into social systems, greatly enhancing the power of individuals selected for the elite. On their own a person can manage the resources necessary to maintain a family. Objective management systems let a single person rule a city, a nation or even an empire.

The basis of Sumerian states was divine ownership. Each city belonged to a particular deity in the celestial pantheon. The concept of an all-seeing celestial landlord, a sky god, gave early states a powerful impulse that continues to this day. Like surveying the sky god was an innovation introduced by civilized societies. Earlier tribal cultures did not assign primacy to a single god, and the sky god embodies the ideological and technical underpinnings of corporate organization. A supreme being, the sky god, who owns everything it can see corresponds to elite rule. This celestial vantage is a metaphor for social hierarchy, but it also represents a strategic position, the aerial view, that has technical implications. An aerial view is required to manage domains, and throughout history surveyors have provided this vantage to elites. Surveying is the vision of the gods, as I have called it elsewhere.

We can use the concept of the sky god to integrate the six thousand years that separate the invention of surveying from the invention of cameras. In fact I can go farther to say that the history of civilization is, to a large degree, the realization of that ancient concept. Alienable property, elite rule, objective legal judgment and management through systems of virtual representation—all these systems derive from the social revolution implemented in the name of these gods, with surveying, the technical embodiment of divine vision, as their basis. The sky god started as concept, but it now functionally exists in the form of the surveillance and geopositioning satellites used to regulate the modern world. The evolutionary path from surveying to cameras to satellites can be summarized as follows.

Surveying led to the development of geometry in Mesopotamia, Egypt and Greece. Greek engineers and artists developed sophisticated instruments for studying geometry, and their investigations led to the discovery of practical optics, in the form of perspectival painting, and theoretic optics, encapsulated in the theorems of Euclid. Optical science reached a high point in the work of Claudius Ptolemy, after which is was forgotten until its revival by the Arab scientist al-Kindi, who introduced the pinhole apparatus, an early form of camera obscura, as a research tool. Investigations into the functioning of the eye and the pinhole effect continued during the Golden Age of Islam, reaching a peak in the work of Ibn al-Haytham, who offered the first mathematically accurate explanation of how a pinhole lens works.

Europeans discovered optics through translations of Arabic works, and the theoretic discipline along with research tools like the pinhole apparatus became standard parts of the European curriculum. At the beginning of the Renaissance, a study group that included Bruno Brunelleschi and Leon Battiste Alberti studied a copy of Claudius Ptolemy's Geography, a treatise that includes a perspectival method for representing spherical shapes in two dimensions. Shortly thereafter, the two introduced the technique of vanishing point perspective to European art, culminating trends that had been brewing in the previous century. A century later the camera obscura was introduced, marrying what had been a research tool to popular representation, and it was rapidly improved with the addition of lenses that had, for two centuries, been used only for the purpose of correcting human vision. During the Industrial Revolution, the inventors of photography devised a way to chemically fix the image in a camera obscura, giving birth to a new form of mass media.

Focusing now on photography, where has the evolutionary convergence of eye and camera brought us? Photography was invented in the 1820s. Within a few decades cameras were being carried by balloons, then by aeroplanes for purposes of aerial surveillance. By the 1960s they had become regular fixtures on orbiting space satellites. Today aerial imagery is a standard element of governance, used for everything from fixing property lines to ocean management. Look at a survey map, then look at an aerial photograph of the same area. They contain much the same information, and it presented in the same geometrically accurate, orthogonal form. We have always relied on eyes in the sky. Like surveyors, cameras realize the sky god through technology, and we use the information they produce to govern our complex societies.

Earlier I noted that corporate societies resembled machines, primarily because both are organized on mechanical principles. Because these mechanisms are embedded in living human societies, they are subject to competition, selection and encouragement. I argued that even a simple technology such as ancient surveying is a form of automation, based on the fact that surveyors apply mechanical processes to their craft. If we accept this argument, then we can comprehend the context for more sophisticated systems of automation to develop, until we arrive at the convergence of technology with nature. The camera is a mechanical eye, and the corporate societies of today have ample uses for it.

Here we have arrived at a boundary condition, a point where biology meets technology, and it is reasonable to ask what comes next. Vision was the first sense faculty to automate, but others, notably hearing, have followed. Thought has been on the engineer's work bench for decades, and today's leaders rely far more on expert systems than is acknowledged. We generally think of machine intelligence, or machinic life, as a reflection of our individual selves, but, should such entities emerge, it would be more accurate to describe it as a descendent of human societies, because we long ago ceased to be autonomous creatures of nature.

Beyond Nature

Optography forces us to consider our nearness to machines. Already we assimilate most of our global experience via cameras, through media like newspapers, magazines, television and cinema. Imagine how little you would know about the world without these products. Cameras now augment our eyes, and they soon could replace them. Crude retinal prosthetics are already available, and they will no doubt exceed natural eyes in power and resolution in the future. Right now prosthetics mimic eyesight. But how convenient would it be to have them swivel around our heads, switch to telescope mode, or take a remote feed from an aircraft? Beyond that we could use visual prosthetics to enter virtual environments. Natural eyesight might one day play a secondary role next to the technologies of perception.

There is another device that has the same structure, but different function, than eyes. That is the projector. Projectors work like cameras in reverse: they generate rather than absorb images. They contain their own light source, and they work better when the conditions of seeing are reversed. Theatres are dimly lit, if at all. Projectors are based in the same apparatus, the camera obscura, as photography, but they were perfected earlier when inventors combined the box with hand-painted slides in perspective. The result was a synthetic environment that delighted audiences and became mass market entertainment in the 18th and 19th centuries. Magic lanterns lost their appeal after the introduction of cinema, but through them motion pictures had a ready audience.

Projectors are late inventions, but like photographic cameras they too have conceptual precursors in the ancient world. As George Wald discusses in "Eye and Camera," many ancient scientists adhered to extramissionism, the idea that eyes project rays into the world. It is these rays that "see," bringing back vital information to the brain. There are many arguments against the theory, notably the fact that we see distant stars, but the ancients associated it with Euclid's Optics (which is otherwise substantially correct), and it persisted until the Middle Ages.

Projection reverses the flow of perception. It doesn't perceive worlds, it produces them, and in so doing captures an essential function of human cognition, one that drove us from biological to technological evolution. Prior to civilization humanity lived in harmony with nature. That harmony was no idyll. Our ancestors lived on the edge of extinction in tiny, scattered populations. In the Paleolithic era they began to innovate, making rather than finding tools, applying cosmetics and keeping records. Agriculture began 11,000 years ago, leading to great population growth, and urbanization about 6,000 years ago, when our story begins. Each of these revolutions gave humanity more control over its environment. From a psychological perspective we see the growing importance of imagination, a faculty that contains our ability to both represent and transform our environment. Technologies of perception contain both of these modalities, and we see them at every stage in the development of optics. Surveying creates an accurate image of land, but it can also be used to project new uses onto that land: roads, farms and buildings. Photography reproduces the visual experience of a place, but it can also be used to stage imaginary experiences.

The projector thus represents the convergence of machines with another human faculty, imagination. Projectors reveal the form of imagination, make it an object to be perceived, and they thus arise from the same impulse—human desire—and technology—practical geometry—as architecture. But in this case the convergence is more poetic than biological. The projector resembles a physical eye, but it functions like our mind's eye, the internal faculty that presents both the material world and the worlds we desire. Imagination is the real force of history, the impulse behind material progress, but unlike perception, it resides firmly within the human. Projectors and architecture reveal a dialectic behind vision: we see in order to remake the world.

* * * *

The boundaries conditions that organize this essay on optography touch on some of the basic questions to confront humanity, issues usually addressed by philosophers. They can be used to illuminate new approaches to these issues, opening the field of discussion beyond the confines of academic philosophy.

- Self and other refers to the problem of truth: how can we know our representations correspond to anything in the world? Does an external world exist?
- Individual and group psychology forms the basis of ethics: how do we behave? How do we judge the behaviour of others?
- Person and machine refers to the problem of existence: what are we? What is the value of human life?

Since the beginning philosophers have posed broad sets of problems around each of these boundaries, treating them as mysteries that can only be solved through specific critical methods. Each generation has rethought them in its own terms, and over time they have moved outside philosophy into disciplines such as physics, psychology, anthropology and cognitive science. Technologies of perception and, more broadly, the scientific culture that has produced them, has largely crossed these boundaries, rendering much of philosophy obsolete.

Think of the broad impact these technologies had, starting with surveying, which enabled architecture, civil design, rational planning, and ending with microscopes, telescopes and digital visualization platforms that are now revolutionizing scientific analysis. Many debates in epistemology and ontology continue only because academic philosophers have not kept pace with science. I would argue that philosophy, and the humanities in general, are in crisis because they have failed to maintain relevance to the topics they purport to study. Yet that need not be the case. Humanity is in the process of a phase shift where we incorporate machinic paradigms, and actual machines, into more intimate settings. Optography heralded the age of the cyborg, an age where the human body could be treated as a machine. With the profusion of prosthetics and externalized cognition in computers, that age is upon us. Our interdependence with machines is far greater than we admit, and philosophers are one of the few groups equipped to discuss the consequences of this evolutionary shift.

Earlier I introduced the notion of the sky god as the paradigm of Sumerian civilization. All-seeing sky gods served as organizing principles for societies that accumulated and managed property, and they represented both the ideology of social hierarchy and the surveillance technology that enabled hierarchies to function. The sky god is a paradigm for a certain kind of social organization, and it neatly embodies the overlapping shade of ideological, legal, social, technological and religious meaning that defines civilisation. To a large degree the history of civilization is the unfolding of the sky god, culminating in the launch of surveillance satellites and the spread of digital information systems in the last decades of the 20th century. No deterministic law governs the spread of these systems, but they have an evolutionary basis because societies that adopt them gain efficiencies and capabilities lacking in their neighbours. But it is clear that we may not like where they lead. The forces that drive progress are powerful, but it remains to see if they are overwhelming, particularly if we start directing the forces of progress on ethical grounds.

At the beginning of this essay I discussed the work of science fiction authors. It is now clear that literary imagination provides more than entertainment. Science fiction has mostly been relegated to the sidelines of so-called serious culture, academic and otherwise, yet its underpaid authors have provided us with more insight than well-respected professors and government commissions. Where are we going? Through thought experiments science fiction writers have provided us with ways to explore the totality of consequences that might arise from one or another technological development. Philosophers, scholars and anyone with an interest in our future could do well by adopting their methods.

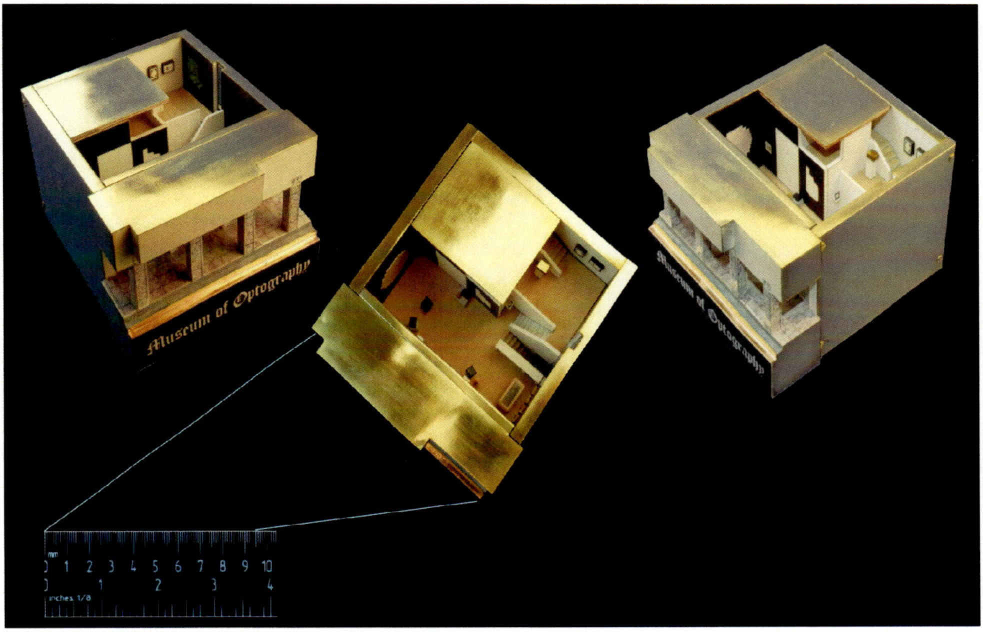

The MicroMuseum of Optography, The College of Optometrists, MusEyEum, September 2008.

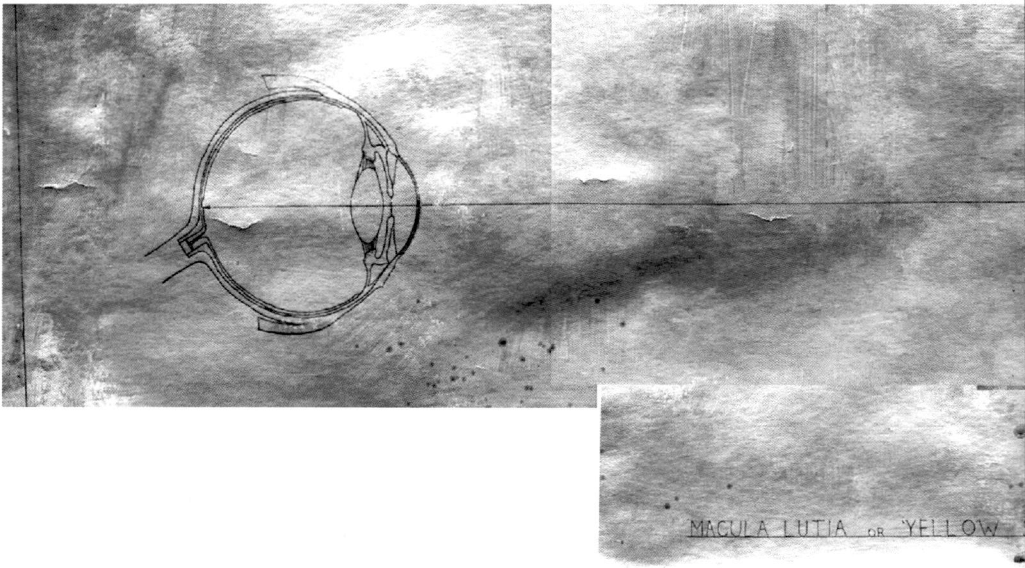

MACULA LUTIA OR YELLOWSPOT WITH FOVIA CENTRALIS , AREA OF ACUTE VISION.

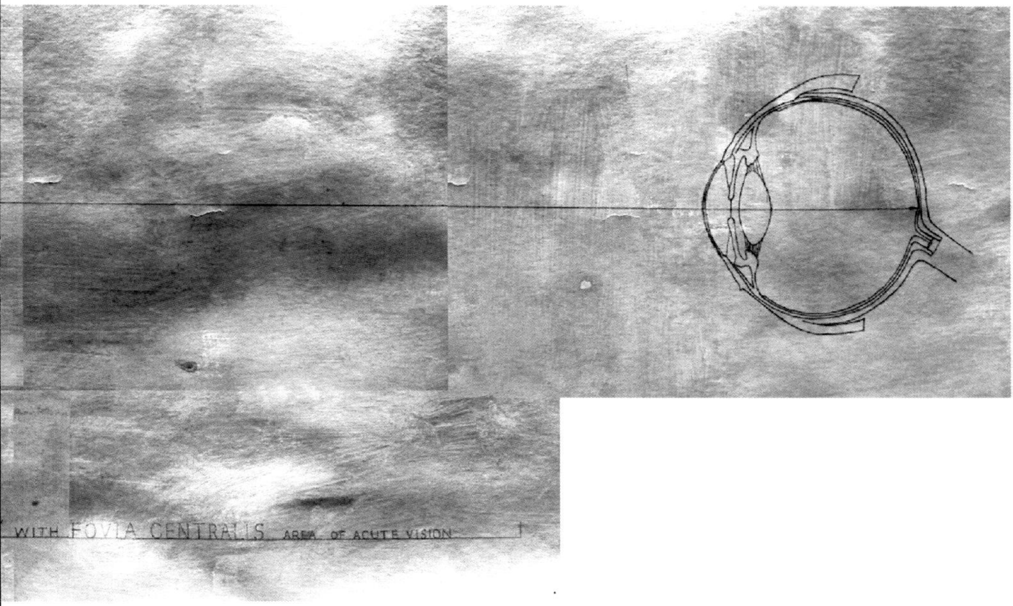
WITH FOVIA CENTRALIS AREA OF ACUTE VISION

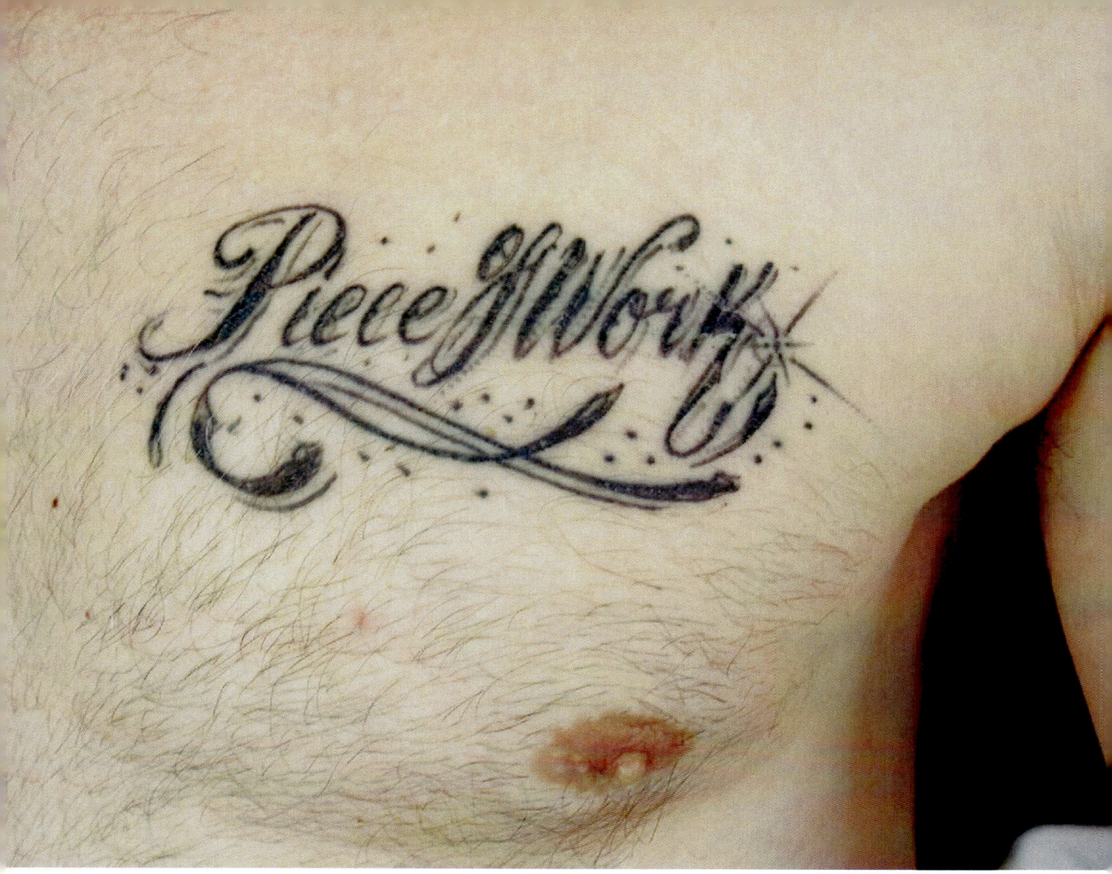

a. piece of work

b. LIMITLESS

instructions:
choose textwork/tattoo ‘a’ and/or ‘b’., typeface & colours/s.
bare skin, feel needles and ink penetrate, become a ‘piece of work’, ‘limitless’, and/or a ‘limitless’/’piece of work’.

paul sakoilsky
30th july 2006

Paul Sakoilsky

Musings on Optograms, the ideal death, the ideal work of art and the 'Museum of Optography': Derek Ogbourne and Paul Sakoilsky, a dialogue, 9.12.06, Kilburn, London.

Introduction.

The thing that struck me about Derek Ogbourne's Optography project, when he first spoke of it, and ever since, having had an ongoing commentary on his developments, was its obsessive nature. Let me say from the outset, I mean this here as a compliment. The desire and application are encyclopedic.

The 'Optogram' and 'Optography', whose history this book and art show delineates, as far as its projected practical usage, in the field of criminology, was a scientific end-game. Yet, as Ogbourne uncovers in his research, taking an arcane subject on which, prior to this project, little was known outside of literary and apocryphal references, Ogbourne has single handedly created what is, what surely must be, the archive on the subject.

One would not want to call this referentiality, so much as hyper-referentiality. Here, everything refers to everything else. One is reminded of Duchamp's Great Glass project: work/text/experiments/research. Ogbourne's Museum Of Optography, is part science, part detective story, part history lesson, part psychogeography, but always already, simultaneously, 'art'. Here one sees at work, an almost Promethean drive to know all, and somehow or other bring all under the gaze, into the praxis/art, which is not to be distinguished from the former, but to be seen as an extension in real space, a pause, a plateau: a book, an exhibition.

One cannot help but love grand ambition and undertaking.

Dialogue ... 9.12.06

Paul Sakoilsky: [...] The show at Galerie Brigitte Schenk, when is that? [Opens March 29th 2007]. So then, Is there a cut-off point, as regards your research?

Derek Ogbourne: It's an ongoing project

[...] Although In the end, the very subject is a dead end; that's why I called it 'The Shutter of Death'. Once it happens, it happens, and that's it. You're left with an image and the aura from its moment of production [...] You know an organic image is caught in flesh. The analogy of the eye and the camera, that kind of intrigues me. The fact that it really is that last retinal glimpse of existence ready for witnesses. When musing or imagining death, your eyes closed, you cut off your visual stimuli. What you then rely on is the memory of what you have last seen - that is the image. But the image is meaningless to you now because you're dead.

[...] The image of Light coming through the window, this was Kühne's main subject for his optograms. It's quite apt, seeing that the first photograph, by Niépce, was of a window. The window, the soul - it's where light comes into a dark box, which is like the eye itself, although the window doesn't have a lens. The camera obscura, and that whole link throughout. It's strange how the idea of the camera and the eye analogy was only really crystallised quite late on in history, that always surprised me. I found out recently that Kühne had an assistant, who also produced over a hundred optograms; and then there was an optographic chamber. (See Richard Kremer, Fig 4 on page77)

It also seems strange to be researching something from the past, something that is in the realm of pseudo-science. This is always something I've been into. I've got a great collection of old pseudo-science books...

Well, I have spoken with you about this before: the in-utility of optography. It's completely useless ... useless in a sense that allies with art. Is the Optogram useless? It's non-utilizable, for what it was meant to be, what it promised for criminology. It's an end-game, a scientific end-game?

Yes, It's of no scientific use, its obsolete science. I'm interested in its utility allied with art but also the vague idea that in the future there might be some application for it. The perfect artwork for me would be to produce a work of art and to win the Nobel Prize for science at the same time. To do good, to make progress for mankind, to get the Nobel Prize for discovering something. I never understood why there isn't a Nobel Prize for art?

For literature ... it must have been how it was set up... Let's return to what you were saying about death a minute ago; and then I really want to bring this round to what's actually going to be shown in the gallery? Obviously, it's going to change in some ways from now till then. You're still processing it all. But how are you going to actually

show it? (Because much of this other stuff will be covered in the rest of the book). Then, to try and talk about some of these topics, in relation to your work, if you see what I mean? But prior to that I'd like to return to what you were saying about the concept of 'death' again. Do you recall? We have said it before, about the shut-off point?
The Shutter of Death? The moment you close your eyes, you enter an internal, mental world that remembers that moment when you had your eyes open. This is imagination. In The Museum of Optography there is a recorded conversation with Salvador Dalí, where Dalí is asked what he would choose for a rabbit to see before it dies. And of course Salvador Dalí, being Dalí, is full of himself, and suggests his own self image, as God. So, the poor rabbit has to look at Dalí before he dies. For me it is fascinating to imagine the last time the world enters your retina. The image might be banal.

The Museum of Optography is to do with this imagination. This is why Retinal 145, the small little retinal drawings, are imagined death scenes. Half of them are romantic landscapes. We don't want to have a violent death, a miserable death; we don't want to have a boring death. We want a near perfect resolution to life. At this very moment I would like to be looking across a beautiful landscape.

I wanted to do this video piece where I collected – a bit like the forbidden kissing montage in the film Cinema Paradiso - endless shots of people saying 'I'm going, I'm going', laying in their death bed, looking out of a window, the sun's rays coming through, and the breeze blowing gently; their last breath. An extended romantic Hollywood death.

What's the name, there's the film of your grandmother, wasn't it? Singing on her deathbed, or very near the end of her life? Convalescing, or not convalescing? I don't know the exact details, she's obviously really, seriously old, singing a hymn in bed [The video is 'Hymn'].
It was one of those readymade bits of found footage. In fact it is the only moving image of her that remains posthumously unbeknown to her. This is a natural wind down to death rather than the sudden optographic death. A moving little video.

'Found'? Did you shoot it then? You did?
Yeah, yeah. I just pointed the camera at her and said, 'Go on sing us a song'. And she sang this hymn. She was singing about Christ being at her side, as though she was going to be taken off to heaven imminently, it was a death hymn, some Christian hymns are like that, she's singing this hymn, almost willing herself to be taken to God. I tried to find her hymn, without luck. I went to different priests, looked in many hymn books and then I found an audio psychic.

An audio psychic?
Yes, they listen to an audio recording and tell you something psychic about it. This particular psychic spoke about my grandmother's dead husband. In the video you get television as backing track - it's a low-quality VHS - a voice saying, 'Life, life is very strange, isn't it?' This TV intrusion is interlaced with her singing, She actually looks like a corpse, she was literally wasting away. (see text and images on page 208-9).

Tell me more about the Show?
Strangely enough, there is a strong surreal element to this exhibition... You could say in many ways, it's not a contemporary show at all. It's like the two drawings I've made are quite surreal, by chance. It's not like I usually do surreal drawings, it's just the guillotined rabbit and the Muybridge bouncing ball drawings; also, the drawing that I've done just now, which is of two men exploring a lump of deformity that is just sitting behind the lens of the eye. It's a drawing I found in Heidelberg's Ophthalmological Library. I just thought it was very beautiful. Instead of the retinal image being cast at the back of the eye, there is this surreal landscape, a cancer or a tumor. I re-drew the drawing adding two explorers that are staking their claim by putting a flag on their conquest. And again, this refers back to film, to Georges Méliès's Journey to the Moon, and even the Fantastic Voyage. It's very much a metaphor for this project really [...] There has recently come to light - on microfilm - the original case notes of the criminal that was beheaded, in the 1880's in Bruchsal, which I visited. (see the Chapter on the Human Optogram). This makes an archival feel for the show, so I'm thinking of installing a microfiche machine, then of course my tiny little retinal drawings will be in the form of a large disk, so they will look like a retina as well. The only way you can inspect them is from a wheeled ladder.

Like a library ladder?
Yes, so that you can reach all the tiny drawings. A lot of the archive material I've collected will be in the show as well, so there's a library feel: a British Library of Optography. Oh, and there's a video documentary I made as well about the hunt for the Human Optogram. The show engages the viewer with the process of looking and finding, deciphering truth from falsehood. You know, finding this elusive thing; the fun is in the hunt. With optography, the product is so fleeting and difficult to produce it is still something that can be rediscovered 120 years on.

It's what's cast on the retina, which is a very different thing from what they're actually seeing, because the act of seeing involves the imaginary, which is cut off at the moment of death. You see what I mean?
Yes there's a separation between the brain and the eye, even though they were once seen as part of the same organ. The optogram is a flesh imprint;

I wonder; when your brain dies does your arm still pick up the imprint of a twig - or anything. The point of my investigation is to extrapolate from the starting point of the optogram; that's why I think photographers of the 19th century were so charmed with the whole idea of the darkroom process where the image appears like magic. You imagine what that white piece of paper's going to bring, even though you know what you've pointed the camera at. And yes, in a sense, the actual optograms the ones made by Alexandridis are not particularly miraculous or that exciting... I've never been into photography at all, it's never really got me excited, it's always been a dead moment, that has a coldness, and limitation of format. Photography is mechanical. It's the same in a sense with the eye. The optogram is the completely objective eye, as it were. You die and you don't necessarily have a choice of where you die.

Surely, you can only choose when you die if you commit suicide?
Well, it's whenever God, or whatever decides when you've got to go, and what you're looking at, whether you're looking at the ceiling or wherever. That's why some of the retinal drawings depict literally the ceiling, some of them are just black, because it would be like that; others are romantic ideas of how you'd die. If your'e lucky and are well supported by those around you, you can choose your last view.

Have you been thinking about mortality while doing this?
All my work is about that. It's about micro moments that separate life from death. The film about going up a mountain, Death and the Monument, is about small moments: the person who edits out the moment before disaster. The fighting one, Struggle, captures the moment of the blink when the fist comes towards you. It is about the very sudden, the separation between life and death. I think Maybe I need to get some humour into my next pieces though. I really do. After finishing Death and the Monument I'm going to probably go a bit wild, make some funny things, something a bit lighter. My work is rather heavy and dark, and sometimes quite violent. It always somehow gravitated towards the eye, and hands. It's all logical really that this has to come now, I mean the optography project. I went from painting, to sculpture to performance, then video, to arrive at this point. But trying to think of what happens next, that's the hardest thing, but it just naturally happens. You do tonnes of thinking, and then you just do it, and it just comes.

Just doing it, yes, exactly - thinking, just seems to get us more confused. But that's part of the whole thing.
You know, being confused, can produce some interesting work about being confused.

Continues on page 194

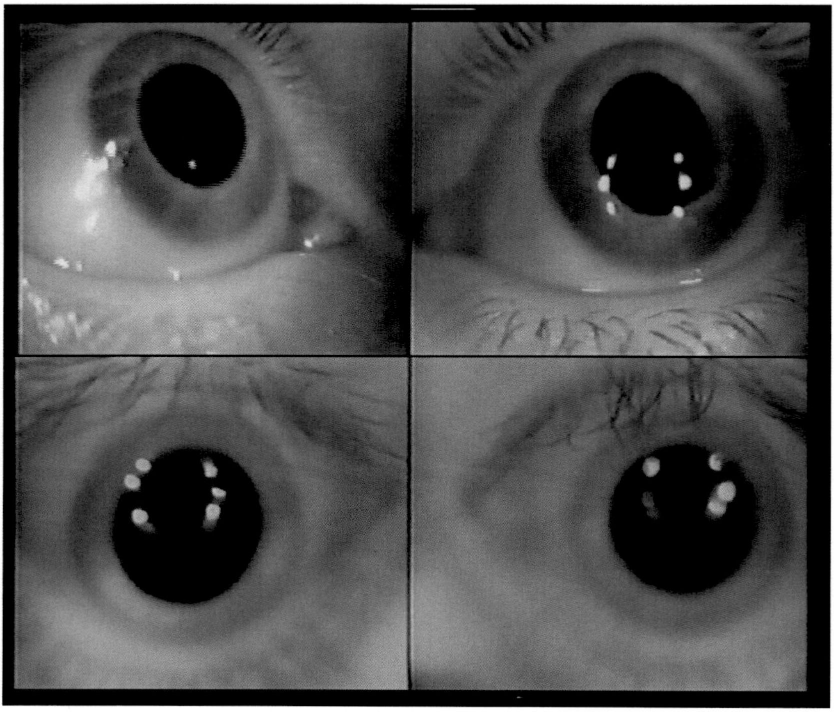

Video still from *Struggle*, Derek Ogbourne, 1997.

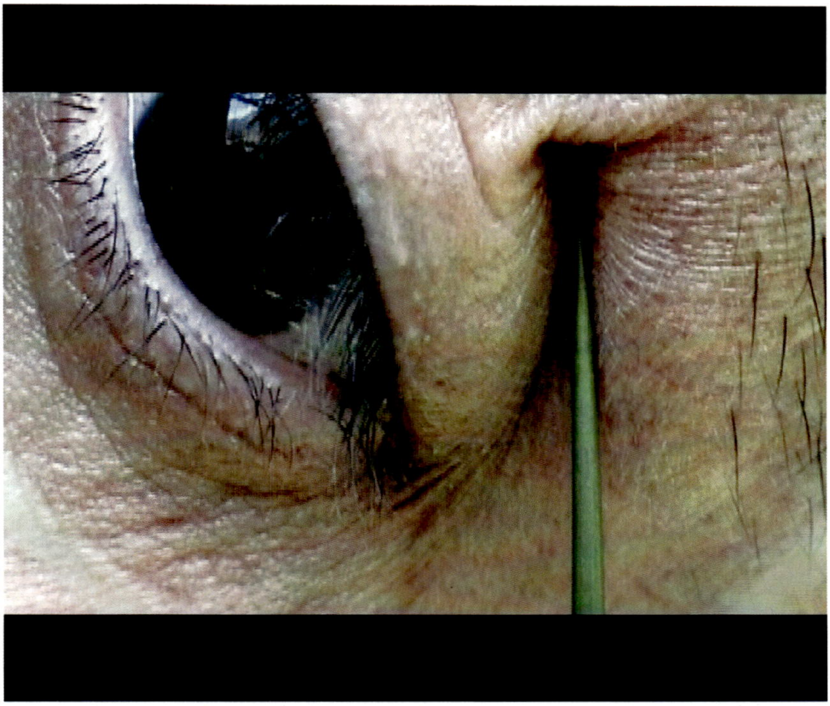

Video still from *Death and the Monument*, Derek Ogbourne, 2008.

Continuation from page 191

Yes, of course.
Years ago I did this Art project called 'Frankenstein's Kitchen' that in the end was about being confused. I Attempted to Create organic Art, that had the properties of life and was dependent upon the viewer or participant to keep it alive. It was a failed project. It was doomed to be. It was more to do with the gallant process of trying to find or discover a way of creating something that was an analogy to a living being, that, literally, if it the object was too hot, or too cold the thing would die. You had to keep the thing alive. Before that, I did this exhibition with huge condom-coloured balloons filled with water, suspending them from the ceiling of a slaughter house in Spain where I in vain tried to keep these things alive, so there's a Frankenstein thing here. You could say there's a 19th century, bodily macabre involved somewhere... Now I've found out that there's another human optogram. I might find out there's a whole lot more. I could travel the world collecting optograms, and this could turn into a bigger adventure, and knowing me I would do this, In the end, you say, why the hell am I collecting? A lot of artwork, and a lot of mine, seems to involve the process of collecting things -- which is I think a very English pastime. I used to collect stamps. Now I collect optograms.

I think that's a good close...

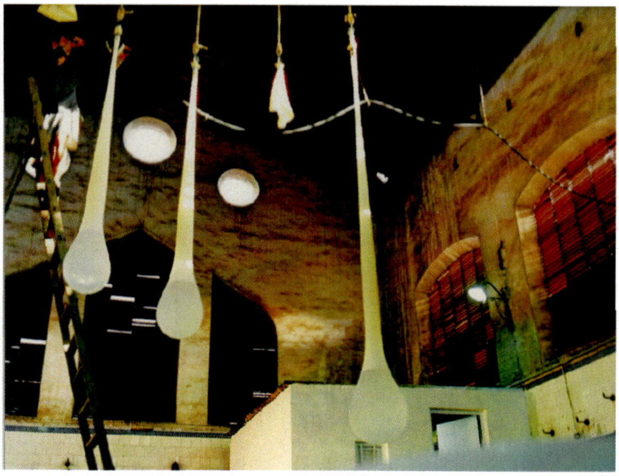

Images from
Space International
Valencia, Spain, 1993

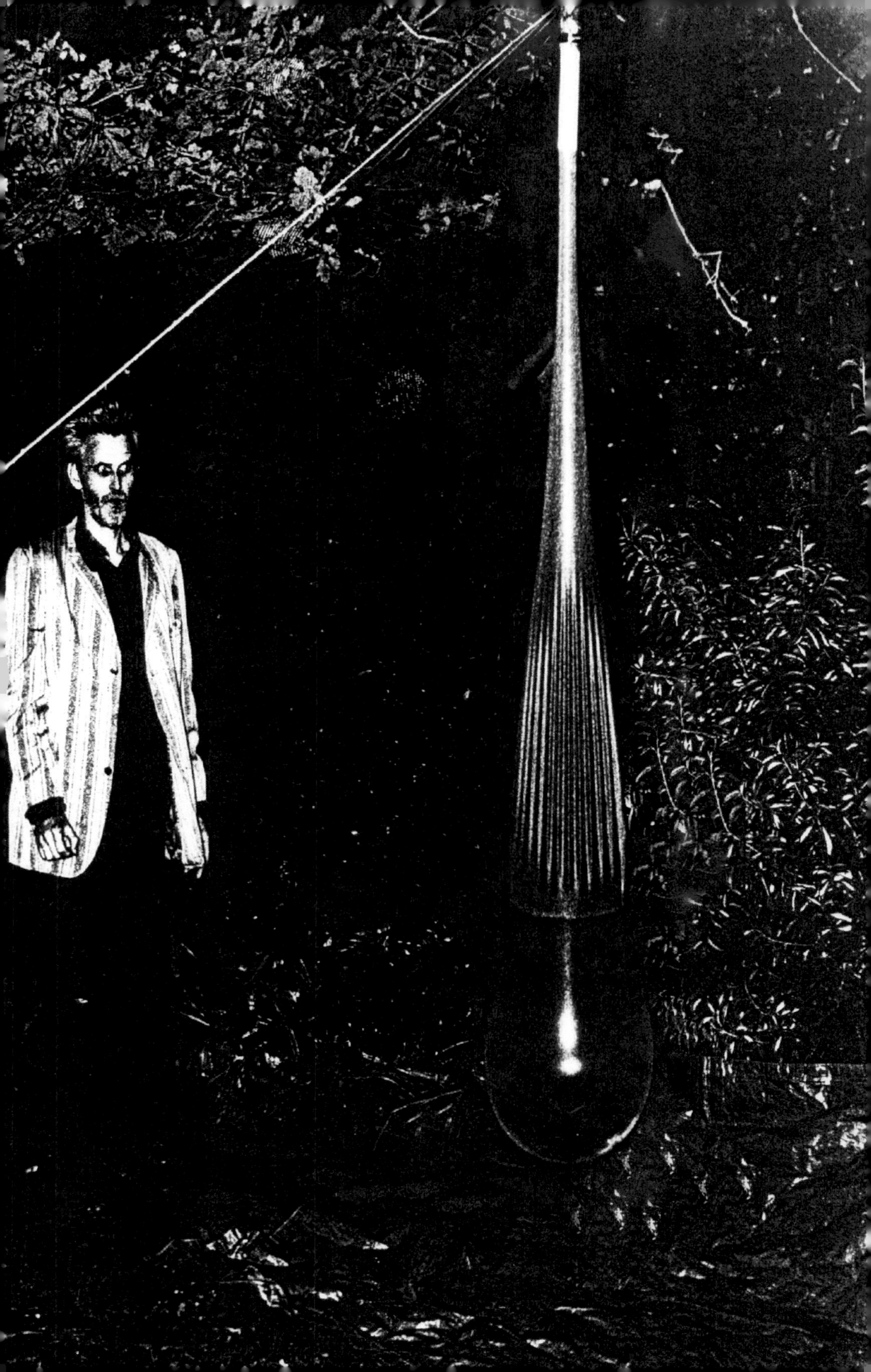

Museum of Optography

Installation Shots

Galerie Brigitte Schenk
Cologne
2007

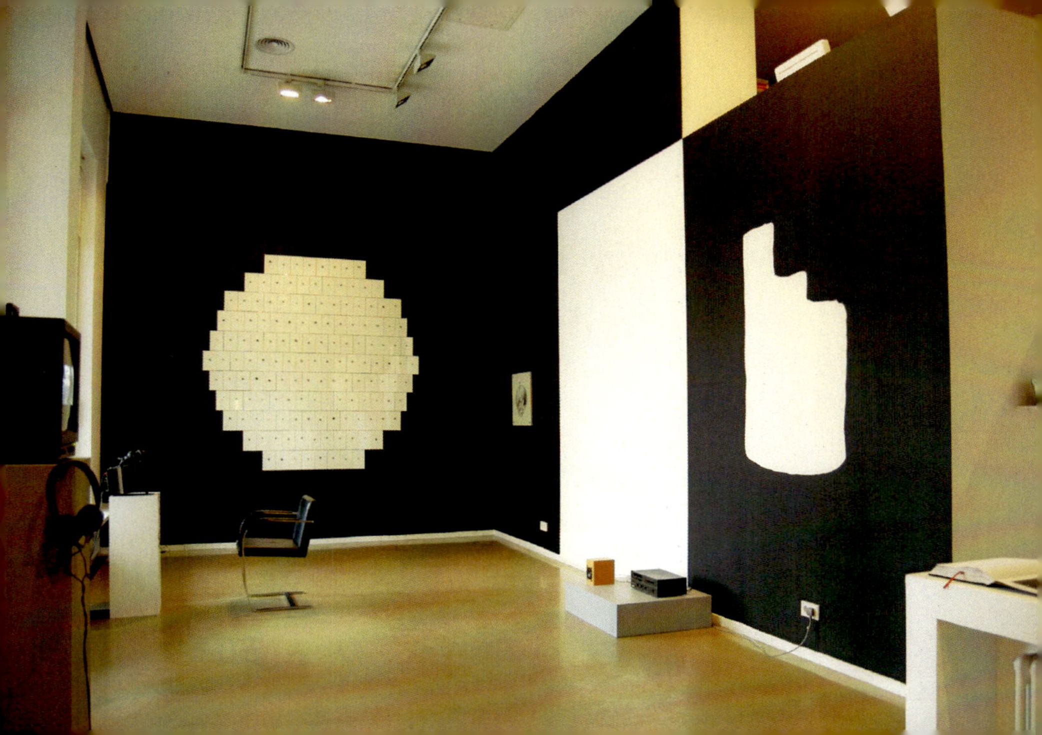

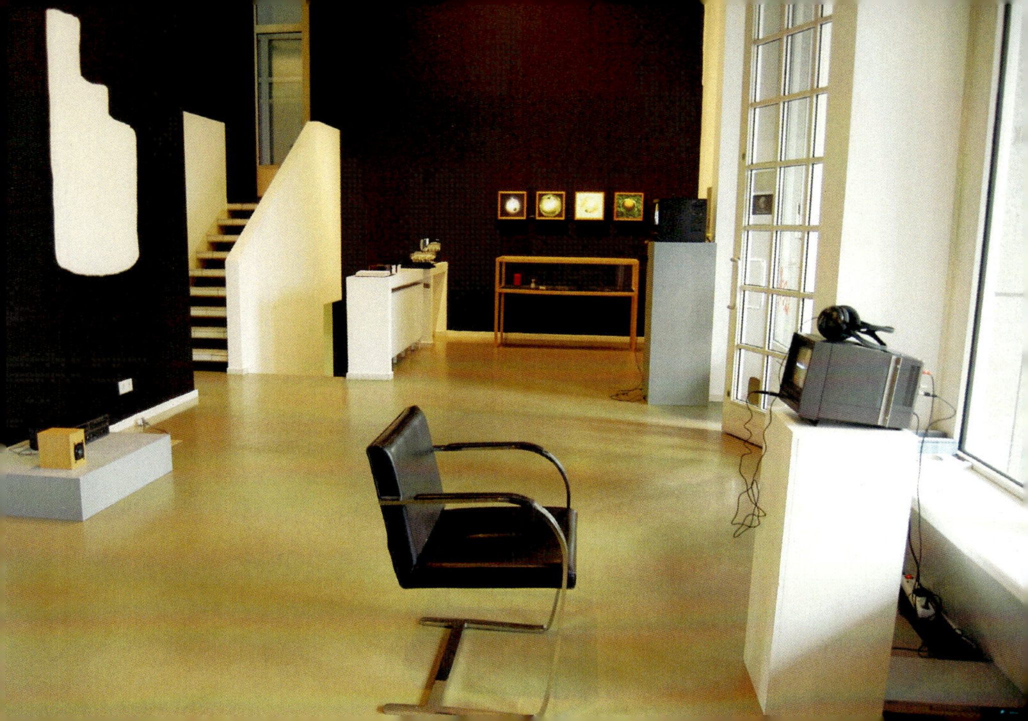

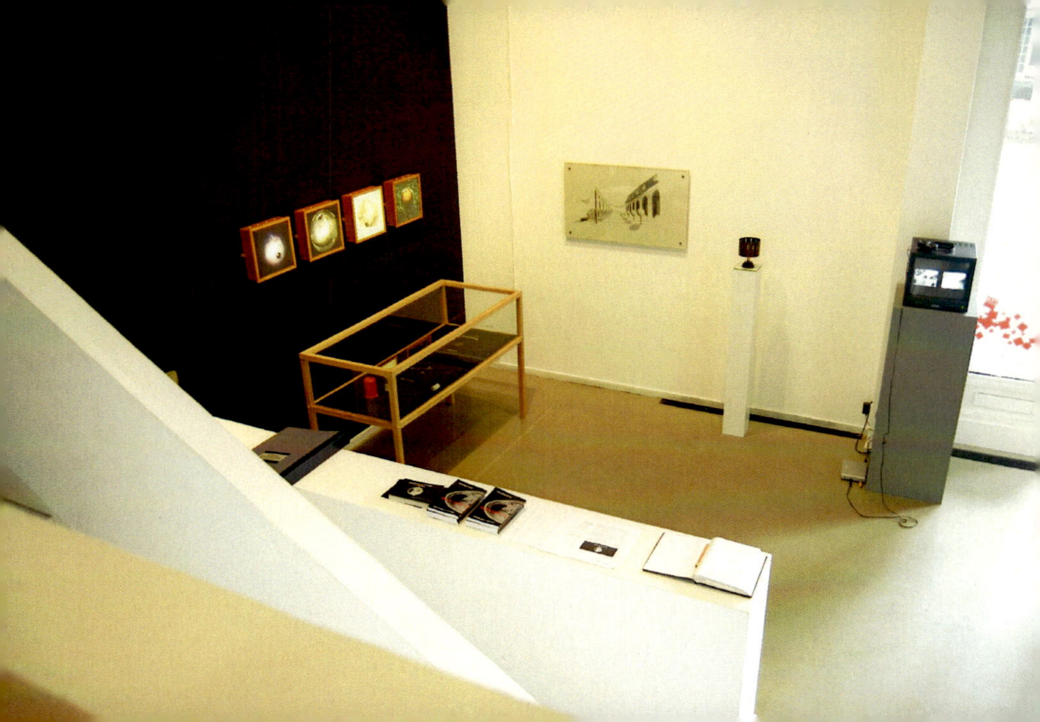

On the Museum of Optography by Susana Medina

Derek Ogbourne's eye is as sharp as a surgeon intent on transmitting the interiority within the physical world, so that its intrinsic poetry is not lost. The persistence of the physical recurs in his work like a chorus, as if he was convinced that art should derive from knowledge of the physical world and create in turn a new world where stripped down layers of reality remove us from the perpetual visual muzak of daily life and take us onto a more intimate dimension. At times Kafkaesque in its claustrophobia, at times Borgesian in its devotion to miniature and the endless, Ogbourne's work often invites us into a parallel metaphysical world, where the physical deftly echoes our inner texture. If some of his video pieces are psychic landscapes that can be seen as metaphysical thrillers with tense but minimal plots, his latest work clusters around some of his recurrent obsessions: the organic, death, the sublime, the eye as a recording device. As usual, a back to basics poetics is employed. In this case, drawing as a bare medium naturally co-exists with organic traces and the first attempts to mechanically reproduce motion, while the video pieces, with their rough-and-ready aesthetics, confirm a raw vision of reality where technology is seen as an extension of what it is to be human. All this, however, has now been re-rendered to form part of a fictional museum where a ghost science is resuscitated as both myth and intriguing fact.

A hundred and forty delicate retinal drawings arranged as a disk that echoes the retina, video, photography, archival material, a documentary and yet more drawings, one of which is accompanied by a zoetrope, conspire to create a tantalising world of pseudo-imaginary science in his latest venture, an installation where art is entangled in a time-warp that is also part detective story, part history lesson, part archive, part psychogeography.

A negative silhouette of an immense optogram welcomes the visitor to the Museum of Optography, a white, mammoth, abstract geometrical shape that emerges from one of the black walls as if insistently asking to be deciphered. It resembles one of those arbitrary shapes that appear in psychology tests. Except that it is gigantic. And haunting. It actually is a glyph from the past that has just emerged into the present. It is the only human optogram in existence. And it has been excavated from an experiment in 1880. Blown up, it gives the gallery space an air reminiscent to one of those Gestalt rooms from the 1950s where perception tests were carried out.

It is followed by a piece of white wall which leaves a gap for the gaze to rest, perhaps to perceive an afterimage. The wall becomes black again and a powerful drawing of an ocular globe affected by some sort of fleshy monstrous growth makes us muse on the fact that disease might take on lush forms. In 'Explorers of Darkness', the carnality of a scientific drawing is displayed for us to gorge upon. Two tiny explorers trek over the disease, trying to conquer it. A historical drawing of eye disease, with a nineteenth century feel about it, it introduces the theme of vision from the point of view of going inside, as well as the artist's interest in growth and movement as characteristics of all living things, which here takes on a different hue: archival material offers him an opportunity for classicism, of the wayward kind.

With '145 Retinal Drawings', we are before a majestic piece. A luminous disk that is monumental and yet precarious looking, it presides over another of the main black walls as if it was a subliminal façade of our last instants of consciousness. Made out of a hundred and forty-five miniature worlds, which are a hundred and forty simultaneous worlds, each drawing is the size of the human retina and takes the viewer into an imagined death scene. Each scene thus entails an observer just before the moment of death. Abstract and figurative, conceptual and sublime, they are coded moments of intimacy that take the viewer inside the last instant of life. Intimately focused, they are delicate statements not only about the vagaries of the field of vision, but also about drawing and touch. Ecstasy is placed alongside the mundane. Upside-down, side-ways or slightly topsy-turvy romanticised landscapes of otherworldly grace and gentleness, give us a glimpse of death as a peaceful end where wonder at the physical world is the last impression we take with us. Other retinal drawings insist on shanty towns or electricity poles or on fleeting images and impressions, while in others, the mysterious geometry of commonplace sights, the hallucinatory hiper-reality of fragments of buildings, rooms, stairways and ceilings, generate private worlds that set us apart from the everyday.

A serial draughtsman, Ogbourne confesses his fascination with what exists within the very fine line between being and not being. Compulsively imagining the last scene before death, armed with pencil and paper, he gives us in this piece an intimate complimentary world suffused with the psychological dimensions of nostalgia, memory and the emotions. These retinal drawings enter the senses slowly and effectively. They are microcosms that resonate within the macrocosm of our psyches. The vulnerability that they convey aptly embodies the fine line between life and death as subject matter. It is as if we were addressed by the interior landscapes of our minds. Immersing ourselves in the detail, the closeness is translated into a sudden intensification of vision, as the miniature drawings cast a spell and a symbolic hold on the psyche and trigger the landscapes sealed within.

Some clues about the Museum of Optography are supplied by an old recording coming from a 70s tape-recorder, which blurs the boundaries between reality and fiction and back again, as a telephone rings with an outdated tone of urgency and a man with a German accent, Dr. Alexandridis, possibly the only person to have successfully produced optograms in the twentieth century, asks to speak to Salvador Dalí. The recording brings a touch of humour into the installation. We are told what optograms are. And true to form, Dalí provides an end to the conversation that is as humorous as it is egocentric.

But what is 'optography'? Did you just say we are told what 'optograms' are? An obsolete science of sorts that deals with the fleeting record of what the eye has been fixed on at the moment of death, that is to say, the fixing on the retina of the last image seen before death, optography was believed to be a new criminologist tool that would help to solve murders, akin to early DNA testing, although so far, it has been of no forensic use. In the nineteenth century, a flurry of articles debated around the subject. Some considered it to be grandiose humbug. While the process of obtaining an optogram is akin to photography, instead of negatives, we get positives made out of light. Instead of paper, we get the flesh of the retina acting both as a camera and a recording surface. Instead of the customary chemical developing, potassic alum solution is used. And instead of a straightforward process, death and the immediate removal of the retina under laboratory conditions are amongst a number of prerequisites for the optogram to appear.

This is part of what we are told by a chilling documentary about the history of optography, which provides further answers to the questions that hover around some of the pieces. The history discontinuously unrolls in Gothic English typeface, as if it was a silent film. The silence is appropriate. As is the drumming that punctuates it, which foretells an execution. Partly a detective story, the documentary covers the quest to uncover the truth and constant fascination behind the myth of optography, beginning with the seventeenth century, when a Jesuit astronomer called Christopher Schiener observed an image laid bare on the retina of a frog. It then travels to the town of Heidelberg (a recurrent topos for optography) where Wilhelm Kühne made the first and most successful visually identifiable optograms recorded as drawings in the late 1870's and also obtained the only known human optogram from a condemned young man who had killed his two children, Edhard Reif. We learn that the arbitrary shape that looms large at the entrance of Museum of Optography is presumably the last thing Edhard Reif saw as he was beheaded. In the documentary, this human optogram spins, pulsates and flashes on the screen creating afterimages and reminding us that the last thing we might see could be a meaningless abstraction that leaves us in suspense for eternity. An interview with Dr. Alexandridis, who made a series of optograms in 1975 for the German police, tells us about the process of obtaining retinal images. The documentary ends with a life-affirming sequence, as a couple of rabbits hop around a landscape covered in snow.

The narrative tone of the documentary is both offset and complemented by a relentless video-piece which shows us a busy hand probing inside some unidentifiable organic matter. Shown on a small monitor on a plinth, the black and white screen is split into four. An exploratory action seen from different angles is taking place. Extreme close-ups of eyes, organic matter, movement and poking take us on a fast journey where the physical world at is most basic is explored through violence. The chaotic humour of this piece is in turn set off against the coolness of the actual optograms we see next.

Vision as a photochemical process reminds us that what we see is enshrined in our central nervous system, not just as memory, but as physical trace, even if fleetingly. Flesh has memory. Tactile memory. As well as memory for illness. Less explored is the visual memory of flesh. This is what the optograms on display eloquently speak of. Back-lit and encased in new hand-made boxes that look as if they had just materialised from the nineteenth century, these visual documents also give us what definitely should be termed 'retinal art'. There is no irony in them though. They are the optograms made by Dr. Alexandridis in 1975. They are presented as scientific facts. Yet one cannot help but see that the rejection of 'retinal' sensations as the basis for art has been turned inside out upon itself. Clinical, beautiful and unsettling, they are now artefacts where images have been preserved post-mortem on the flesh of the retina. They are quietly anxious objects, reminders of the bodily macabre. The number '75' imprinted in red, a drawing of Dalí's face and a checkerboard pattern, are presented as evidence of the retina as camera. They are accompanied by a vitrine lined in black felt, which displays the tools necessary for the optographic process to take place: potassium hydroxide, a scalpel, pins, a magnifying eyeglass, tweezers, a glass ball and a red photographic safe light.

Poetic as the idea of preserving the last image before death in the retina might be, the optograms are a crude reminder that scientific knowledge, whether successful or not, is sometimes dependent on cruelty to animals. And that no satisfactory alternative has been found as yet to this unsavoury fact. Death and violence, even if it is painless, are at the basis of much medical research. So far, our physical survival might depend on factories of death. And thus the optograms oscillate between a metaphysical shudder and a sublime poetics of the trace.

The act of seeing is also explored in 'Homage to Eadweard Muybridge', in which a zoetrope is placed next to a surrealist drawing of archive feel, where an endless row of rabbits held in guillotines look at a set of lined up balls. A ludic piece, it is both humorous and troubling: the beautiful wide-eyed innocence of the rabbits, the man-made guillotines, the classical façades and the bare outline of mountains in the background configure a perfectly ambivalent landscape. The drawing captures the illusion of a rapid succession of images about to be set in motion, which is emphasized by

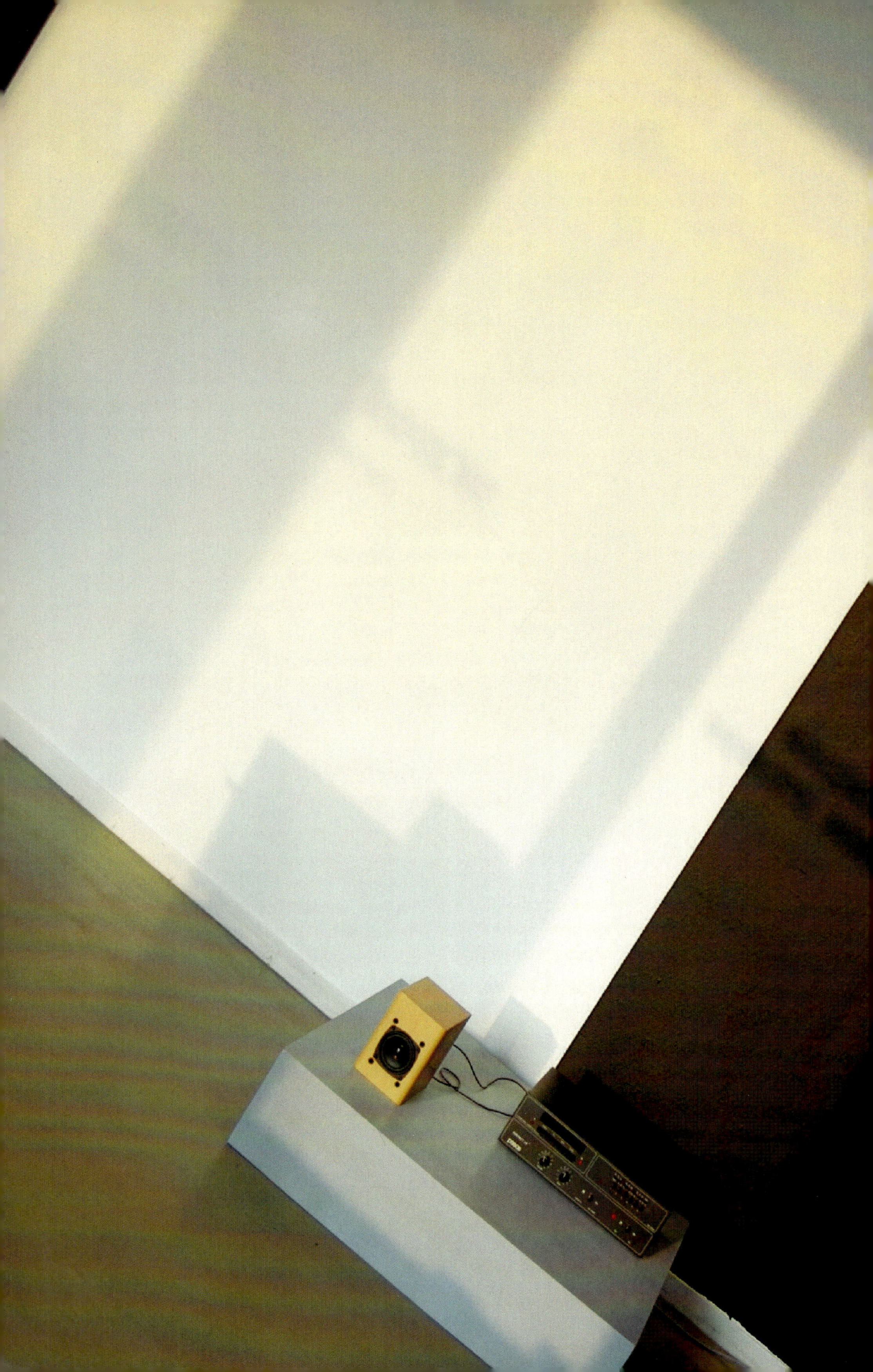

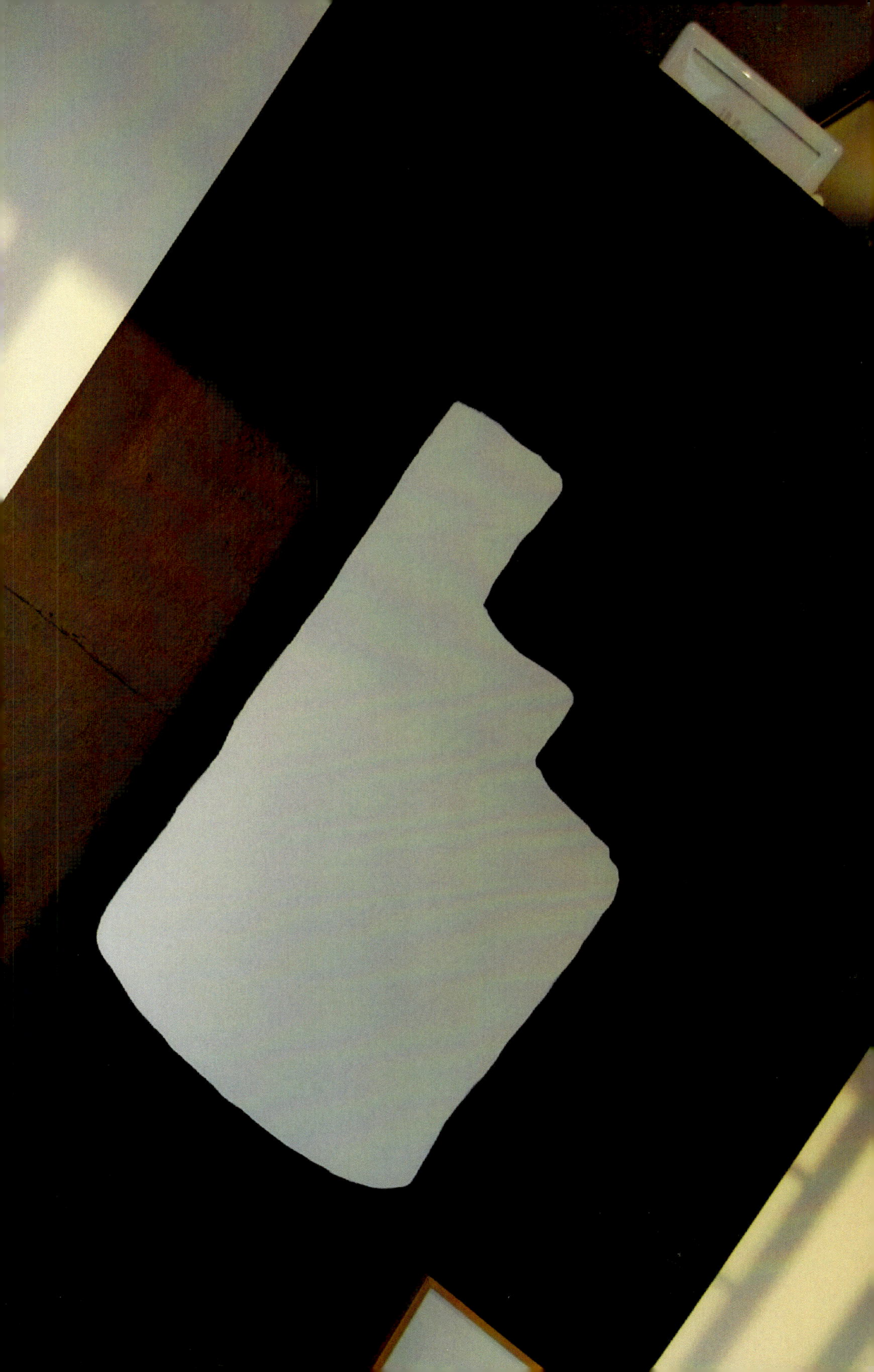

placing the zoetrope next to it. A device that produces an illusion of action from a rapid succession of static pictures, the zoetrope belongs to the class of 'philosophical toys' which provide entertainment while also illustrating scientific principles. Consisting of a cylinder with slits cut vertically in the sides, it is a precursor of cinema, as were Muybridge's pictures of horses airborne during gallop, which through his invention of the zoopraxiscope, a machine similar to the zoetrope, are also part of the history of the motion picture. This is cultured black humour of an interactive kind: if you spin the zoetrope after seeing the drawing, you have just playfully set the guillotines off and you can observe a ball bouncing, which is the set of optograms that the rabbits' retinas would have produced. However, if you spin it and then see the drawing, the suspended moment portrayed in the drawing prevails and the rabbits remain forever intact, albeit under guillotines.

The artist's preoccupation with ghostly traces also appears in a small piece that provides a passage to the next floor. A delicate trace on paper, fossil-like and framed by a Venetian mirror frame, it could have been purloined from a cabinet of curiosities. It could be an optogram. It is certainly a modern fossil, an unusual coffee stain on an envelope that has crystallized into an amber outline providing an organic resin-like trace that looks as if it could be millions of years old. While in this piece coffee time becomes geophysical time, in the next set of drawings, a different strand of time is introduced, one where computer diagrams of contraptions to hold rabbits prefigure their future obsolescence.

Over the last fifteen years Ogbourne has developed a remarkably coherent body of work. Museum of Optography offers us another coherent turn of the screw. One where science, optics and an erratic taxonomy of visual organic traces in different media conjure up a humanised world which speaks in a babble of languages and temporalities. Life and death, permanence and transience, mourning, melancholia and a playful tragicomic tone permeate the space. There is no referencing to the vanitas still life tradition. And yet it is implicitly there. But there is no moralistic message, just a stating that 'death' is a fact of life. Best known as a video artist, his video 'Hymn' is, however, a rescued home video that provides a poignant conclusion to Museum of Optography. Preserving a real life moment in real time, the subject might be an intimation of death, but there is no death of affect. In 'Hymn', an emaciated and frail old woman, who is probably in her late nineties, looks at the camera with sunken eyes while slowly singing a hymn as if postponing her fate through song. The poor quality of the recording aptly lends the old woman an appropriate spectral patina. TV background noise interlaces her song and mumbled forgotten lyrics:

... If he be my guide
In his hands and feet are imprints
And his side ...

...Finding, following, ...ing
He's sure to bless
Life is martyred in ...

As she sings, a much louder TV voice intrudes into her song providing an aside comment, which is at once counterpoint and truism:

LIFE IS VERY STRANGE, ISN'T IT?

It is indeed. We leave Museum of Optography, transformed by Ogbourne's meditation on the utterly time-tangled, tragic and sublime nature of human life, taking with us powerful symbols of beauty and dismay, ready to embrace life's music, with its dreams and nightmares.

Exact transcript of 'HYMN' video loop
[Blue indicates background TV]

Edith Elisabeth Ogbourne (1898 - 1996)

Hymn

...Fe...marks to lead me to him
if he be my my guide
[To the bedroom, Don't you dare]
In his hands and feet are imprints
and his side
[I just don't know where to begin]

(Something like)......Finding following......ing..
[It will be if you don't worry about it]
He's sure to Bless.
(Louder) [Life, Life is very strange]
Life is martyred In he.....

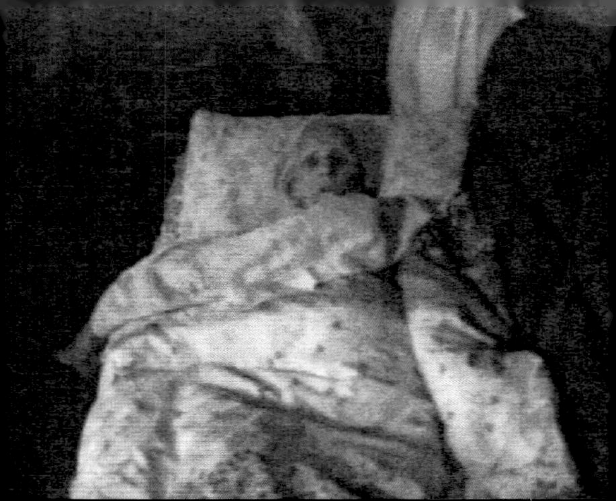

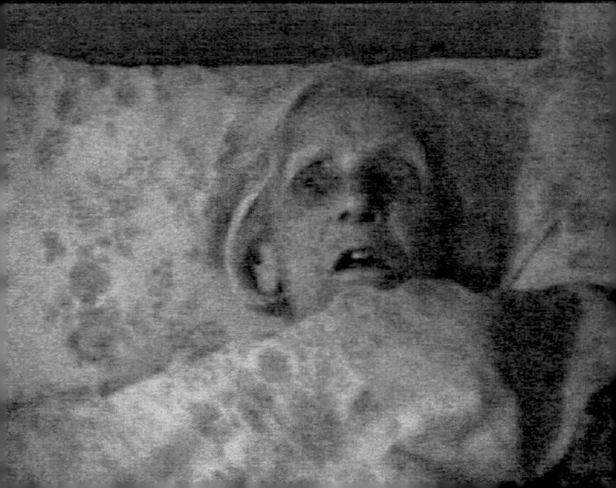

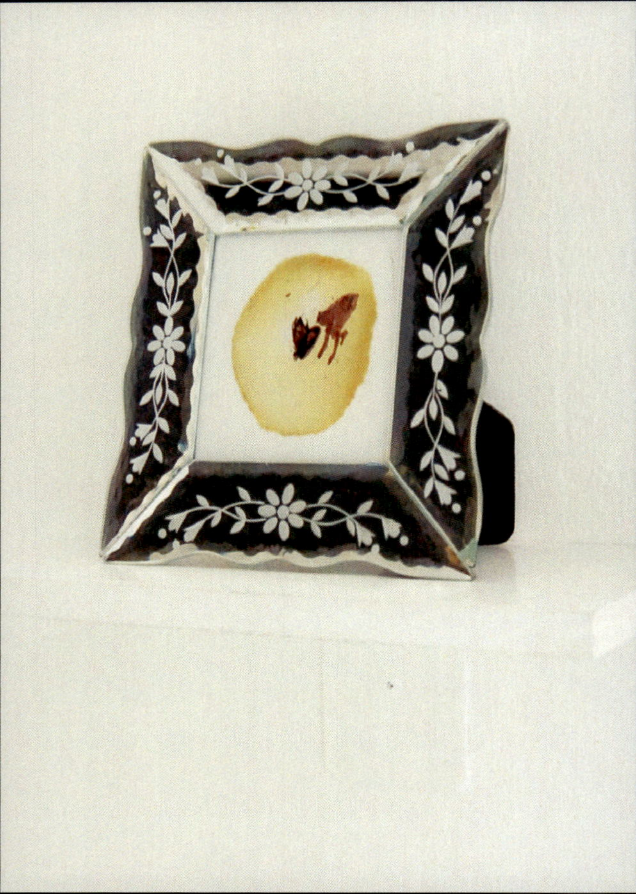

A Million years ago large stands of forests in some parts of the world began to seep globs of sticky resin. This aromatic resin oozed down the sides of trees, as well as filling internal fissures, trapping debris, such as seeds, leaves, feathers and insects. As geologic time progressed the forests were buried and the resin hardened into a soft, warm, golden gem, known as amber. Amber is the fossilized resin of ancient trees which forms through a natural polymerization of the original organic compounds. Most of the world's amber is 30-90 million years old.

Acknowledgments

Alexandra Veith, Thom Kubli, Bruce Ogbourne, David Ryder, Brigitte Schenk, Brigitte Schenk Gallery, Bill Cisneros, Hoor Al Qasimi, Ruth Boswell, Dr. Erich Veihofer, Francesca Piovano, Dory Lama, Richard Niman, Peter Evans, Prof. Uday B. Sheorey, Hannelore Medina, Dr. Richard Kremer, Dr. Arthur B. Evans, Maria Vila, Bill Jay, Dr. Evangelos Alexandridis, Paul Sakoilsky, Jamie Robinson, Carter Presents Gallery, Simon Worthington, Mute Magazine.

Kind permission from

BMJ Publishing Group, British Journal of Opthalmology, 1976; Vol 60, p. 8
Dr. Uday B. Sheorey, p.135
Elijah Wald (Son of George Wald), p. 9
Dr. Evangelos Alexandridis, p.11-17
Dr Veihofer, The Prison museum, Ludwigsburg, Germany, p. 26-27
Arthur B. Evans, p. 37
Copyright Elsevier Pocket Companion to Guyton & Hall Textbook of Medical Physiology, 11th Edition, John E. Hall, PhD, p. 61
Frog's eye, untraceable image, p.76
untraceable press image, p. 77
The newspaperarchive.com and The Dothan Eagle, p. 78-79
Hans Richter Estate, p. 148-149
George Wald – Ali Hossaini, p. 168
Paul Sakoilsky, p. 185

Note: It is hoped that further edition of this volume will be printed contain ing two further essays by Margarida Medeiros and Andrea Goulet, entitled respectively *Body, mind, machine: 19th century ideas of automation* and *Death and the Retina*: Claire Lenoir, *L'Accusateur*, and *Les Frères Kip.*

Special thanks to
Susana Medina and Jan Woolf
for their editorial
contributions to
this book

Dedicated to Pamela and Bruce Ogbourne